TO KATE

Things fall apart; the centre cannot hold;

Mere anarchy is loosed upon the world,

The blood-dimmed tide is loosed, and everywhere

The ceremony of innocence is drowned;

The best lack all conviction, while the worst

Are full of passionate intensity.

.   .   .   .

And what rough beast, its hour come at last,

Slouches towards Bethlehem to be born?

—Yeats, "The Second Coming"

Contents

Tables and Figures

Tables

Figures

Illustrations

Acknowledgments

Many people have encouraged us. We would particularly like to thank Rick Teichgraeber of the Murphy Institute for giving support to the presentation of our research from the beginning, Paul Lewis of Tulane Studies in Political Science for his sponsorship and continual encouragement, and the Amistad Research Center and the Louisiana Coalition against Racism and Nazism for the use of their materials on David Duke. For extra effort during analysis and the creation of the manuscript, we thank Joan Dee, Geoff Garin, Bill Gwyn, Harrison Hickman, Rosemary LeBoeuf, Jo Ellen Miller, Bob Robins, and Kate Rose. At the University of North Carolina Press, David Perry has nurtured this project from the beginning.

Douglas D. Rose

Introduction

Responses to David Duke

It is Thursday night in Baton Rouge, Louisiana, in January 1991.
I am behind one-way glass looking in as eleven supporters of David Duke sit
around a table discussing their views. Despite the week-old Iraqi war, it is not
hard for the participants to focus their sense of concern and uncertainty on the
domestic situation.

They are talking about hard times—low pay, scarce jobs, few benefits, and
short hours on the income side, and high prices, catastrophic health care
costs, and increasing taxes on the outgo side. College graduates have to leave
the state to get a job. What do you need to get a job? One says qualifications,
others say political connections, and still others say to be a woman or a
minority.

They feel squeezed from above. Employers squeeze them for a buck. Oil
prices go up, oil companies pocket the profits. Companies dump waste,
ruining the environment, for profit; S&Ls are looted by their officers. The
government helps the "big boys" out through tax breaks, because politicians
are influenced by lobbyists and campaign contributions. This goes on, they
say, but it is sort of invisible—they are bleeding but they never saw the knife.

Their outrage comes from the squeeze from below, from welfare and
affirmative action. There is little dissent on the main points. Free tax money

is going to people who could work and do not, who spend the money on drugs and feel that the world owes them a living. Who pays the tab? The middle and working classes—the rich get tax breaks. Yet it is the middle and working classes who are barred from an opportunity to better themselves by affirmative action, which gives any decent job to minorities, whether qualified and hardworking or not. They perceive the whipsaw: affirmative action on the income side and welfare abuse on the outgo side.

Most people in the room think they know why these unfair, antiworker, antiwhite policies persist. The beneficiaries of affirmative action and of welfare abuse are supported by minority group racial solidarity. Because all blacks support the same candidates, politicians support the policies to get bloc votes and stay in office. Thus, politicians get campaign contributions from the rich (who get tax breaks) and votes from minorities (who get minority programs) and rip off the white middle class. Then they raise their own salaries and use their connections to get benefits for their friends and families.

Other politicians who represent the interests and values of Duke supporters are mentioned. For working-class Duke supporters these politicians include Louis Lambert, a populist "watchdog" against high utility rates, and Woody Jenkins, a conservative antiabortion advocate. Middle-class Duke supporters prefer Buddy Roemer, the "scrub-the-budget" and anti–special interest governor, and George Bush, the stern enforcer of a line drawn in the sand.

David Duke, however, satisfies both groups. First, he speaks out against welfare abuse and affirmative action, whereas other politicians seem afraid to. Second, as a candidate he perhaps can rally enough votes on these issues to outweigh minority bloc voting. Third, he proposes what they see as universally fair policies, stressing individual equality and strict guidelines. Most of the anti-Duke campaign information and media coverage they dismiss as just more negative political campaigning from the same people who are already abusing the public trust. Supporters identify with David Duke: once convinced—often by his TV messages—they may not say anything, but when he is attacked or insulted, they feel offended.

Are they racists? They do not think they are. Yet their admiration of blacks is slow and grudging, while their criticism is fast and free. All say that blacks take away more than they contribute to contemporary American life. Though some are bothered by Duke's Ku Klux Klan background, they agree with his issues, and because they feel more strongly about the issues than about the background, they are prone to give their man the benefit of a large doubt. The KKK is not part of their lives, except when someone uses it to attack Duke. They feel less racist than victimized: they are not to blame for slavery, they support civil rights—so why must they either submit to blatantly unfair policies or be labeled racist?

Duke's U.S. Senate campaign has brought their feelings out of the closet. They do not even know what other Duke supporters think on many issues because they have never talked politics as a group. They have learned to support Duke. Half plan to vote for him in the gubernatorial election in 1991, and many more would support him for the U.S. Senate against John Breaux in 1992. Perhaps a third say they would prefer him to George Bush in a bid for the White House.

David Duke, a state representative, garnered these supporters in his run for the U.S. Senate in the fall of 1990. He lost, taking 44 percent of the vote cast, but received 57 percent of the white vote. Duke then contended for the governor's office, making the runoff, which he lost in a blaze of national publicity. Duke subsequently turned to the presidential primaries. Though many people became aware of him during the gubernatorial runoff campaign in October and November 1991, David Duke had been emerging for several years. On election, he was perhaps the best-known state legislator in America. By the middle of the Senate campaign, his name recognition in Louisiana was unexcelled. Duke draws attention as a black hole absorbs light. He is noteworthy, less for what he is than for the responses he provokes—among supporters like those described here, among opponents, among political elites, and among people like me, a scholar who now studies David Duke.

I

Since July 1990, I have been coordinating the research project on David Duke that produced this book. It started, in effect, early in 1989, during Duke's runoff for state representative, with calls from journalists wanting material. Other than anecdotes about his early escapades, I found we had little of value to offer. We could provide information on Duke's past associations with fringe neo-Nazi and racialist groups, but only limited insight into his present political success.

After the election, Lawrence Powell's initial regression analyses of the vote—indicating that Duke's voters were largely registered Democrats, for example—illustrated what could be done. When the need for information increased with Duke's run for the U.S. Senate, and when Paul Lewis promised support, I put together a research plan to uncover reliable information about David Duke.

Nine of us—professors, journalists, consultants, and activists—divided up the work. The diversity of our backgrounds reflected the diversity of insights and approaches that might be employed to accomplish our goal. I wanted to provide the best information that could be collected and analyzed in a short period of time. I called on people familiar with Metairie and southeastern Louisiana who could place Duke in perspective given recent local history and long-standing local custom. The crucial expertise is not always evident from contributors' biographies. Gary Esolen, for example, is the expert on television techniques because he is a star political debate coach by avocation.

We took on the subject of David Duke as a political phenomenon. Conversely, our research is not about David Duke as a person—we do not try to answer questions such as "is he normal?" As we see it, Duke qualifies as a political sensation both for his performance and for how others treat him.

We focus both on the public and on political elites. Lawrence Powell, Douglas Rose, and Susan Howell and Sylvia Warren describe the public reaction to David Duke—in the 1989 state legislative contest, the 1990 Senate race, and the 1991 gubernatorial campaign—and consider public opinion about Duke in addition to voting behavior. Why do people support him? Why do they oppose him? What explains his success? William McMahon, Gary Esolen, and Elizabeth Rickey study how political elites— the legislature, the media, and Republican party officials—deal with Duke. Ferrel Guillory, William Moore, and Lance Hill put Duke into contexts—the changing South, American right-wing extremism, and opportunistic Nazi racial thought. Ronald King ties together our findings into themes.

The theme we all came to understand, the one that underlies our varied results, is this: David Duke is not just a phenomenon that happens in that weird state of Louisiana. He is not just a passing fad, and leaders who do nothing special to counteract him will fail.

II

The chapters of this volume are self-contained yet meant, in combination, to provide a broad understanding of the David Duke phenomenon. The main conclusions of one chapter can form a starting point for understanding the implications of the next. Together, they make a story that goes like this.

In America, in the South, in Louisiana, in Metairie, lived David Duke.

Ferrel Guillory sets the stage, recounting the changes in the South in the past twenty-five years that provide the context for David Duke. Mostly the

South's changes are America's changes, stretched out or speeded up, yet the changes involving party, race, and leadership are more dramatic in the South. Only Duke carries on the southern tradition of world-class demagoguery. Yet Duke is, more than a southerner, a Louisiana boy, raised on populist politics.

Louisiana is populism's only success, the only state where a populistic program was enacted—under the Longs—and retained as public policy to the present day, including the exemption of homeowners from property taxation. Originally, only Louisiana had enough mineral resources per capita to afford populism, and only Louisiana had the politics to enact it. The voters of Metairie grew up with a peculiar brew of Earl Long, segregation, Edwin Edwards, and soak-the-rich mentality.

Duke was elected as a Republican to the state legislature . . .

Lawrence Powell explores Duke's victory in the runoff for an open state legislative seat in House District 81. Though weak opposition and weak party ties play a role, Powell locates the main thrust of Duke's appeal in traditional populist politics—the right-wing version—and points to the key role of the Louisiana oil recession in alienating blue-collar workers from mainstream candidates. Seymour Martin Lipset's working-class authoritarians would be at home in District 81's Bucktown. Duke's appeal is neither local nor unique in Powell's analysis.

Powell shows that Duke's voters have in the past supported Democratic populist candidates, such as Edwin Edwards. The populist appeal has worked in Louisiana and elsewhere for one hundred years and it is not going away. Duke is following where others have gone before. Basically, that means that the audience is receptive to the messenger.

. . . despite his racist past . . .

William Moore recounts how Duke has been trying to combine mainstream and extreme for some time. This, however, has been more a matter of style and tactics than of substance. Moore traces Duke's political career over two decades, from raw media events and crude mailers to a few believers to slick television spots, from neo-Nazi youth groups to the electoral arena. Moore notes early aspects of Duke's movement of racial themes to the mainstream. Duke sought respectability for the Ku Klux Klan by avoiding violence and bringing in the middle class and women, and he continues to seek respectability for his themes: respectable techniques, racial themes.

. . . and his continued associations, which embarrassed other Republicans.

Elizabeth Rickey examines the response of the Louisiana Republican party. David Duke posed problems for a party that had stressed putting candidates in office without concerning itself about orthodoxy. Rickey details the celebration of Duke's state House victory at the neo-Nazi Populist party convention, her purchase of Nazi books at Duke's legislative office, and her attempt to have the Louisiana Republican State Central Committee censure Duke. Her conversations with Duke, in which he applauds the heroism of Rudolph Hess and argues that the Nazi extermination camps were a myth, leave little doubt about his racial ideas. Rickey shows that when state Republican leaders tried to avoid offending Duke supporters, they offended the national Republican leadership, they double-crossed members of the State Central Committee, and they left registered Republicans—the white voters who are least supportive of Duke—a choice between Duke and a Democrat. After the 1990 Senate election, the state Republican party was not in very good shape. After the 1991 gubernatorial election, the party was in shambles.

Duke attacked blacks for holding to the wrong values . . .

What is Duke's message? Susan Howell and Sylvia Warren identify the content of his appeal as "symbolic racism," a campaign theme used nationwide. Howell and Warren, in examining public opinion and voting preferences in District 81 and the surrounding area, show that support for David Duke rests on the symbolic racism that worked for Republican candidates throughout the 1980s. It worked for several candidates in the U.S. Senate contest in Louisiana. Symbolic racism blames blacks for cultural failure—the lack of an appropriate work ethic—using themes that are at once racist and embodiments of traditional American folk culture, including populism. The appeals of Duke in District 81 have worked, and will work, elsewhere. Although voters have additional reasons to support or oppose him, the core appeal is symbolic racism. This is the current version of right-wing populism among white voters. It differs from the segregationist themes of a quarter century ago in its stress on culture rather than genetics.

. . . whereas he used to attack blacks for carrying the wrong genes.

Symbolic racism is at odds with the message David Duke first espoused. Lance Hill shows that Duke, when not on the campaign trail, proclaimed a different type of racism, the genetic racism embraced by Adolf Hitler. Duke's Nazism goes beyond wearing a uniform or lighting birthday cakes for Hitler —it is an ideology. Hill's analysis of the place of Nazi race doctrine in Duke's political thought shows just how essential racism has been to Duke's thinking and appeal. Even if his voters are responding to a modern symbolic racism, Duke himself has espoused genetic racism from the beginning. Hill,

by comparing Hitler's speeches from his preofficial days with Duke's publications, demonstrates a similarity of concept and program. Ironically, he
shows Duke as truest to Nazism in his use of symbolic racism to acquire
political power, the opportunistic tactic that Hitler employed in Nazism's
electoral period.

Duke found an audience for his new message . . .

How do voters get the revised message? Gary Esolen recounts the success
of television in winning support for David Duke. Duke was successful because he created a technique of attention getting and message delivery that
exploited weaknesses in TV news coverage. Esolen shows that Duke uses
controversy to get media attention, then delivers the message to his audience.
Controversy attracts television coverage, which, in turn, gives Duke an audience. Ignoring Duke does not work either, as that leaves his message
unchallenged. Esolen, a former talk-show host, also reviews the difficulties
most interviewers have with David Duke and explains why a few questioners
have been successful.

. . . because political elites couldn't make up their minds what to do.

William McMahon's report of the legislature's response to David Duke
indicates a less-than-heroic grappling with the issues. Republican leadership,
television editors, and the legislature all were ineffective in handling Duke.
Duke provoked controversy in the legislature from the first day, but the
members largely tried to treat him as just another representative. McMahon
points out that, in the end, David Duke severely polarized the state House
along racial lines, something that body had never previously experienced.
While Duke was not an accomplished policymaker, he was an accomplished
newsmaker. He also took the heat for legislators with similar views.

If the political elites—who, in some models of American politics, protect
us from the weaknesses of the mass mind—were vulnerable to Duke's appeals, how about the voters?

Supporters liked his message, opponents didn't like his past.

Douglas Rose examines the many explanations offered for white voter
reactions to Duke's U.S. Senate campaign and finds them all true in part. But
the main division is simple. According to Rose, the contrast between Duke's
past associations and views and his current positions is central to support and
opposition. In the Senate race Duke split the electorate into ardent factions,
supporters upholding his positions on issues and opponents condemning his
Klan background. The issue became Duke himself, and it was difficult to
change views about him once they were formed. If Duke appealed to voters

before opponents had a chance to communicate facts about his background, he won support.

Voters, the press, the party, the policymakers, and his opponents did not know what to do about David Duke . . .

In the Louisiana gubernatorial election of 1991, Duke and former governor Edwards defeated the Republican incumbent Roemer. Douglas Rose and Gary Esolen show that the media and the opposing candidates largely kept quiet about Duke's past in the primary campaign, during which Duke successfully targeted supporters with his direct mail appeals. In the nationally covered runoff, anti-Duke sentiment carried Edwards to a landslide victory. Yet the media coverage helped launch Duke's 1992 candidacy for the Republican presidential nomination.

. . . and uncertainties remain.

Ronald King reexamines the questions animating this study: Is Duke a Louisiana oddity or part of a national phenomenon? Are Duke's supporters racists? Are television newscasters dupes? Does the electorate learn from press coverage of the candidates? As King points out, the chapters do not contain everything we might wish to know about the David Duke phenomenon. Even the central, consensual points—Duke is not an isolated phenomenon, Louisiana's response is not unique, and political elites do not handle Duke well in their normal routines—leave question marks. This is not everything there is to know; it is what we know now.

Ferrel Guillory

1 | David Duke in Southern Context

On the day after David Duke's fourteenth birthday, President Lyndon Baines Johnson signed the Civil Rights Act of 1964. "I think we just delivered the South to the Republican Party for a long time to come," White House aide Joseph A. Califano, Jr., recorded Johnson as saying on the evening of the signing ceremony.[1] As clearly as anyone, LBJ saw that his presidential signature on that law would send long-lasting political ripples across the South.

Only months later, the teenaged Duke made his first visit to the New Orleans Citizens Council office and began his odyssey through the American far right. Twenty-five years later, as a Republican, he would hold a state legislative seat in Louisiana from a major metropolitan area, pose a powerful challenge to a veteran U.S. senator who exemplified the modern South, and contribute to unseating an incumbent Democratic-turned-Republican governor.

Especially from beyond the Louisiana state line, it is tempting to see Duke's emergence—however long it eventually lasts—as yet another manifestation of the state's penchant for political idiosyncrasy. But Louisiana exceptionalism represents only one dimension of many in the explanation of why Duke has become a political factor in late twentieth-century America.

David Duke is, to be sure, a Louisiana product. He was reared mostly in its largest city. He studied at its flagship university, whose campus he used as a forum for articulating his radical views. And ballots cast by Louisiana voters made him a public officeholder. But while Duke is a Louisiana boy, he is also an example of a broadly national phenomenon. From time to time, the United States has seen radical-right movements and personalities flash on the scene like shooting stars. Duke serves as a reminder of forces that can be set loose when the center does not hold.

Duke is something else, too. He is an outgrowth of the stresses and strains felt in the wake of an extraordinary era of change in the states of the old Confederacy. The search for a full, multidimensional explanation of how it was possible for Duke to have become a political force in Louisiana leads through old byways and new thoroughfares of the American South.

The Changing South

The South's passage into a postdesegregation era took place amid powerful social and economic forces that both lifted many southerners up and left many behind. These forces helped create a remarkable period of political growing up. But change brought a certain instability as well—an instability that Duke has exploited.

Currently, the South manifests itself as two Souths—that is, dual realities, contrasting, yet genuinely southern. "Shadows in the Sunbelt," a report issued in May 1986 by a group of southerners, identified two economic Souths—a booming urban South and a declining rural South.[2] Culturally, too, there are the Souths of rootedness and rootlessness—the South that looks behind and the South that looks ahead, the South of illiteracy and the South of learning, the South that elects Jesse Helms and Strom Thurmond and the South that elects Terry Sanford and Dale Bumpers. After decades of what C. Vann Woodward described as "daily change of the 'unchangeable,'" the South now presents itself as a landscape of change—of sunlight and shadows, of growth and stagnation, of progress and alienation.[3]

Immense change was already under way when LBJ put his signature to antidiscrimination legislation in 1964 and again in 1965. As C. Vann Woodward wrote:

In the 1940s the South suddenly entered a period of nearly three decades filled with more shocks of discontinuity than any period of its history, with the possible exception of the 1860s. Part of them are caught in the familiar litany—cotton moving west, cattle moving east, blacks moving north, Yankees moving south, everybody moving to town, and towns and industries growing faster than ever before. Old monuments of continuity disappeared in rapid succession: one-party politics, one-crop agriculture, one-horse farmers, the white primary, the poll tax, Jim Crow signs, disenfranchisement laws. Out they went. In their place came the Brown decision in 1954 against segregated schools, the Civil Rights movement and black nationalism, the collapse of massive resistance, and at the demand of a Southerner in the White House a new and comprehensive Civil Rights Act and a Voting Rights Act.[4]

From the mid-1960s to the 1990s, the South felt even more "shocks of discontinuity": blacks moved back south, small-town southerners moved to southern cities, city dwellers moved to the suburbs, cities grew cosmopolitan and their roads became clogged, low-wage manufacturing moved offshore, oil prices moved—up and down—at the bidding of Middle Eastern sheiks, and more and more southerners moved into services. This was the southern experience because it was the American experience. Yet in the South it was a more dramatic break with the past, more of a change.

Further political "discontinuity" followed the voting rights law, which parted the curtains of the ballot machines for millions of blacks and opened the doors to public office for thousands of them. Almost all black voters entered the Democratic party; as they did so, millions of white voters departed, some converting outright to become Republicans, many others drifting about in an I-vote-for-the-person independence. At historically breathtaking speed, the "solid South" of the Democratic party was replaced by the South that gave Republicans a "lock" on the electoral college.

The New South—For a Moment

For a time it seemed that the dissolution of white-Democratic, one-party rule would permit the flowering of refreshing, reformist politics that could be carried out by both Democrats and Republicans. Hints of new possibilities came in the 1960 election of Democratic governors Leroy Collins in Florida and Terry Sanford in North Carolina, who sought to turn their states away from racial segregation and "fergit, hell" politics. In 1966 Arkansas rejected a segregationist Democratic candidate and elected Republican Winthrop Rockefeller governor. And in 1969 Virginia turned away from the Byrd machine and elected a Republican governor, A. Linwood Holton, who took his daughter Tayloe by the hand into a desegregated public school.

And yet, as President Johnson accurately sensed, the liberation of both black and white southerners from the shackles of segregation did not put the region on quite the political path that the civil rights movement and its Democratic allies wished. Though Johnson won a full presidential term in a national landslide in 1964, his Republican opponent, Arizona senator Barry Goldwater, carried Mississippi, Alabama, Georgia, South Carolina, and Louisiana. In every former Confederate state except Texas, Goldwater won a majority of the votes of whites.[5]

In a 1961 speech in Atlanta—well before the signing of the Voting Rights Act and well before Richard Nixon's "Southern strategy"—Goldwater signaled that the Republican party would seek to build itself up in the region by targeting white voters. "We're not going to get the Negro vote as a bloc in 1964 and 1968," he said, "so we ought to go hunting where the ducks are."[6] Through much of the 1960s, Alabama governor George C. Wallace gave voice to white resistance to pressure for racial change, running for president both as a Democrat and as a third-party candidate. In doing so, he influenced southern and national politics. As a third-party presidential candidate in 1968, Wallace won the electoral votes of five Deep South states. His candidacy served to loosen further the ties of white southerners to the Democratic party. Then, in 1972, Republican Richard Nixon swept the South as he won the presidency in a landslide. His victory was accompanied by the election of six southern Republican senators, including the hard-right Helms of North Carolina.

Before and after Watergate, which interrupted the Republican surge in the South, the region experienced another kind of surge in the 1970s. In state after state, moderate-to-progressive Democrats won governorships on the strength of biracial coalitions. The nation hailed these New South governors: Reuben O. Askew in Florida, James B. Hunt, Jr., in North Carolina, John C. West and Richard Riley in South Carolina, William Winter in Mississippi, Dale Bumpers in Arkansas, and Jimmy Carter in Georgia, who after one term as governor went on to bring the South back into the Democratic fold when he won the presidency in 1976.

Louisiana, too, was touched by the trend. When the Democratic gubernatorial primary in 1971 ended up with Edwin Edwards, J. Bennett Johnston, and Gillis Long as the top three candidates—each of whom played down racial divisiveness and played up economic development—the state was galvanized with a sense that it had made a break with the past. Edwards defeated Johnston in a runoff and became governor with a strong political base among blacks, Cajuns, and those whites who were ready to have Louisiana participate in the New South then ablooming. A constitutional convention produced a new, short and snappy, state constitution, which the voters adopted.

But time and troubles eroded this progressive spirit, not only in Louisiana but also across the region. Hardly anyone talks or writes these days about a "New South." The Carter presidency, buffeted by inflation and Iran, lasted only one term. Edwards, though winning three terms as Louisiana's governor, fell victim to the collapse of an oil-driven economy and dwindling public confidence in his personal integrity. In South Carolina, a Democratic party that produced two New South governors in the 1970s practically disintegrated in the second half of the 1980s.

Two-party competition did not bring the South the burst of creativity from a clash of ideas that its proponents hoped. Instead, the South shifted not so much from a one-party system to a two-party system as from a weak-party system to a weaker-parties system. It succumbed to image-conscious, television-oriented politics—and it even helped give birth to the modern brand of negative, personal-attack campaigning. By the presidential elections in the 1980s, the region had become reliably Republican. In statewide, congressional, and legislative elections, the South's voters frequently turned to Republicans, more often to Democrats, even more often to incumbents. State-level Democrats proved resilient, especially in nonpresidential election years.

In the Vacuum, Distrust and Embarrassment

The South was no longer fertile ground for world-class demagogues. By the end of the eighties, said Roy Reed, a writer and journalist based in Arkansas, there were only "small pockets of demagoguery" to be found. "In an exhaustive survey of the old Confederacy, conducted as the sap was rising this spring and politics was approaching the boil, not a single Southern demagogue of national stature could be found," Reed wrote just before the 1988 Democratic National Convention in Atlanta. "Not only is demagoguery on the ropes, but there has been a general blanding of the politics of the South."[7]

Along with that "blanding" has come a void in leadership. No mourning is now heard for the passing of demagoguery. But, as the South heads toward the twenty-first century, change seems to have outpaced the ability of the South's politicians and institutions to cope with it. Stalemate abounds. Where is the strong, compelling leadership that defines issues and points the way to a better future? Why do so many southerners still feel uneasy about their state and local governments—even finding themselves faintly embarrassed by their politics and politicians?

The South, to be sure, has no monopoly on alienation. The "American electorate . . . presents a disquieting picture of political gridlock," said a report on the findings of a massive national public opinion survey in 1990. "Despite the popularity of President Bush, cynicism toward the political system in general is growing as the public in unprecedented numbers associates Republicans with wealth and greed, Democrats with fecklessness and incompetence."[8] But if there is a place where political alienation is especially intense, it is Louisiana. A loud echo of the national poll findings rings out from a post-1990 election survey that found that 52 percent of white Louisianians say they are not represented well in government. "David Duke's Senate candidacy," pollster Geoffrey Garin wrote, "was played out against a backdrop of broad political discontent. Indeed, voters' feelings of political alienation were a far better predictor of support for Duke than their feelings of economic hardship."[9]

Economics and Race in the Post–New South

If alienation is fundamental to explaining late twentieth-century American —and southern—politics, it is also necessary to look at economic stress and racial friction. When his polltakers asked Louisiana whites to explain what their representatives in Washington should be doing better, Garin found a substantial outpouring of sentiment in favor of protecting the middle class and reflecting its values. "The single most important cause of voters' political alienation is a very strongly held perception that government is no longer concerned about the needs of middle class people," Garin asserted. "While racial considerations were clearly part of David Duke's appeal, the racial issues raised by Duke hold a secondary place at best in voters' own definition of what it means to be 'for the middle class.' "[10]

As Earl and Merle Black have explained, it was one thing for the South to penetrate the "outer color line," but it has been another thing for the South to confront the "intermediate color line." The outer line buckled under the weight of legislation and court decisions that gave blacks legal access to public accommodations, schools, and the ballot box. The inner line, in the Blacks' analysis, marks personal black-white relations. The intermediate line forms a zone of friction, producing controversies over schools, jobs, and housing. It is a zone in which blacks and whites perceive themselves in competition over reaching and climbing the ladder of success. It is the zone in which David Duke operates. "Vast differences in the living conditions and socioeconomic status of blacks as a group and whites as a group provide abundant material for bitter and protracted interracial conflicts," the Blacks wrote.[11]

It has been widely recognized that in the 1980s the gap between rich and poor widened. But what is especially significant—well documented but perhaps less recognized—is the economic stagnation afflicting the American middle class that developed from the mid-1970s to the mid-1980s. Frank Levy, a professor of public affairs at the University of Maryland, has explored this phenomenon extensively. Levy divided the years since World War II into two economic eras. The first, running from the end of the war to 1973, featured steady expansion in inflation-adjusted wages. Most Americans had reason to believe that they could advance beyond their parents economically. But from 1973 to 1985, said Levy, inflation-adjusted wages stagnated. "This stagnation," he wrote, "has led to a kind of quiet depression that is responsible for many of our current problems." And, he added, "there is a rapidly increasing inequality of prospects, an inequality in the chance that a family will enjoy the middle-class dream."[12]

Friction at the intermediate color line, middle-class economic stagnation, public alienation and faltering leadership, weak political parties, and a generation of discontinuities—all of these provide the context for today's southern politics and help account for the emergence of David Duke. If Louisiana is different, it is more in degree than in kind: middle-class economic stagnation was exacerbated by the plunge in the oil industry, and racial friction intensified from deep divisions between city and suburbs, especially in the New Orleans metropolitan area, as the city became predominantly black and as white flight drove suburban growth. Louisiana also exemplifies the weakness of political parties with its open primary system, in which all candidates run, regardless of party. Such a system does not permit parties to deflect a Duke-type insurgency.

Parties and the Future

However unlikely it is that Duke would win the sanction of a mainstream party, his candidacies surely raise questions for—and challenges to—the Republican and Democratic parties. How the two major parties respond to those questions and challenges will go a long way toward shaping the future, both of the South and the nation.

The growth of the Republican party in the South has been fueled by many factors. The southern GOP entered its modern era composed only of Civil War–era mountain Republicans and post-office Republicans (the small band awaiting patronage when its party won the White House). To that base the party has recently added immigrants from the North, religious fundamentalists, and southern suburbanites, professionals, and businessmen for whom

President Ronald Reagan's antigovernment, antitax, and antiregulatory policies had strong appeal. But it is an inescapable fact of history that the Republican party surged in the South also by willingly serving as a vehicle for white resistance and disaffection. Sim A. Delapp, a Lexington, North Carolina, attorney who was active in Republican campaigns from 1920 to 1966 and who has since died, put it to me bluntly in a 1973 interview: "The leadership hasn't brought this party to where it is now. I can tell you what's brought it—and any man that knows politics knows. The race question brought it. The Democratic Party leaned toward the liberals and the dissident elements of the population so much that North Carolinians got tired of it and came over to us."

"Exploiting racial fears and hostilities of white voters became a key factor in building a Republican majority in the South," Thomas B. Edsall wrote in the *Washington Post* obituary of Lee Atwater, a South Carolinian who rose to the chairmanship of the Republican party.[13] In 1988 Willie Horton, a black criminal, became a powerful symbolic weapon hurled by Republicans against Democratic presidential candidate Michael Dukakis. When President George Bush vetoed an antidiscrimination bill in 1990, he tagged it "quota" legislation. (In November 1991, in the wake of Duke's showing in the Louisiana governor's race, the Republican president signed into law a similar bill.) In 1990, in North Carolina as well as Louisiana, Senate contests featured race-tinged themes. A Jesse Helms campaign commercial depicting a white worker being rejected for a job as a result of a racial quota put into video much the same message that David Duke delivered in words. Even more than the Louisiana campaign, the North Carolina contest illustrated the two Souths: the Republican Helms, a longtime foe of the civil rights movement and its legislative goals, versus Democrat Harvey B. Gantt, the first black student at Clemson University who later was elected the first black mayor of Charlotte.

Before being stricken with the cancer that eventually took his life, Atwater proclaimed a Republican policy of seeking greater black participation and support, and the national party orchestrated an effort to banish David Duke from its midst. Nevertheless, in the context of recent history, Duke was following a well-worn path in selecting the Republican party. The GOP's alternative to Duke in the state legislative race was John Treen, himself a switchover from the old States' Rights party. And, while national Republicans have sought to push Duke away, many Louisiana Republicans have treated him more gingerly. Duke puts southern Republicans face-to-face with a moral challenge: Do they persist in seeking political advantage from lingering racial disharmonies, or do they turn their energies to healing wounds and thus remaking the South?

For the Democratic party, the persistent dilemma is this: How can it remain loyal to its progressive values and still reach out to the middle class, to the growing suburbs of the South? This dilemma, of course, has a racial dimension; white southern voters have turned away from the Democratic party because it has become the principal vehicle for black participation and advocacy in politics and government. But the challenge is not only how to hold together a biracial coalition; it is also whether Democrats reconnect to the middle class both economically and culturally.

Ever since Richard Nixon tarred George McGovern in 1972 as the candidate of the three As—amnesty, acid, and abortion—the public has seen the Democrats at least as much through Republicans' eyes as through the Democrats' own. Even when Democrats nominated sons of ministers, like McGovern and Walter Mondale, for the presidency, the party came off as aloof from religion and from mainstream values. In North Carolina, for example, the Helms "white-hands" commercial surely had an effect, principally in driving up white voter turnout. But the election-day exit poll by Voter Research and Surveys provided evidence that other factors were at work. Helms led his black opponent, according to the exit poll, by a 59–41 margin among voters describing themselves as regular churchgoers.

While professing, rightly, their belief in pluralism, in the great American right to believe what you want to believe, Democrats have often been squeamish about talking about religion, about what they as individuals believe about right and wrong. While professing their dedication to the rights embedded in the Constitution, Democrats have often left the impression that they do not care enough about personal safety, about the drug menace, about the nagging insecurity fostered by crime. David Duke says that hard work is better than welfare. Surely Democrats can meet the challenge of showing themselves both compassionate to the poor and dedicated to fostering the basic values and aspirations of the middle class.

The Louisiana poll by Geoffrey Garin speaks directly to Democrats, saying that their "failure to fulfill their historic role as champions of the middle class created the opening for Duke's success."[14] He has pointed Democrats toward filling the vacuum that Duke has sought to occupy, and he detects an opening for progressive politicians. While Garin's focus is on Louisiana Democrats, his message has broader implications.

As a result of civil rights protests, court rulings, acts of Congress, and Lyndon Johnson's signature, de jure segregation has ceased to exist. And yet the South remains a place in which some of America's most sensitive frictions—racial, religious, cultural, and economic—are played out. While David Duke has sought to exploit those frictions, his success casts light on

them. Examining Duke the phenomenon—as well as the successes and failures of political, governmental, media, and other institutions in dealing with
it—leads to a deeper understanding of the forces and attitudes at work in
southern politics. As paradoxical as it might seem, understanding why so
many Louisianians voted for Duke may well contain lessons about how to
bring about a reassertion of the progressive spirit in the South.

The potential for progressive politics in the South indeed can be uncovered
anew. The antidote to Dukedom is leadership—leadership that restores confidence that government stands on the side of families struggling to make ends
meet, leadership that focuses on education and opportunity, leadership that is
laden with values and understands the culture, and leadership that offers a
sense of hope for the future.

NOTES

1. Califano, "Tough Talk for Democrats."
2. MDC Panel on Rural Economic Development.
3. Woodward, *Thinking Back*, 68.
4. Ibid.
5. Grantham, *Life and Death of the Solid South*, 161.
6. Quoted in Bass and DeVries, *Transformation of Southern Politics*, 27.
7. Reed, "Southern Demagogue," 76.
8. Times Mirror Center, "The People, the Press, and Politics 1990."
9. Garin, "How 'It Can't Happen Here' Almost Happened in Louisiana," p. 2 of executive summary.
10. Ibid., p. 3.
11. Black and Black, *Politics and Society in the South*, 152–71 (quotation, 170).
12. Levy, *Dollars and Dreams*, 4, 6.
13. *Washington Post*, March 30, 1991, A1, Final edition.
14. Garin, "How 'It Can't Happen Here' Almost Happened in Louisiana," p. 7 of executive summary.

REFERENCES

Bass, Jack, and Walter DeVries. *The Transformation of Southern Politics*. New York: Basic Books, 1976.
Black, Earl, and Merle Black. *Politics and Society in the South*. Cambridge: Harvard University Press, 1987.
Califano, Joseph A., Jr. "Tough Talk for Democrats." *New York Times Magazine*, January 8, 1989, 28–29, 38, 43.

Garin, Geoffrey. "How 'It Can't Happen Here' Almost Happened in Louisiana: A Study of the David Duke Phenomenon in the 1990 Senate Race." Garin-Hart Strategic Research Group of Washington report to the Center for National Policy, Washington, D.C., March 1991.

Grantham, Dewey W. *The Life and Death of the Solid South*. Lexington: University Press of Kentucky, 1988.

Levy, Frank. *Dollars and Dreams: The Changing American Income Distribution*. New York: Russell Sage Foundation, 1987.

MDC Panel on Rural Economic Development, MDC Inc., Chapel Hill, N.C. "Shadows in the Sunbelt." Report, May 1986.

Reed, Roy. "The Southern Demagogue: Death of a Breed." In *The Prevailing South: Life and Politics in a Changing Culture*, edited by Dudley Clendinen, 24–27. Atlanta: Longstreet Press, 1988. Originally printed as *Decision '88, the Prevailing South*, Atlanta Journal/Atlanta Constitution, July 18, 1988.

Times Mirror Center for the People and the Press. "The People, the Press, and Politics 1990." September 19, 1990.

Woodward, C. Vann. *Thinking Back: The Perils of Writing History*. Baton Rouge: Louisiana State University Press, 1986.

Lawrence N. Powell

2 | Slouching toward Baton Rouge

The 1989 Legislative
Election of David Duke

Attracting worldwide news coverage, David Duke's 1989 election
to the state legislature from the New Orleans suburb of Metairie encouraged
the media myth that Louisiana's exotic politics have little relevance for the
rest of the nation. That was a reassuring thought for distant observers accustomed to viewing racial politics as peculiarly southern. But the late Walker
Percy, who lived across Lake Pontchartrain from New Orleans, came closer
to the mark: "If I had anything to say to people outside the state," he told a
New York Times reporter, "I'd tell them, 'Don't make the mistake of thinking
David Duke is a unique phenomenon confined to Louisiana rednecks and
yahoos. He's not. He's not just appealing to the old Klan constituency, he's
appealing to the white middle class. And don't think that he or somebody like
him won't appeal to the white middle class of Chicago or Queens.' "[1]

As this chapter and later research will show, Percy's warning is well taken.
Duke won because he was able to add a substantial segment of his district's
white middle class to his blue-collar base. The conjunction of declining
income, growing political cynicism, and intensifying racial polarization in-

clined those voters to embrace an insurgent alternative to politics-as-usual. Duke became the preferred protest candidate because of his ability to convince angry whites that blacks were the source of their problems, which enabled him to deflect old-fashioned Longism into the channels of reactionary populism.

By reawakening the furies of racism, Duke has disrupted the New Deal party alignments that tenuously emerged in Louisiana following the civil rights movement. And because the forces driving Duke's political movement —declining living standards, voter cynicism, fear of crime—reflect national trends, the lesson of his legislative victory is that it could happen elsewhere.

Duke, the Far Right, and the Media

Duke ran in a special election to fill the vacancy in House District 81 created when the four-term incumbent moved on to a state judgeship. In Louisiana's open primary system, the top two vote getters, regardless of party, go into a runoff in the event no candidate fails to receive a majority ballot. Duke surprised everyone by coming in first with one-third of the votes in the January 21 primary. (Local pollsters as recently as Christmas had him running a distant third among seven candidates.)[2] His opponent was John Treen, a local home builder and brother of David Treen, the first Republican governor in Louisiana since Reconstruction. Both Duke, who established residency in the district after the official filing deadline, and Treen ran as Republicans. After a campaign based on attacks on affirmative action, on objections to forced integration, and on the need to curtail the growth of the black "underclass," Duke emerged triumphant.

The runoff on February 18, 1989, was exceedingly close. Out of nearly 17,000 ballots cast, Duke eked out a 227-vote victory, a 50.7–49.3 percent margin. The turnout was extraordinary. Almost eight out of every ten (77.8 percent) registered voters trekked to the polling places that day. Not even the presidential election three months earlier, or the heated governor's race of 1987, had aroused as much voter interest in the Eighty-first.

Duke made a handsome, poised, almost picture-perfect candidate. Long before the primary, the surgically transformed, well-groomed former grand wizard of the Knights of the Ku Klux Klan had turned in his hood for a pinstriped suit, moved his rallies from the cornfields to hotel meeting rooms, and abandoned the Klan for a "white rights" organization he had founded in 1981 called the National Association for the Advancement of White People (NAAWP). The candidate's new look was in keeping with the far right's attempt to mainstream its movement through the channels of electoral poli-

Contact sheet of Duke photographs for campaign material in 1989 election, Louisiana House of Representatives. (Courtesy of Jackson Hill)

tics, a tactical shift that Duke himself had helped to pioneer. Yet even his Republican credentials were part of a quick political makeover. He had run as a registered Democrat in the 1988 presidential primaries, then as an Independent in the general election on the right-wing Populist party ticket in eleven states; he finally changed his registration to Republican to run in the special election in House District 81.[3]

Duke's agenda, as expressed in the *NAAWP News*, belies his appearance as a mainstream conservative politician, however. Philosophically a National Socialist who has never wavered in the racist belief that culture and character come from genes, Duke—whether as a Republican, Populist, or Democrat—wants to create a "White Christian Republic." His goal is to build a social movement, not merely advance a political career. The media, which might have been expected to make some capital of all this, did not. Expecting to find a frothing racist, national reporters were thrown off guard by the pat answers Duke had fine-tuned during years on the electronic talk-show circuit. When pressed to explain his extremist past—which included parading in a Nazi uniform with a sign calling for the gassing of the Chicago Seven—Duke smilingly attributed his behavior to the follies of youth, and it stuck. Meanwhile, the local daily, the New Orleans *Times-Picayune*, covered a nonstory about a one-man crusade by a New York Jewish activist to derail Duke's campaign. Almost as if to compensate for a failure of investigative journalism, commentators and columnists from around the country found it easy to discount Duke's election as a localized resurgence of the Klan. It became simply more political entertainment from America's northernmost Banana Republic.[4]

But this is a profound misreading of the meaning of Duke's political breakthrough, based on the false assumption that his voters were old-fashioned racists. They look a lot like white suburbanites elsewhere.

Racism and the Eighty-first District

Duke's appeal to white resentments against racial preferences was unchanged. Ten years earlier, while still in the Klan, he had run for the state Senate from a district that overlapped House District 81, and his platform was the spitting image of the one he stood on in 1989: stop reverse discrimination, encourage welfare mothers to have fewer children, end forced busing, replace welfare with workfare, and so on. Duke ran second to a popular incumbent who won reelection outright in the first primary. He polled only 26 percent of the vote—roughly the proportion of the district's electorate that had moved to Jefferson Parish during the 1960s and 1970s to escape integration in New Orleans. This "white flight" population forms a strong base in a House district that is practically the political equivalent of a bar of Ivory soap (99.6 percent white). And, as the strong positive correlation in Figure 2.1 clearly indicates, Duke had no trouble holding on to that vote in the primary leg of his 1989 race for the House seat.[5] But why was he able to expand beyond his consolidated base during the runoff?

It is only partly because Duke got rid of his sheets and retailored his image to suit 1990 fashions. The makeover admittedly made him more palatable to white suburbanites who, even in the Deep South, today reject the *overt* racial extremism of the segregationist past. (As a University of New Orleans poll conducted shortly after Duke's election showed, the racial attitudes of white Jeffersonians mirror the nation's in accepting racial equality in principle but opposing implementation measures like affirmative action.)[6] But something is also inclining those same voters to flirt with *covert* racial extremism. That is the meaning of the "hidden vote" Duke has received in nearly every election since 1989: it comes from whites who want to cast a racial protest ballot in spite of contemporary sanctions against openly expressing antiblack views. Duke's recent electoral breakthrough probably has less to do with changes in Duke than in the white electorate.[7]

Although there is now a broad consensus for the principle of black equality, white racial attitudes have definitely hardened during the Reagan-Bush era. Duke is the beneficiary of twenty years of Republican bottom fishing for Wallace votes. Relentless Republican attacks against affirmative action as "reverse discrimination" have conditioned whites to believe they have legitimate grievances against black people and the federal agencies championing their interests. Suggested by the 1968 and 1972 third-party bids of then Alabama governor George Wallace, these themes of the "southern strategy" have helped the GOP build a top-down presidential majority favoring the wealthy by siphoning votes from the low-status New Deal coalition. Race was the wedge that disrupted Democratic solidarity, converting Wallace Democrats into Nixon, Reagan, and Bush Democrats. Antipoverty and affirmative action programs pitted southern populists and blue-collar ethnics against the black community. Conservatives exploited racial resentments to make "liberal elites" and big government, rather than big business, the new target for right-leaning populist ire.[8] That intensifying sense of racial grievance among whites lent legitimacy to Duke's pseudo-egalitarian slogan of "equal rights for all, special privileges for none."

Heightened anxieties concerning black crime in neighboring New Orleans have also hardened white attitudes in suburban Jefferson. Parish politicos have been quick to exploit these racial fears for political gain. Two years prior to Duke's election, Sheriff Harry Lee, a Chinese-American who had cast

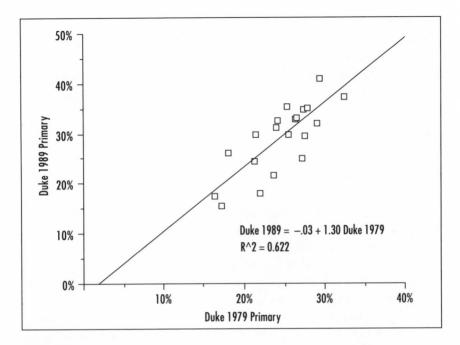

Duke 1989 = −.03 + 1.30 Duke 1979
R^2 = 0.622

Figure 2.1
Support for Duke in the 1979 and 1989 Legislative Primaries

himself in the image of a good old boy, made national headlines by ordering his deputies to pull over blacks driving through white neighborhoods in "rinky-dink cars." Under fire for allowing a white convicted rapist to roam the parish as a trustee, Lee won reelection by a landslide after issuing the directive. Not to be outdone, the Jefferson Parish council dealt with a local crime wave by barricading two streets connecting a black neighborhood in New Orleans and a white working-class Jefferson community, only to have the city's black mayor, Sidney Barthelemy, make a great fanfare of tearing the roadblocks down.[9] This linkage in voters' minds between race and crime received powerful reinforcement, of course, from the 1988 Bush campaign commercials about black rapist Willie Horton.

Racial tensions were close to the surface by the time of Duke's legislative election. Midway through the campaign they exploded when black teenage rowdies disrupted a downtown New Orleans Martin Luther King Day march by assaulting white onlookers and smashing storefront windows. Television cameras captured the violence for a local news audience already made fearful by nightly stories of a spreading epidemic of crack-related murders in New Orleans's poorer black communities.[10]

As racial tensions were rising locally, permissions to scapegoat African-

Americans continued to pour in from Washington. The latest authorization arrived just after the turn of the year and right in the midst of the Duke campaign, when the Supreme Court handed down its sweeping ruling against minority set-asides in *Richmond v. Croson*. Asked by a radio reporter about charges that he was a white supremacist masquerading as a traditional conservative, Duke coolly answered, "If I'm a racist, then so is the United States Supreme Court."[11] For a candidate who symbolized white racial fears and resentments, the timing of current events seemed like manna from heaven: first, a sensationalized outburst of black violence reminiscent of the urban riots of the sixties; then, a controversial decision suggesting that blacks were receiving unfair advantages.

As one Duke supporter explained to a *Times-Picayune* columnist at the height of the campaign, "We need him now. . . . We have to send a message to the blacks."[12] But, again, the messenger was the message. That is the only plausible rationale for choosing an ex-Klansman to send a signal that any Republican conservative could transmit just as easily. Analysts who argue that Duke's past hurts his electoral chances overlook that his extremist history ironically renders him a more powerful voice for "white people" than anyone without his baggage could possibly become. His Klan antecedents, as his finance manager later observed, tell white and black voters alike that "he means business."

The new recruits to Duke's 1989 "white rights" campaign came from Metairie's bungalow belt, the blue-collar and lower white-collar neighborhoods in the Eighty-first District. But their newfound readiness to embrace a symbol of racial extremism was only partly due to Republican racial policies. Republican economic policies that have helped shift wealth and opportunity upward played an important part in preparing the ground for Duke's racist insurgency.

Social and Political Geography

As recently as the 1940s Jefferson Parish—"da Parish," to old-timers— was largely made up of truck and dairy farms, vestiges of the sugarcane and plantation agriculture that had been economic mainstays since before the Louisiana Purchase. But the coming of oil and gas and suburbanization remade the landscape, and today that portion of the parish encompassed within the Eighty-first could stand as a microcosm of the new, middle-class South that emerged following World War II. Most residents earn their living as technicians, salespersons, and service industry workers. There is also a substantial concentration of blue-collar workers. The only unusual thing

Table 2.1

Median Family Income and Occupational Structure in District 81,
Jefferson Parish, and Louisiana, 1980

	District 81	Jefferson	Louisiana
Median Family Income			
All precincts	$21,108	$22,875	$18,088
Poorest precincts	$13,750	NA	NA
Richest precincts	$37,500	NA	NA
Occupations			
Managers	16.0%	13.4%	9.6%
Professionals	15.5	11.8	11.7
Technical/sales	39.7	37.7	29.9
Services	8.7	8.6	13.7
Crafts	12.0	16.1	16.1
Operators/laborers	8.1	12.5	18.9

Source: U.S. Bureau of the Census, *1980 Census of Population and Housing . . . : Louisiana*
(Washington, D.C.: GPO, 1982).

about the community is its many professionals and managers.[13] They bulk larger in the social structure than blue-collar workers, reversing the usual occupational distribution within the state at large. (See Table 2.1.)

The residential areas bordering the posh Metairie Country Club along the district's southern boundary are some of the most affluent neighborhoods in the metropolitan area. Partners of downtown New Orleans law firms, local manufacturers, wealthy physicians, and big developers live in baronial splendor along its tree-shaded lanes. Near Lake Pontchartrain to the north lies the old fishing village of Bucktown, well known for its oyster houses. In between sprawls a crazy-quilt pattern of apartment complexes for young singles, clapboard bungalows owned by skilled craft workers, and the Levittownish Creole cottages (in brick, not cypress) of salesmen, technicians, and lower-level administrators. About 61 percent of the residents are homeowners. One marks his social bearings according to whether pleasure boats or shrimping trawlers are parked in the driveway.[14]

Older than the parish's zoning code, the "Old" Metairie section of the district dates back to the 1940s, when Jefferson was a rural enclave notorious for wide-open gambling. Some residential streets still have backyard chicken coops. Mom-and-pop Italian grocery stores stand on several corners, often but a stone's throw from working-class taverns and auto repair shops more commonly seen along seedy Airline Highway (where Jimmy Swaggart was caught sinning in one of the strip's no-tell motels). Grandfathered in as "nonconforming uses," these symbols of an older middle- and working-class community are today being crowded by the upscale home building under way on the fringes of the district's wealthier neighborhoods.

And it is a community of sharp economic contrasts. The median family income of white Jeffersonians as of 1980 was slightly less than $23,000. That is about what it was for the Eighty-first in 1989 ($21,108). Yet the district has some voting precincts where the median income is almost double the parish average.[15]

The Eighty-first's social makeup, moreover, has made it a happy hunting ground for Republican vote seekers. To begin with, the large country club element provided party managers a substantial foundation on which to build. To become competitive, all they had to do was add recruits from the growing middle class that has been fueling GOP growth everywhere in the former Confederacy. Sunbelt prosperity has made their job easy. Increasingly wary of federal programs that seemingly offer them few direct benefits, the district's middle-class residents generally incline toward the upper-class view that a family's economic well-being is a matter of individual, not governmental, responsibility—an entrepreneurial outlook that can easily translate into a top-down consensus for limited government and low taxes.[16]

Consequently, the area now comprising District 81 has been reliably Republican for over two decades. Ronald Reagan won smashing victories here in both 1980 and 1984, and George Bush did nearly as well four years later. In David Treen, the district furnished Louisiana with its first Republican congressman since 1888 and its first governor since Reconstruction.[17] Local Democratic incumbents—including Duke's predecessor in Baton Rouge—have made showy demonstrations of changing their affiliation to the Republican party. They have merely been following their constituents into the GOP, which saw its share of registered voters nearly triple during the Reagan presidency (see Table 2.2). In a state where Republicanism has yet to filter much below the presidential level, the Eighty-first stands apart by virtue of its head-to-toe support for GOP candidates—notwithstanding nominal Democratic majorities on the registration rolls.[18]

Buried under the avalanche of Republican voting majorities lies a substratum of Democratic working-class populism. It is thin, however, because of the comparative smallness of the blue-collar base. The best showing by Democratic presidential candidates in recent years was the 31 percent captured by Jimmy Carter in 1976. His votes came preponderantly from precincts with heavy concentrations of craft and semiskilled workers and high school graduates.[19] By 1984 over half of these Democratic voters had

Table 2.2

Republican Registration in District 81, Jefferson Parish, and Louisiana, 1980, 1984, and 1989

	District 81	Jefferson	Louisiana
1980	12.4%	10.6%	7.4%
1984	20.2%	13.0%	11.3%
1989	36.6%	27.4%	17.4%

Source: Registrar's Office, Jefferson Parish.

jumped to Ronald Reagan (see Table 2.3). Charismatic economic populists like Edwin Edwards can still bring these downscale Reagan Democrats back to the fold. But the problem for local Democrats is that there are not very many low-status voters to work with.

Populism itself, parties aside, is a deeply ingrained Louisiana tradition that influences the political expectations of even the state's middle classes. The Bayou State is sui generis in combining a low personal tax burden with an activist government. Blessed with mineral riches, Baton Rouge until recently has been able to offer a wide range of social welfare services and particularized benefits through the Huey Long formula of taxing large oil and gas corporations. Average Louisianians have grown accustomed to having their government furnish jobs for friends and relatives—in the school system, the sheriff's department, the state bureaucracy—plus social welfare benefits if they are poor, or indirect subsidies for private and parochial education (where most of the largely Catholic middle class in southern Louisiana has parked its children) if they are middle-income wage earners. But they are not used to high taxes. Reform governors from Sam H. Jones through David Treen have adapted to this post-Long world by calling not for "limited" but "good" (read: honest and effective) government, and then finding ways to pay for the high level of services that even the middle class has come to regard as a political birthright. Oil and gas companies usually picked up much of the tab.[20]

This redistributive populism, at least on the tax side, has worked out especially well in Jefferson. Long ago the parish earned the sobriquet *The Free State of Jefferson* partly because of the something-for-nothing mentality of its voters. Two successive elected tax assessors, the father-and-son combination of "Big" and "Little" Lawrence Chehardy, have used the "poor man's" homestead exemption first introduced by Huey Long to build a king-making family dynasty on shielding the middle class from property taxes. Largely due to their pressure the homestead exemption, which is now embedded in the state

Table 2.3

Where the 1976 Carter Voters of District 81 Went in 1980 and 1984

1980

Carter voters	69%
Reagan voters	15
Anderson and nonvoters	14

1984

Mondale voters	30%
Reagan voters	66
Nonvoters	3

Source: OLS regression estimates, precinct data.

constitution, covers homes valued at $75,000 or less. Only upper-income residents pay any property tax, but even they pay comparatively minimal rates because their residences are chronically underassessed.[21]

The low-tax culture nourished by the Chehardys has enabled Jefferson Republicans to build their coalition from the top down, welding the country club set together with the broad middle. Conservatives have done this by successfully blending appeals for good government with business-oriented programs of economic development and support for various middle-class entitlements. The practical political result until recently has been a reliable coalition of upper- and middle-income voters on behalf of traditional Republican conservatism. It is a marriage between classes that works smoothly so long as everyone receives a free ride, economic growth continues, and bruising battles do not erupt over who gets what and at whose expense. In the meantime, the district's blue-collar residents have moved in and out of the Republican presidential column, voting for tall-in-the saddle candidates like Ronald Reagan and economic populists like Edwin Edwards.

Enter David Duke

Although nominally a Republican, Duke did not win by assembling the pieces of a traditional Republican coalition. Instead of going from the top down, he built his political base from the bottom up, mixing working-class Democrats with white collarites that he sheared from the lower end of the Republican coalition.[22] Duke's political foundation was Democratic, not

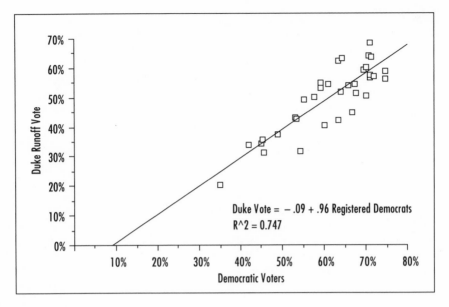

Figure 2.2
Democratic Support for Duke in the 1989 Runoff Election

Republican. Registered Democrats went for Duke, and Republicans went solidly for John Treen, the former governor's brother (see Figure 2.2). The regression equations in Figure 2.2 suggest that, in a district with a three-to-one Republican registration advantage, Duke would have received 15 percent of the vote to Treen's 85 percent, whereas a reversed registration advantage would have meant a 63–37 percent victory for Duke. Moreover—and perhaps not surprising—the Duke vote in 1989 also overlaps that for Jimmy Carter in 1976, Louis Lambert in 1979, Edwin Edwards in 1983, and John Breaux in 1986, the last three of whom carried populist credentials (see Table 2.4). In other words, Duke prevailed partly because of his powerful draw among traditional southern Democratic populists.[23]

All of the elections described in Table 2.4 were extremely polarized, especially the Duke election. For example, according to the regression estimates, Duke received 157 percent of the votes cast for Carter in 1976—or, to state it differently, for every vote received by Carter in that year, Duke received 1.57 votes in 1989. What actually happened is that both the Carter and Duke races were polarized along the same cleavages, except that the Duke election was even more polarized. Suffice it to say that the results indicate a strong overlap in the vote of Duke and the various Democratic candidates.

Table 2.4

*Distribution of the Carter, Lambert, Edwards, and Breaux Voters in the
1989 Legislative Runoff*

	Carter 1976	Lambert 1979	Edwards 1983	Breaux 1986
Duke voters, 1989	157%	139%	125%	170%
Treen voters, 1989	−56	−52	−37	−80
Nonvoters, 1989	2	13	12	10

Source: Regression estimates. The percentages refer to precinct-level voting behavior. That is, they
summarize, not the behavior of individual voters, but the electoral tendencies of precincts composed
of certain voter types. This is one reason for the negative and 100+ percentages. The negative
percentages also indicate a high degree of polarization in all of these elections. This is a statistical
exaggeration of the fact that the Carter electorate was an even stronger Duke electorate.

The district's class divisions mirror these political cleavages. Duke did
extremely well in precincts with large concentrations of skilled blue-collar
workers; analysis of the data indicates that he would have captured all the
votes in an imaginary neighborhood made up entirely of individuals employed in precision production, the crafts, or as repairmen. He also ran
strongly among machine operators, drivers, and fabricators, the core groups
comprising the semiskilled occupations.

Among higher-status groups, however, Duke's vote fell off sharply. He did
poorly in the oak-shaded precincts where attorneys, physicians, and other
professionals tend to reside. John Treen captured these areas handily. An
imaginary precinct comprising nothing but lawyers, for instance, would have
cast two-thirds of its vote for Duke's opponent. Managerial precincts of the
same social purity would have gone for Treen in even more pronounced
numbers. But much of the variation among precincts in support of David
Duke is not due simply to occupation but depends on other social, economic,
and political factors as well.

The district's educational variables show a sharper voting cleavage, as
Figure 2.3 demonstrates. Precincts with large numbers of college graduates
favored Treen, while those where high school graduates predominate strongly
supported Duke.

Insofar as they can be measured by SES census categories, therefore, the
central tendencies of the electorate are fairly clear: upper-status Republicans
supported John Treen in preponderant numbers, whereas registered Democrats and blue-collar workers went solidly for Duke. It is possible that the

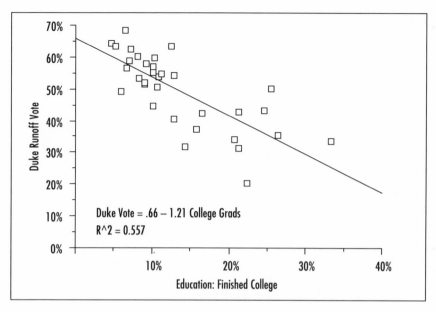

Figure 2.3
College Graduates' Support for Duke in the 1989 Primary Election

latter group alone, though comprising merely one-fifth of the households, provided Duke with about 40 percent of his final vote.

Duke's swing vote came from the lower end of the middle class—technicians, sales personnel, lower-level administrative workers—who comprise, as we have seen, the largest occupational groupings in both parish and district. Treen drew votes from the same category (see Table 2.5). Yet regressing the runoff vote on family income categories shows that middle-income groups, when separated out around the median income, voted solidly for Duke. An imaginary precinct consisting only of families earning in the $10,000–35,000 range would have given Duke 80 percent of its vote.[24]

Duke won, in short, because he was able to forge blue- and white-collar workers into a protopopulist coalition, shattering the top-down coalition that had been producing safe Republican majorities for over two decades. The only other time Republicans lost their stranglehold on the Metairie area was when Wallace's American Independent ticket carried Louisiana—and Jefferson Parish—in the 1968 presidential election, apparently by fusing low-status blue and white collarites into a backlash coalition that typified the Wallace vote nationwide.[25] Now Duke, who for years had striven to cast himself as the legitimate heir of the Wallace movement, was pulling together the same social elements.[26]

Table 2.5

Distribution of Education, Income, and Occupation in District 81, by Candidate Choice

Precinct Characteristic	One-half College Ed.	No College Ed.	>$35,000	<$35,000	Mgr. Prof. Tech.	All Others
	Education		**Income**		**Occupation**	
Duke voters	2%	52%	1%	47%	21%	87%
Treen voters	70	27	77	20	54	–9
Nonvoters	28	22	22	23	24	22
Total	100%	101%	100%	100%	100%	100%

Explaining the Duke Vote: Mediagenics or Radical Protest?

Professional pundits and political handlers involved in the election like to attribute Duke's 1989 success to the mechanics of the campaign and the quality of the candidates. Duke is an adept vote getter, arguably the most adroit political operative coming out of the far right today. Knowing his strength was in the grassroots, Duke rang doorbells and blanketed the district with multiple mailings; most of his electronic advertising was on the radio talk shows popular in working-class markets. His shoe-leather campaign had much better voter contact than Treen's. He raised most of his campaign funds in small donations, albeit from outside the district and the state.[27] He launched preemptive counterstrikes, accusing his enemies in the press of smearing his name even before his political and ideological extremism received much exposure. The effect was to neutralize the most damaging revelations in advance, which the Treen campaign publicized in tabloid form only days before the election. To an electorate grown cynical about the state's loose electoral ethics, the last-minute charges of neo-Nazi activities seemed like traditional Louisiana mudslinging.

Duke drew on political cadres from the outside but in a way that did not detract from his image as the champion of the little man and woman. Treen, by contrast, may have played into Duke's hands by calling in the heavy artillery. Both George Bush and Ronald Reagan made personal endorsements, along with the state's Republican leadership. Lee Atwater of the Republican National Committee sent funds and personnel to assist the Treen campaign. The effort seems to have backfired. An improvised yard sign appearing next to the interstate that bisects the district defiantly declared: "No One tells District 81 How to Vote!" The outside intervention likely fueled the already strong flames of antielite resentment burning in the district. A pro-Duke flier put out during the campaign by so-called Democrats for Duke played brilliantly on the "Rocky" theme by skillfully mixing together appeals to the politically alienated, Longite disgust with monied interests, and localistic resentments of outside interference:

> John Treen has a huge amount of money from political action committees (PACs). He has Northeastern media experts conducting a vicious smear campaign of lies that could make traditional Louisiana dirt-throwers blush! But David Duke is going to win because he really stands up for us! He has had little money, but a big heart and [a] great deal of courage. And when he wins for us, Louisiana politics will be changed forever. David Duke is a truly independent, courageous man who with our help will beat the big money and the old-line forces. . . . David Duke is a modern *David* versus the *Goliaths* of money, power, media, and political corruption. When he wins this race, *we all win.*[28]

Facing the tall and handsome Duke was an old and slightly rumpled John Treen. Where Duke was "mediagenic," Treen was dull and phlegmatic. A political maverick by temperament, Treen had been a Republican long before the Reagan revolution had made it popular for local Democrats to switch to the GOP. Jefferson politicos who were beginning to wrest control of the Republican organization from "good government" diehards regarded Treen as arrogant and aloof. Only late in the campaign did they issue a grudging endorsement of Treen. Democratic Sheriff Lee could not bring himself to support either candidate. "You know what it gets down to, David?" he told Duke in a telephone conversation during the campaign: "A choice between a bigot and an asshole." Laughing, Duke admitted that Lee was probably right.[29]

But for all of his shortcomings, Treen waged an effective come-from-behind campaign that saw him add thirty percentage points to his vote, capture most of the nonvoting population, and come within an ace of winning the runoff. Habitual nonvoters, who would not ordinarily be expected to turn out for a special legislative election, were moved by Duke's candidacy to go to the polls—to vote against Duke (see Table 2.6). Duke's personal attributes admittedly had an impact on all this, but more was obviously shaping the election outcome than Duke's electioneering skills or the likes and dislikes of local leaders. As for Sheriff Lee's fence straddling, doubtless the real expla-

Table 2.6

Distribution of Nonvoters from the 1983 Gubernatorial, 1986 U.S. Senate, and 1987 Sheriff's Elections in the 1989 Legislative Runoff

	1983 Governor	1986 U.S. Senate	1987 Sheriff
Duke voters, 1989	4%	10%	29%
Treen voters, 1989	40	41	28
Nonvoters, 1989	56	49	43

Source: Multiple regression estimates.

nation is that he shared voting bases with Duke. And through the grapevine of his deputy sheriffs he had ample opportunity to learn that those voters were volatile and restless.

One of them, a Duke supporter, told a local reporter: "When you saw Mr. Treen on television, he looked like he was around Metairie Country Club all the time. . . . I really didn't think he had my best interest at heart."[30] Such simmering class resentment, rather than the byplay of professional handlers, held an important key to Duke's election. Jefferson Parish, along with the rest of southern Louisiana, has been economically decimated by the collapse of oil prices. The depression only began to lift in its fifth year. The state's 1982 unemployment rate of 13.1 percent almost doubled the national figure. Per capita income, having reached parity in 1981 with the rest of the country's, declined to less than 75 percent of the national average by 1988.[31]

Jefferson Parish has shared in these economic misfortunes. While registering modest employment gains, from 1982 to 1987 the parish lost many high-paying positions: 38.2 percent of its oil and gas extraction jobs, 27.4 percent of its construction jobs, and 16.8 percent of its manufacturing positions. The growth industries are in the service sector. But these white-collar opportunities do not pay as well as the vanishing blue-collar jobs. Overall, between 1978 and 1987, Jefferson Parish experienced a net loss of 47,806 high-wage jobs while adding 31,538 low-wage positions.[32] Those grim statistics translated into declining living standards for many of the parish's residents.

The economic pain has not been equally distributed, however. Since 1982, wage earners have seen their living standards shrink by 6.5 percent. By contrast, real income deriving from dividends, interest payments, and rents has grown by 19 percent over the same period. For example, the real income of oil and gas workers has almost been cut in half; that of construction workers has fallen by about one-third. Small repair shop owners have experienced a 55 percent drop in income. (See Table 2.7.)

Table 2.7

Changes in Real Personal Income in Jefferson Parish, 1982–1987

% Change

Wages and salaries	–6.5%
Dividends, interest, and rent	19.0%
Construction	–31.5%
Heavy construction	–38.0%
Oil and gas extraction	–45.0%
Services	22.0%
Miscellaneous repair services	–55.0%

Source: U.S. Department of Commerce, Bureau of Economic Analysis. Recalculated by James Bobo, University of South Alabama.

Not merely the localized depression but the widening gap between rich and poor in the United States as a whole has produced this bleak economic reality. Top corporate CEOs today receive ninety-three times as much compensation as the average factory worker, an income spread that has more than doubled since 1960. Moreover, as a recent report by the House Ways and Means Committee has made clear, in the last ten years the top fifth of American families has improved its living standards by 17 percent, while the economic position of the bottom fifth has fallen by a tenth. The biggest losers have been low-income black and minority families, especially those headed by single mothers. But middle-income white families—whose mean income ranges between $21,000 and $34,000 per year, the income band embracing the Duke electorate—have also been buffeted by economic ill winds: their share of total white family income has shrunk by 12 percent in the last decade. (See Table 2.8.)[33]

Unhappily, national income and wealth data are not broken down by state or county/parish, so it is impossible to ascertain changes in income distribution for Jefferson Parish. But it is obvious that economic conditions in District 81 today are custom-ordered for the kind of populist insurgency David Duke is trying to lead on the right. Working- and middle-class voters, reeling from the bad hand dealt them by modern market trends, are upset that the federal government is making them fend for themselves.

What makes Duke's candidacy all the more appealing to the little man and woman is the fact that the two major parties are failing to give articulate voice to their economic grievances. Democrats have been trying to recast themselves as a second business party, forgetting Harry Truman's memorable

Table 2.8

Changes in the U.S. Distribution of White Family Income, 1978–1988

	Lowest Quintile	Second Quintile	Third Quintile	Fourth Quintile	Fifth Quintile	Top 5%
1978	5.6%	12.0%	17.6%	23.9%	41.0%	15.5%
1988	5.1%	11.1%	16.8%	23.7%	43.3%	17.0%
Rate of change	–8.9%	–7.5%	–4.5%	–0.8%	5.6%	9.7%

Source: U.S. Department of Commerce, Bureau of Economic Analysis. Recalculated by James Bobo, University of South Alabama.

advice that if you give the voters a choice between a Republican and a Republican, they will choose a Republican every time. Meanwhile, the GOP itself has been pursuing tax policies that favor upper-bracket voters.[34]

Louisiana state politics in the late eighties fit the popular perception that the two parties are too busy looking out for big business or "special interests" to heed the problems of the average citizen. Buddy Roemer was one of the more conservative "boll weevil" southern Democratic congressmen sent to Washington with the Reagan landslide of 1980. His gubernatorial victory in 1987 was made possible by the blessings of the state's leading newspapers and only one-third of the vote (the second-place vote getter in the primary, Edwin Edwards, withdrew before the runoff election). Four years later Roemer left office with a record of environmental and educational reform and a reputation for honesty. But when he first arrived in Baton Rouge he championed the trickle-down economic development strategies favored by LABI (Louisiana Association for Business and Industry), the chief business lobby in Louisiana. To offset the budget deficits stemming from a sour economy (and overreliance on oil and gas taxes), he kept social expenditures level. Tuition and fees at state colleges and universities tripled in seven years at the end of the eighties, a growth rate far above the regional average. To create a more favorable business climate, Roemer pushed for cuts in unemployment payments and for tort reforms, limiting the amount of damages that could be paid in workmen's liability cases. But the centerpiece of his program was "fiscal reform," aimed at easing business's tax burden by shifting it to homeowners who were shielded by the $75,000 homestead exemption. Meanwhile, regressive sales taxes were taking up more and more of the revenue slack. In effect, Louisianians accustomed to having their cake of low taxes and eating their cake of affirmative government were suddenly being asked to pay more for less.[35]

The legislature balked at the "Roemerista Revolution," particularly efforts to tilt the tax system toward business and industry. But after the freewheeling Edwin Edwards was forced into the political shadows by the collapse of the state's economy and his own personal scandals, no strong leader stepped forward to champion the economic populism that was Huey Long's legacy to state politics.

The voters made known their feelings concerning Roemer's "fiscal reform," however, and the results illuminated the underlying forces driving the Duke phenomenon. Less than three months after the special legislative election, a statewide referendum was held on a package of tax and business incentive measures favored by the Roemer administration. The administration's proposal was solidly defeated. In District 81 it was trounced, 60–40 percent.

As Figure 2.4 indicates, Duke's victory and fiscal reform's defeat were so closely correlated that the House election was practically a dress rehearsal for the referendum itself: Duke supporters who went to the polls in April cast nearly 90 percent of their votes against "fiscal reform." A top-down consensus in favor of conservative economic growth policies, low taxes, and affirmative government was breaking up over elite efforts to make the financially strapped middle class bear the costs of economic restructuring. The very coalition that had sent Duke to the state House was now protesting the probusiness austerity policies of the Roemer administration.

Equity and fairness had become uppermost in the average voter's mind, as they usually do when the pie starts to shrink. Six months after being defeated at the polls, in October 1989, fiscal reform was back before the voters. Jettisoning the omnibus approach used in the April referendum, the administration this time unbundled the constituent elements into separate propositions, and the results are instructive. The voters predictably defeated a proposal for shifting the tax burden onto local governments, but they approved other tax-raising measures. The key winner was a highway trust fund scheme linking a one-cent gasoline tax increase to an ambitious program of highway and bridge construction. District 81 voters supported the pump-priming highway program by roughly the same margin they had defeated the omnibus reforms in April, and even some Duke voters supported it. What remained consistent, however, was stiff opposition to trickle-down approaches to fostering economic development. Very few of the Duke voters casting ballots in the low-turnout October 1989 election favored a proposal to grant tax exemptions for business inventories. The measure lost handily (see Table 2.9).

It was on the waters of economic and political frustration that David Duke

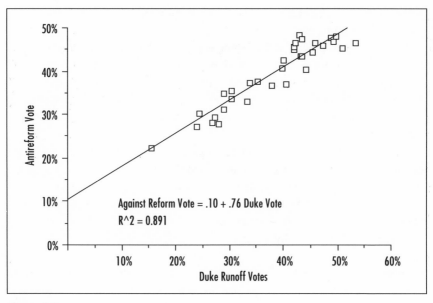

Figure 2.4
Duke Voters in the Fiscal Reform Election, April 29, 1989

launched his successful 1989 campaign for the legislature. He exploited the antitax mood by promising to defend the homestead exemption against any and all comers (yard signs proclaiming "Save Our Homestead Exemption" went up in the closing days of Duke's runoff race) and pledging to oppose a tax increase. He called for further spending cuts. And he successfully focused blue- and white-collar economic resentments on programs of racial preference and the black "underclass." The true explanation for the ailing economy and the empty state treasury, Duke argued, was affirmative action, minority set-asides, and the social ills of the black poor. The way to bring the economy back was to end "reverse discrimination" and reduce "the illegitimate welfare birthrate that is bankrupting us economically and is the source of much crime and social ills."[36] This Duke message, hammered at repeatedly in campaign mailers and broadsides, addressed white working-class economic grievances, gave vent to resentments against "special interests" (read: blacks), and legitimized the furies of white backlash by wrapping it in the shibboleth of "equal rights for all, special preferences for none."

The overriding issue for working- and middle-class voters in Louisiana House District 81, in other words, seems to have been "fairness." As one state employee living in Jefferson Parish explained to a *New York Times* reporter two days before the election, "He [Duke] is appealing to a frustration that is pretty deep. . . . They're angry about minority set-asides, affirmative

Table 2.9

Fiscal Reform Voting by District 81 Precincts Favoring Runoff Candidates

	Duke Voters	Treen Voters	Nonvoters
Highway Trust Fund			
Vote for	23%	54%	–21%
Vote against	24	13	3
Nonvote	53	33	118
Total	100%	100%	100%
Business Inventory Tax Exemption			
Vote for	12%	60%	–21%
Vote against	36	8	6
Nonvote	52	31	115
Total	100%	99%	100%

action, busing. I think they feel the fairness of society is being tampered with."[37] The "special interests" were being looked after. Who was looking out for the little man and woman?

American populists during tough times traditionally harbor resentments of the classes above and below, which is why they are capable of swinging right or left. Duke gave them a backlash target in the form of America's ancient scapegoats, and they went right. He was helped in part because the political system was not paying close attention to the economic grievances of District 81's white working and middle classes. From that base, Duke came close to unseating U.S. Senator J. Bennett Johnston in the October 1990 open primary election. It is unclear whether he will ever muster enough white support to win statewide office; as the recent governor's election has shown, Louisiana's sizable black electorate (27 percent) is a major stumbling block to his larger political ambitions. Nonetheless, Duke does possess the power to influence the agenda for the next decade. The American two-party system has historically defeated third-party challenges (which is what Duke's candidacies represent in all but nomenclature) by simply appropriating their issues. Duke has already scored a classic "success-in-failure" by giving welfare reform an ugly racial spin.[38] After Wallace left the scene, it looked as though the race-driven conservative realignment in presidential politics might take place without a nativist insurgency materializing on the extreme right. But Duke's 1989 success in the economically depressed Eighty-first District was perhaps the first indication that the GOP's maneuvering room was beginning to contract.

Both parties in Louisiana have felt the brunt of Duke's insurgency. The makeshift Louisiana Republican party depends on episodic middle-class Republican voters shoring up the bottom end of its coalition. From the looks of Republican Ben Bagert's (the regular nominee) poor showing in the 1990 U.S. Senate primary, Duke has separated this group from traditional conservatism in much the same way he did in the smaller arena of Metairie—and George Wallace did in the Deep South. But state Democrats also have reason for concern. Duke has driven a wedge into the low-status, New Deal alignment of Cajuns, labor, and blacks that gave Edwin Edwards his first three terms in the governor's mansion. This unstable Democratic-populist coalition took shape only after the race issue was muted in state politics. But Duke, having raised that issue once again, is determined to keep it paramount. "For years and years, all these legislators . . . always voted with the minority-liberal programs because they're afraid of this 25 or 30 percent black constituency going against them and raising hell with them," Duke told a national Populist convention shortly after his election in 1989. Duke wants to force Louisiana lawmakers to start "worrying about the 70 percent." That has spelled trouble for white politicians who have made a career of balancing biracial constituencies by carefully blending progressive and conservative appeals.[39] Edwards captured his historic fourth term in 1991 only because an odd assortment of professional politicians, reformers, business people, and African-Americans hastily pulled together to defeat a common threat to their economic well-being, a defensive coalition unusual in Louisiana politics.

The economic and political conditions that produced David Duke are hardly peculiar to the Bayou State. Nationwide, the deepening gulf between rich and poor, coupled with the ideological incoherence of the American left, are inflating the ranks of Walter Dean Burnham's "party of the nonvoter" and are creating political openings for the white racist right. The public's confidence in national institutions is plunging. Doubtless, a Duke-style campaign has stronger prospects in the South, where the white working class, as Earl and Merle Black have shown, have a greater affinity for ideological conservatism and where progressive electoral coalitions are more difficult to assemble.[40] But Walker Percy was doubtless right to warn us that conditions are ripe for David Duke, or those like him, elsewhere in the country.

NOTES

1. Quoted in King, "Bad Times on the Bayou," 120.
2. Berry, "White Lies," 6.
3. *Ballot Box Bigotry*.

4. *Ballot Box Bigotry*, 1–2; Louisiana Coalition against Racism and Nazism, "Media Resource Packet"; Hill, chap. 6, this volume; DuBos, "David Duke's Nazi Books"; Berry, "White Lies." See also Sternberg, "Role of the New Orleans Media."

5. In the scattergram (Figure 2.1), each dot represents a precinct, positioned on the graph according to the percentage of the vote received by Duke in 1979 and 1989. Read down the *y* axis to determine his 1979 voting percentage for each dot (precinct); read across the *x* axis to determine his 1989 percentage. Called the *least squares regression line* because it represents the minimum squared distance of all dots from any line, the upward slanting line running through the dots is also mathematically expressed in the form of the $y = a + bx$ equation—here written out on the graph. To give two examples of how to read the equation: (1) according to the regression line, a precinct that cast 10 percent of its votes for Duke in 1979 delivered the same percentage to him in 1989 $[-.03 + 1.3(.1) = .1]$; and (2) a precinct casting 33.3 percent of its vote for Duke in 1979 delivered 40 percent of the vote to Duke in 1989 $[-.03 + 1.3(.333) = .4]$. The R^2 answers the question "how closely do the data, the dots, cluster around the line?" or "how good an explanation is this?" With an R^2 of 0 percent, the dots fall randomly around the line and the explanation explains nothing; with an R^2 of 100 percent, all dots fall right on the line and the explanation is perfect.

6. Howell, "UNO Poll," esp. table 2 on p. 8. See also Morgan, "Put Up Your Duke," 63, tables 17 and 26.

7. Duke supporters, it now seems clear, were trying to screen out information about Duke's extremist ties. One-fifth of his 1989 runoff voters said they had not heard about his past involvement with the neo-Nazi movement, yet one-half of them were clearly lying about what they knew and when they knew it. Of the remaining 80 percent who admitted knowledge of Duke's controversial politics, nearly all chose to take him at his word when he claimed to have turned over a new political leaf. Morgan, "Put Up Your Duke," 47–48, 62, 72–73, tables 5–9.

8. Edsall and Edsall, *Chain Reaction*, 3–46.

9. Eig, "Lee: Will Stop Blacks in White Areas"; Rhoden, "Jeff to Set Barricade on Crime"; Donze, "City Crew Bulldozes Jeff 'Wall,'" A1.

10. Philbin, "Police Caught Unprepared after Parade," B1.

11. Author's recall of WWL News Radio interview, January 1989.

12. Kelso, "Message Senders."

13. For a perceptive analysis of political and social developments in the region since World War II, see Black and Black, *Politics and Society*, 3–74 and passim.

14. O'Byrne, "Anatomy of an Upset," A1.

15. U.S. Bureau of the Census, *1980 Census of Population and Housing: . . . Louisiana*, table P-13; O'Byrne, "Anatomy of an Upset," A1. Census precinct and block data were provided by Division of Business and Economic Research, University of New Orleans.

16. Black and Black, *Politics and Society*, 213–31, 259–316; Lamis, *Two-Party South*, 20–43, 108–19, 212–15.

17. Alarmed by Republican inroads in East Jefferson (where District 81 is located), the late majority whip Hale Boggs arranged in 1969 to have this part of his

constituency gerrymandered out of his district. See Engstrom, "Hale Boggs Gerrymander." Richard Nixon received 80.5 percent in 1972, Gerald Ford 73.5 percent in 1976, and Reagan 73.6 percent in 1980 and a commanding 84.5 percent in 1984.

18. Registration figures understate the real growth of Republicanism in the district. Most voters still register as Democrats while favoring Republican presidential candidates, a pattern that has been common in the region and the state since 1952. Partisan identification is a better gauge of Republican strength, but that information is not available on the district level.

19. There is a moderately positive correlation between the Carter vote and the percentage of households headed by craft workers ($r = .43$), by operators ($r = .4$), and by high school graduates ($r = .61$), which is an even better proxy for social class. The correlations are stronger between the vote for Gerald Ford and SES indicators of upper-status households. For a more in-depth explanation of the methodology on which the voting analysis of this chapter rests, see n. 22.

20. Sindler, *Huey Long's Louisiana*, 152, 160–61; Landry and Parker, "Louisiana Political Culture," 7–13; Grosser, "Political Parties," 274–79; Theodoulou, *Louisiana Republican Party*, 72, 131–32; Maginnis, *Last Hayride*, 48–51. See also ACIR, *Significant Features of Fiscal Federalism*, 128–29, tables 77–78); Public Affairs Research Council of Louisiana, "Government Spending."

21. Little Lawrence succeeded his father by waiting to qualify until minutes before the deadline expired, after all potential challengers had been scared off by the fact that his politically invincible father was going to stand for reelection. After his son qualified, Big Lawrence withdrew and his son ran unopposed. The father recently stepped down as a state appeals court judge. Cunningham, "Free Ride" and "Chehardy Comes of Age."

22. The findings below are based on Ordinary Least Squares (OLS) bivariate regression analysis of selected aggregate data (raw census and voting returns), because adequate survey research data are not available. The unit of analysis is the voting precinct. The estimated percentages are extrapolations and therefore susceptible to some estimating error; that is why a few of the estimates are negative numbers or totals greater than 100.

The voting returns have been made available by the Jefferson Parish registrar's office. Registration data furnished by the office are broken down by race, party, gender, and age. For information relating to occupation, income, and education, I have resorted to the computerized census block data available from the Division of Business and Economic Research at the University of New Orleans. Because the census blocks seldom coincide with the voting precinct boundaries, I have had to do some adapting. The decision rule was to average the percentages of census blocks that overlap a voting precinct, taking the resultant score as the average for that electoral unit.

23. The Democratic nature of Duke's electorate is also indicated in Morgan, "Put Up Your Duke," 58.

24. Polling data corroborate the findings of OLS regression analysis: 61 percent of respondents reporting incomes below $25,000 voted for Duke, whereas 64 percent who said they earned more than that voted for Treen. Morgan, "Put Up Your Duke," tables 22–23.

25. The area now encompassed by District 81 may have remained in the Republican column, but only barely; the rest of Jefferson Parish voted for Wallace. Precinct boundaries were different then, so it is impossible to ascertain the social composition of the Alabama governor's vote; but it seems to have been located in precincts that Duke carried in 1989. The returns are available in the New Orleans *Times-Picayune*, November 6, 1968. See also Public Affairs Research Council of Louisiana, "General Election, November 1968"; Converse et al., "Continuity and Change in American Politics"; Black and Black, "The Wallace Vote in Alabama"; Crespi, "Structural Sources of George Wallace's Constituency"; Lipset and Raab, *The Politics of Unreason*, 338–427.

26. "Watch for Far Right," 4–5.

27. Morgan, "Put Up Your Duke," 58. Duke benefited from his access to the substantial mailing list of Willis Carto's Liberty Lobby magazine, *The Spotlight*. According to the Anti-Defamation League of B'nai B'rith, Carto is a notorious anti-Semite.

28. Parent and Mott, "Politics of Resentment"; "Democrats for Better Government," campaign flier, [January 1989].

29. O'Byrne, "Anatomy of an Upset," A14.

30. Ibid., A15.

31. Data sheet from Oakland Econometrics, New Orleans, La., August 30, 1989.

32. James Bobo to author, November 15, 1989.

33. U.S. House of Representatives, *Background Material*; Goffman, "Income Gap," 8; Phillips, *Politics of Rich and Poor*.

34. I am obviously influenced by Robert Kuttner's analysis of the condition of the national Democratic party. See his *Life of the Party*. See also Edsall and Edsall, *Chain Reaction*, 159–63.

35. Public Affairs Research Council of Louisiana, "Gist of It"; Hill, "Curious Rise of Buddy Roemer"; Ruth, "La. Leads South in College Tuitions"; William G. Black, "Louisiana State Expenditures"; Weber, "Historical Development." In 1990 the state ranked third nationally in its reliance on total sales tax revenues. Public Affairs Research Council of Louisiana, *PAR Legislative Bulletin* 38.

36. "Democrats for Better Government," campaign flier, February 1989.

37. Applebome, "Klan's Ghost Haunts G.O.P.," A1.

38. Lipset and Raab, *Politics of Unreason*, 59–61 and passim.

39. Johnson, "Duke Tape"; Black and Black, *Politics and Society*, 308–16; Lamis, *Two-Party South*, 226–32; Wildgen, "Voting Behavior."

40. Burnham, *Current Crisis*; Black and Black, *Politics and Society*, 66–72; Lewis, "Poll Finds Public Lacks Confidence"; National Election Studies, 1984, 1986, 1988, ICPSR.

REFERENCES

Advisory Commission on Intergovernmental Relations (ACIR). *Significant Features of Fiscal Federalism: 1984 Edition.* Washington, D.C.: GPO, 1984.

Applebome, Peter. "Klan's Ghost Haunts G.O.P. on Louisiana Political Trail." *New York Times,* February 16, 1989.

———. "Ex-Klansman Puts New Racial Politics to Test." *New York Times,* June 18, 1990.

Ballot Box Bigotry: David Duke and the Populist Party. Atlanta: Center for Democratic Renewal, 1989.

Berry, Jason. "White Lies: David Duke in the Media Mind." Paper, October 1989.

Black, Earl, and Merle Black. "The Wallace Vote in Alabama: A Multiple Regression Analysis." *Journal of Politics* 35 (August 1973): 731–36.

Black, Earl, and Merle Black. *Politics and Society in the South.* Cambridge: Harvard University Press, 1987.

Black, William G. "Louisiana State Expenditures: An Overview." In *Louisiana's Fiscal Alternatives: Finding Permanent Solutions to Recurring Budget Crises,* edited by James A. Richardson, 27–42. Baton Rouge: Louisiana State University Press, 1988.

Burnham, Walter Dean. *The Current Crisis in American Politics.* New York: Oxford University Press, 1988.

Converse, Philip E., Warren E. Miller, Jerrold G. Rusk, and Arthur C. Wolfe. "Continuity and Change in American Politics: Parties and Issues in the 1968 Election." *American Political Science Review* 43 (December 1969): 1103–5.

Crespi, Irving. "Structural Sources of George Wallace's Constituency." *Social Science Quarterly* 52 (September 1971): 115–32.

Cunningham, Lynn. "Chehardy Comes of Age." New Orleans *Times-Picayune,* April 19, 1981.

———. "The Free Ride: Louisiana's Property Tax Mess." New Orleans *Times-Picayune,* September 25–26, 1988.

Donze, Frank. "City Crew Bulldozes Jeff 'Wall.'" New Orleans *Times-Picayune,* February 22, 1987.

DuBos, Clancy. "David Duke's Nazi Books." *Gambit,* June 13, 1989.

Edsall, Thomas, and Mary Edsall. *Chain Reaction: The Impact of Race, Rights, and Taxes on American Politics.* New York: W. W. Norton, 1991.

Eig, Jonathan. "Lee: Will Stop Blacks in White Areas." New Orleans *Times-Picayune,* December 3, 1986.

Election Returns. New Orleans *Times-Picayune,* November 6, 1968.

Engstrom, Richard L. "The Hale Boggs Gerrymander: Congressional Redistricting, 1969." *Louisiana History* (Winter 1980): 59–66.

Goffman, Ethan. "The Income Gap and Its Causes." *Dissent* 37 (Winter 1990): 8.

Grosser, Paul. "Political Parties." In *Louisiana Politics: Festival in a Labyrinth,* edited by James Bolner, 255–83. Baton Rouge: Louisiana State University Press, 1982.

Hill, Lance. "The Curious Rise of Buddy Roemer." *The Nation*, March 12, 1988, 333–35.

Howell, Susan. "The UNO Poll: Racial Attitudes Survey, Orleans and Jefferson Parishes." Unpublished paper, March 1989.

Johnson, Allen, Jr. "Duke Tape: Blacks Argued for Racial Discrimination in B.R." *The Louisiana Weekly*, March 18, 1989.

Kelso, Iris. "Message Senders." New Orleans *Times-Picayune*, January 29, 1989.

King, Wayne. "Bad Times on the Bayou." *New York Times Magazine*, June 11, 1989, 56–59, 120–25.

Kuttner, Robert. *Life of the Party: Democratic Prospects in 1988 and Beyond*. New York: Viking, 1987.

Lamis, Alexander P. *The Two-Party South*. New York: Oxford University Press, 1984.

Landry, David M., and Joseph B. Parker. "The Louisiana Political Culture." In *Louisiana Politics: Festival in a Labyrinth*, edited by James Bolner, 1–13. Baton Rouge: Louisiana State University Press, 1982.

Lewis, Robert. "Poll Finds Public Lacks Confidence in Institutions." New Orleans *Times-Picayune*, June 10, 1990.

Lipset, Seymour Martin, and Earl Raab. *The Politics of Unreason: Right Wing Extremism in America, 1790–1970*. New York: Harper and Row, 1970.

Louisiana Coalition against Racism and Nazism (LCARN). "The Politics and Background of State Representative David Duke," edited by Lance Hill. 1990. Available in biography section, LCARN Collection, Amistad Research Center, Tulane University, New Orleans.

Maginnis, John. *The Last Hayride*. Baton Rouge: Gris Gris Press, 1984.

Morgan, Donald H. "Put Up Your Duke: Racism, Extremism, and Politics in the Election of David Duke to the Louisiana State Legislature." M.A. thesis, Tulane University, 1989.

National Election Studies, 1984, 1986, 1988. ICPSR, University of Michigan, Ann Arbor.

O'Byrne, James. "Duke: Anatomy of an Upset." New Orleans *Times-Picayune*, March 5, 1989.

Parent, Wayne, and King Mott. "The Politics of Resentment: An Examination of Two 1989 Elections in the Deep South." Paper presented at the 1989 Annual Meeting of the Southern Political Science Association, Memphis, Tenn., November 1989.

Philbin, Walt. "Police Caught Unprepared after Parade." New Orleans *Times-Picayune*, January 18, 1989.

Phillips, Kevin P. *The Politics of Rich and Poor: Wealth and the American Electorate in the Reagan Aftermath*. New York: Random House, 1990.

Public Affairs Research Council of Louisiana. "General Election, November 1968." *PAR Analysis* 154, December 1968.

———. "Government Spending: Louisiana Tops the South." *PAR Analysis* 279, December 1985.

———. "The Gist of It." *PAR Analysis* 282, January 1988.

————. *PAR Legislative Bulletin* 38, no. 1, April 29, 1990.

Rhoden, Robert. "Jeff to Set Barricade on Crime." New Orleans *Times-Picayune*, February 11, 1987.

Ruth, Dawn. "La. Leads South in College Tuitions." New Orleans *Times-Picayune*, February 18, 1990.

Sindler, Allan P. *Huey Long's Louisiana: State Politics, 1920–1952.* Baltimore: Johns Hopkins University Press, 1956.

Sternberg, Julie. "The Role of the New Orleans Media in the Election of David Duke." Senior thesis, Princeton University, 1991.

Theodoulou, Stella Z. *The Louisiana Republican Party, 1948–1984: The Building of a State Political Party.* New Orleans: Tulane Studies in Political Science, 1985.

U.S. Bureau of the Census. *1980 Census of Population and Housing: Summary Characteristics for Governmental Units and Standard Metropolitan Statistical Areas: Louisiana.* Washington, D.C.: GPO, 1982.

U.S. House of Representatives. *Background Material and Data on Programs within the Jurisdiction of the Committee on Ways and Means*, app. I. Washington, D.C.: GPO, 1989, 939–1064.

"Watch for Far Right to Try a Larger Strategy in '88 Elections." *The Monitor.* Center for Democratic Renewal, August 1987.

Weber, Ronald E. "Historical Development of the Louisiana State Tax Structure." In *Louisiana's Fiscal Alternatives: Finding Permanent Solutions to Recurring Budget Crises*, edited by James A. Richardson, 43–61. Baton Rouge: Louisiana State University Press, 1988.

Wildgen, John. "Voting Behavior in Gubernatorial Elections." In *Louisiana Politics: Festival in a Labyrinth*, edited by James Bolner, 330–39. Baton Rouge: Louisiana State University Press, 1982.

William V. Moore

3 | David Duke

The White Knight

David Duke is an unusual extremist. He strives to make extremism acceptable. Avoiding violent methods, though not flamboyant ones, he has learned to expand support of his extremist causes by appealing to supporters not previously associated with extremism. When presented to a mass audience, the Duke message now is offered as mainstream Americanism, while his earlier leadership in racist and anti-Semitic causes is described as youthful posturing. Duke the candidate has parlayed the backing of an extremist core into broad support with legitimate methods and covert racism but without ending his interaction with neo-Nazis and Ku Klux Klansmen. Duke's political campaigns are an extension of his characteristic eagerness and ability to attract large numbers of supporters, some of them disappointed "once-hads," few of whom would consider themselves extremists. In Duke's hands, such an approach works.

David Duke: A Personal and Political Profile

Duke was born on July 1, 1950, in Tulsa, Oklahoma, the son of David H. Duke, an engineer for Shell Oil Company and a major in the U.S. Army Reserves. In 1954 his father accepted a position with Royal Dutch Shell at the company's headquarters at The Hague in the Netherlands. In 1955, however, the family moved to Louisiana, first to Lake Charles and then to New Orleans, which for the next fourteen years provided the background for Duke's developing political beliefs.

Duke's family had a strong orientation toward education. His grandfather attended the University of Kansas for three years; his grandmother taught chemistry there, and one of his aunts was a surgeon in Chicago. At an early age Duke wanted to be an anthropologist, an archaeologist, or some sort of natural scientist. According to Michael Zatarain, Duke's father wanted to raise his children with strict, conservative Christian values and made young David sit and read for an hour a day. The elder Duke wielded great influence in the household.[1]

Although much of David Duke's family life would seem to have been uneventfully middle class, it was not. By the late 1950s his mother had developed a drinking problem, for which she was hospitalized unsuccessfully. Duke's way of dealing with his mother's alcoholism was to go to his room when he returned from school and read or delve into some other project.[2] In 1966 his father left home to work for the U.S. Agency for International Development. During this period Duke began to drift into the world of racial politics.

Duke's first exposure to the racial right occurred during the 1964–65 school year, when he visited the office of the Citizens' Council, a segregationist group founded in 1954. The Council advocated the use of education and legal methods to resist integration. The New Orleans chapter, one of the strongest in the United States, had as one of its founders and leaders Judge Leander H. Perez, the head of neighboring Plaquemines Parish's political machine. At the Council's headquarters, Duke was introduced to segregationist literature, including Carlton Putham's *Race and Reason: A Yankee View*. This work presented various arguments—biological, cultural, historical, and psychological—that integration would not only fail but would also lead to increased crime and poverty. According to Duke, the book changed his perspective: "I wasn't even half convinced, but I was convinced enough to say, 'My gosh, this man does have some reasonable arguments.' So then I started reading everything I could get my hands on [about] race and things like that."[3]

Throughout that school year, Duke spent more and more time at the Citizens' Council's office. After his father left in the fall of 1966, he immersed himself in the Council, only to be sent off to Riverside Military Academy, a military boarding school in Georgia. Returning to New Orleans for his senior year, Duke was enrolled at John F. Kennedy High School, where he encountered public school integration. At Kennedy, a schoolmate introduced him to the Ku Klux Klan and he became a member at age seventeen.

The Klan den that Duke joined had about thirty-five members, most of them businessmen and Catholic. The leader and financial backer of the group was Jim Lindsay, a successful businessman and resident of the uptown section of New Orleans, who used the pseudonym, Ed White, in the KKK. According to Zatarain, White had an enormous influence on Duke, eventually becoming a surrogate father. (Lindsay, who was known by the police by still another alias, James Lawrence, was mysteriously murdered in 1975.) Duke regularly attended bimonthly meetings of the Klan and became, in the words of one former Klansman, "a model member."[4] But his Klan activities were not highly visible and his membership did not become public knowledge until 1974.

"THE NAZI OF LSU"

In the fall of 1968, David Duke enrolled at Louisiana State University (LSU) in Baton Rouge. During that year he found another mentor, a Catholic priest and strong anti-Semite, Father Lawrence J. Toups, whom Duke had first met through the Citizens' Council. According to Zatarain, it was Toups who transformed Duke from an ordinary southern racist into a hardened anti-Semite. Duke now waded into anti-Semitic publications, including Gerald L. K. Smith's *The Cross and the Flag*. Smith, a longtime extremist, had belonged to the Ku Klux Klan in the 1920s, had worked for William Dudley Pelley's Silver Shirts in the 1930s, and had been one of Louisiana governor Huey Long's chief advisers. Described by Seymour Martin Lipset and Earl Raab as the dean of anti-Semitism, Smith pictured the United States as a victim of complex conspiracies, with the twins of the Antichrist, Zionism and Communism, "seeking to destroy not only the foreground of our tradition, but the background of our tradition."[5]

While a sophomore at LSU Duke became involved with the National Socialist Liberation Front (NSLF), an arm of the National Socialist White People's party (NSWPP) created for college students in 1969. The NSWPP, in turn, had been organized from the American Nazi party by Matt Koehl, who assumed control when its leader, George Lincoln Rockwell, was killed by a party dissident. Koehl changed the name of the party to the NSWPP and moved its operations into a new headquarters in Arlington, Virginia. Duke now sought publicity for his views, telling a crowd at LSU in 1969: "I am a National Socialist. You can call me a Nazi if you want to." He was photographed with a copy of George Lincoln Rockwell's book *White Power* at

LSU's Free Speech Alley, where he often spoke, and he handed out copies of the NSLF newsletter, *The Liberator*, on campus. He once rebuked a professor in class for criticizing *Mein Kampf*, which Duke called "the greatest piece of literature of the twentieth century."[6]

At the same time, however, Duke portrayed his position as moderate. In a November 1969 letter to the editor of the campus newspaper, *The Daily Reveille*, he declared that his goals were not to bash minorities but to open dialogue and build leadership:

> Exterminate all Jews, and with more efficient methods than Hitler used! Ship all of the Negroes back to Africa in cattle boats! Exterminate all people who politically disagree! According to Mike Connelly these are the aims and objectives of the National Socialist Liberation Front. What has Connelly been reading—Argosy Magazine? If he or anyone else can prove that this is what I and the NSLF have advocated, I will quit.

> The NSLF has different views from the run-of-the-mill political groups on campus, whether they support the right or the left. Their approach to the problems confronting our civilization is completely mechanical, economic, and materialistic. National Socialism, on the other hand, is unique! Instead of stressing materialistic economic dogma as democratic-liberalism has in its Eastern version or Western version, we believe that the quality and spirit of our people are by far the most important issues of our time.

> What are the goals of the NSLF? Our first goal is to break through the communication barrier in this country and to let the people know exactly what we stand for instead of what certain people say we stand for. Then we will express to them why we believe as we do. Once the people hear both sides, we are confident that they will choose ours; then we can proceed to build the leadership we need to liberate our people so that they can determine their own destiny.[7]

Duke's venture into the world of National Socialism culminated on July 23, 1970. Dressed in a Nazi uniform with a swastika armband, and carrying a sign that said "Gas the Chicago 7" and "Kunstler Is a Communist Jew," he picketed a speech by lawyer William Kunstler at Tulane University. Since then, Duke has tried to downplay the incident. In an interview with Patsy Sims, he said "that was clear back when I was eighteen. Maybe I was twenty. [He was twenty.] I was just a kid. I just didn't know how to combat William Kunstler."[8] Dismissing his Nazi ties and his title "The Nazi of LSU," Duke said:

You're very naive when you're starting your political activity, and you don't realize the lowness of these people. I've passed out all sorts of stuff, but that's the kind of thing they pick up on. They say, "well, you're a Nazi"; or you make a statement like I did about World War Two that we should have fought against communism instead of with communism. You could have said a hundred other statements, but they pick this out and call you a Nazi, which is an age-old Jewish thing, anyway. But I *didn't* have a name at LSU as a Nazi. Like I say, that was just the first semester.[9]

Duke's activities—and some of his associates—dispute these assertions. For example, the September 1, 1970 *N S* (National Socialist) *Bulletin* stated that Duke spoke at the NSWPP annual meeting in Washington, D.C., in August of that year. According to Bill Jackson, then an LSU student, Duke had a Nazi flag in his dormitory room; a high school classmate claimed that she had seen a Nazi flag in his New Orleans home. Art Jones, a longtime Nazi, said Duke is rewriting history by claiming that he was not associated with the American Nazi party. Jones stated: "(NSWPP Commander Matt) Koehl wanted someone to be an agitator on college campuses, and Duke was that man. He was an NSWPP organizer for two years. He wasn't a full party member, but he was definitely affiliated with us." Another former NSWPP member, Rick Cooper, supports Jones's assertion: "For Duke to say he was never a Nazi is a lie. Duke is trying to turn around and deny that he knew people who were friends in the past."[10]

A GROUP OF ONE'S OWN

The Kunstler picketing prompted a rebuke by Duke's father. Duke then told friends he would no longer support the NSLF,[11] and in the fall of 1970 he started his own group on the LSU campus called the White Youth Alliance (WYA). The substantive change was slight. The design symbolizing the WYA was a cross inside a circle; it looked somewhat like a swastika and was the original Klan symbol. (Members could purchase armbands with this symbol.) The national mailing address for the organization was the post office box in Arlington, Virginia, of the National Socialist White People's party, and Duke's pamphlet, "The White Power Program," which outlined the program and goals of the White Youth Alliance, copied passages verbatim from the already-published "Goals and Objectives of the NSWPP." Yet the intent was both personal and local: the front page of "Goals and Objectives" features a picture of David Duke holding a copy of George Lincoln Rockwell's book, *White Power*.

Duke also published a new paper, available to WYA members and subscribers, which he called *The Racialist*. It advertised for sale various books and tapes, including *Our Nordic Race*, *Behind Communism* (Zionist forces), *The Protocols*, and *Mein Kampf*. Tapes for sale included speeches of George Lincoln Rockwell entitled "Rockwell at Brown University," "Rockwell vs. Carmichael," and "Rockwell vs. NAACP."

Activities of the White Youth Alliance generally centered around Duke's speeches at Free Speech Alley. In addition, members picketed a speech by black activist Dick Gregory in November 1970. An antiwar rally on March 5, 1971, marked the group's last major activity at LSU; Duke's association with it had lasted approximately one school year. At the end of the spring semester, subscribers received a special edition of *The Racialist* in which Duke, now a junior, told them that he would be moving out of academe into the real world. He had received a short-term employment offer, he said, that would enable him to further the cause. "In every White Nation I will visit," he noted, "there will be Racialists waiting to greet me. I can promise you that this will be one more step toward world-wide White racial unity. . . . Next fall when I return, I will not resume a full-time school curriculum because I feel that I have the knowledge and ability to devote all my energy to this cause."[12] The job was a position with the State Department teaching Laotian military officers English at the American Language School in Vientiane, Laos. It had been secured for him by his father. Apparently, the State Department was unaware of his political activities. Duke remained in the post for five months.

THE REAL WORLD

By December 1971, when David Duke returned to the United States, the White Youth Alliance was out of business. A month later he formed a new organization in New Orleans called the National party. In a letter addressed to members and supporters of the WYA, Duke boasted that the "anti-white government paid my way to Laos and back, and made possible an organizational tour for the leader of the White Youth Alliance around the globe!" He then explained to his followers why the National party had been formed: First, more than just a student organization was needed. Although such a group should be youth-oriented, all people were required in the struggle. Second, any organization that wanted to bring about a change in government must be political and must contest elections. Finally, he stated, the organization had to maintain close contact with the people; its ideology had to be immutable while its tactics were flexible.[13] (Duke later described the National party as "kind of a jump from just college students to general [people]" and as "an organization that was based on Klan principles, Klan symbols.")[14] While his peers pursued their studies at LSU, he set up headquarters in New Orleans and began publishing a new magazine, *The Nationalist*. Within a month, he claimed a following of six hundred.

The magazine preached to the true believers. In the April 1972 issue, for instance, Duke talked about the need to build a white political machine and said that "the Jewish dominated MINORITY MACHINE must go": "The Jews dominate the whole apparatus by their money power, and by their control of the mass media. By simple use of their power, they control the corrupt, self-serving whites like [Richard] Nixon, and through their media control, they produce a small but significant number of brainwashed white liberals. As for the primitive Blacks, it takes very little to manipulate them. Even today, after 60 years as the top Negro organization in America, the NAACP still has a Jewish president: Kivie Kaplan."[15] But local activities were limited. Although the National party held a march in January 1972 that attracted several hundred people and worked on behalf of George Wallace's campaign for president, it generally maintained a low profile.

THE BIG TIME

In September 1972 David Duke married and moved to Seattle, Washington, where his mother and sister now lived. After a few months as a bellhop at a motel, he came back, reentered LSU, and returned to the fold of the Ku Klux Klan. At first he organized for the Klan in the Baton Rouge–New Orleans area and edited its publication, *The Crusader*. Soon he became Louisiana grand dragon (state leader) and national information director.

Following his goals for the National party—to make it youth-oriented but broad-based, political, and pragmatic—Duke changed the focus of his Louisiana-based Klan. He recruited high school and college students and created youth organizations. He allowed the admission of women as equals as well as Catholics. He also worked the military bases; in the 1970s, Klansmen were found at Camp Pendleton, California, at Fort Hood, Texas, and on Navy bases in Norfolk, Virginia, and Charleston, South Carolina.[16] Defense policy toward Klan activities was as follows:

> While Department of Defense and military service regulations generally prohibit KKK activity on Federal property, we are restricted by First Amendment Constitutional considerations, from interfering with KKK or other organizational activity which takes place on private property. Legally, we cannot prohibit military personnel from joining the KKK. We can, however, take action to insure that their KKK activities do not

materially interfere with our military mission or otherwise pose a clear danger to the loyalty, discipline or morale of military personnel. Consistent with these standards, service regulations now restrict the distribution of literature on military reservations and provide Commanders with the authority to place "off-limits" sanctions on any facility in the surrounding civilian community which adversely affects the health, welfare or morale of the troops. These are some of the tools that Commanders can use to restrict the influence of the KKK.[17]

According to at least one estimate, Duke increased the size of his Klan from several hundred to three thousand within a year. Racial and anti-Semitic themes continued to appear in the Duke-edited *Crusader*. Its readers were offered the same Nazi literature that Duke had advertised in *The Racialist* and *The Nationalist*: George Lincoln Rockwell's *White Power*, Hitler's *Mein Kampf*, *The Hitler We Loved and Why*, and *Herman Goering: The Man and His Works*. Trying to make the Klan a viable political force by making it more respectable, Duke continued to deny that he was aiding neo-Nazis by selling such literature: "This is America and people should have the right to read anything they so desire. . . . You can go into any bookstore in the United States and find copies of communist books or pro-Zionist material, but I'm criticized for allowing free speech to occur."[18]

The company he kept disputed his disclaimer, as several of his key lieutenants were veterans of neo-Nazi groups. One was James K. Warner. Warner had been an officer in George Lincoln Rockwell's American Nazi party in the early 1960s; later he was involved in anti-Semitic organizations such as the Christian Defense League, the New Christian Crusade Church, and the Sons of Liberty. Karl Hand, Jr., had been active in the National Socialist Party of America and later served as a leader of the National Socialist Liberation Front. William Pierce, whom Duke promoted in an article entitled "Masters of the Media," was a former physics professor at Oregon State University who had joined the American Nazi party in 1966 and was editor of the *National Socialist World*. Later, he served as an executive officer in the National Socialist White People's party and in 1970 became affiliated with a neo-Nazi organization called the National Alliance.

Despite these Nazi links, David Duke's career and reputation as a Klansman flourished in the seventies. After Jim Lindsay's death in 1975, Duke became grand wizard of the Louisiana Knights of the Ku Klux Klan. Young, articulate, and good-looking, Duke presented a new image for the Klan; one writer called him "The Image-Maker of the Klan."[19] He appeared on a variety of local and national TV talk shows—including "Today," "Tomor-

Duke speaking to a Klan rally in 1979. (Courtesy of Michael P. Smith)

row," and "A.M. America"—and became a regular on the college lecture circuit. His ability to attract publicity led to an increase in the size of the Klan during the last half of the decade: in 1975, when Duke held a Klan rally in Walker, Louisiana, he drew an estimated 2,700 spectators. In the late 1970s, Klan membership nationally peaked at approximately 10,000.[20]

In 1980 David Duke severed his ties with the Ku Klux Klan. He then established a new organization, which he called the National Association for the Advancement of White People (NAAWP) so its "name and clear purpose made it impossible for minority racists to condemn us without exposing their hypocrisy." He described it as "primarily a white rights lobby organization, a racial movement, mainly middle class people."[21] As with his other groups, Duke created a subsidiary newspaper—the *NAAWP News*. In addition to printing articles comparable to those that had appeared in his earlier publications, Duke continued to advertise a variety of racial, anti-Semitic, and Nazi publications. Readers could join the NAAWP for twenty-five dollars a year; for an additional ten dollars, they could become official organizers.[22]

While the NAAWP lacked the drawing power of the Ku Klux Klan, the organization did allow Duke to claim that he had distanced himself from his previous associations and to woo the larger constituency he sought. It is from this base that he built an electoral following.

David Duke and the World of Electoral Politics

David Duke's first attempt to affect electoral politics came in the fall of 1975, when, as Louisiana's grand wizard and a Democrat, he ran against a one-term conservative incumbent, Kenneth Osterberger, for the state Senate seat of the Sixteenth District near Baton Rouge. Duke's campaign never mentioned his Klan connections. His advertisements showed him opposed to increased taxes, gun control, the welfare state, forced busing, and reverse discrimination against white people in employment, scholarships, and promotions. The overt racism of his other publications was singularly absent, though he played to the virtually all-white constituency of his district in a campaign ad asserting that many white politicians were "slaves to the black vote." ("Give the Majority a Real Voice," the headline said.) Duke supporters came from other states to campaign on his behalf; Osterberger noted that it was not uncommon "to see cars with Pennsylvania, California and New York plates covered with Duke for Senate signs."[23] Although defeated, Duke received 11,079 votes or 33.2 percent of the total cast in the November first election.

For David Duke, the defeat represented a step toward greater public acceptance. After continuing his Klan activities, and even establishing contacts with extremists in the United Kingdom and Canada,[24] he reentered the political arena in 1979, running as a Democrat for another state Senate seat, this time from suburban New Orleans. As was the case four years earlier, Duke's opponent was an incumbent, Joseph Tieman. Tieman, who had strong ties to the Jefferson Parish political machine, easily withstood Duke's challenge. In a four-man race, Tieman received 21,329 votes (51 percent), while Duke, campaigning once again as a moderate conservative, came in second with 9,897 votes (26 percent).

Although Duke said he thought he would never run for political office again, in 1988 he entered the presidential primaries race as a Democrat. In an announcement made before 150 supporters on the steps of the Georgia state capitol, Duke laid out his plans for the presidency, attacking affirmative action, illegitimate welfare childbirths, government set-asides, income taxes, the Supreme Court, and "Zionist control over the media." Among those present were Daniel Carver, grand dragon of the Invisible Empire, KKK; Edward Fields of the white supremacist National States' Rights party; and Don Black, Duke's successor in the Knights of the Ku Klux Klan. Duke's campaign manager was Ralph Forbes, a member of Rockwell's American Nazi party from 1959 to 1967, the prime mover in the Sword of Christ Good News Ministry (an anti-Semitic movement in Arkansas), and a featured speaker at the North Midwest Conference of the Aryan Nations in 1985.[25]

Distancing itself from Duke, the Democratic party did not allow him to appear in Democratic-sponsored debates. He did not receive matching funds from the government. At the polls, he captured only 22,000 votes in the states where he ran. But Duke changed parties and saw the presidential race through as the Populist candidate. The Populist party, created four years earlier, had brought together a number of racial extremists; Willis Carto, the head of Liberty Lobby, an organization the Anti-Defamation League called "the most active anti-Semitic organization in the country," was its founder.[26] The campaign raised over $500,000, publicized Duke, and garnered approximately 150,000 votes.

Less than two months later, in January 1989, Duke switched parties and elections again, this time running as a Republican in a state House race. In short order he campaigned and won a third of the primary election vote for the Eighty-first District, a largely white suburb of New Orleans. In the February runoff election that followed, Duke defeated John Treen, brother of a former Republican governor and a local home builder, by 227 of the nearly 17,000 votes cast. Once again, Duke portrayed himself as a moderate conservative who opposed affirmative action, welfare spending, and increased taxes. However, within a month Duke spoke at another meeting of the Populist party in Chicago, and he continued to sell neo-Nazi and racist literature through his Metairie legislative office.

Then in November 1989 David Duke announced that he would challenge Democrat and longtime incumbent, J. Bennett Johnston, for his U.S. Senate seat. Duke again downplayed his extremist past, noting in a *New York Times* interview: "There are many liberals today who were radical leftists in their younger days. I'm a conservative who might have been considered a radical rightist in my younger days."[27] This approach clearly worked: though Duke lost the primary election the following October, he gained 44 percent of the vote. The Senate election marked a high point of Duke's political career, yet it was topped the next year by the publicity he received during his gubernatorial campaign. Although Duke was defeated by Edwin Edwards in the runoff for governor by a 61 to 39 percent margin, the contest gave him national publicity. Subsequently, he announced that he would campaign for president as a Republican in 1992.

SUPPORTERS OF RIGHT-WING MOVEMENTS

What attracts voters to David Duke? We are beginning to find out. Duke's electoral success resulted in the creation of the Louisiana Coalition against Racism and Nazism (LCARN), a New Orleans–based group that organized to expose Duke's past. A July 1990 poll commissioned by the coalition revealed that the typical Duke supporter was a white Democrat between the ages of thirty-five and forty-nine, a high school graduate with no college education, a parent of public school children, a Catholic, and a male with a total family income between $20,000 and $40,000.[28]

One source of information about Duke's core supporters can be found in letters to LCARN protesting the coalition's opposition. The letter writers are not necessarily average Duke supporters—their intensity moved them to write. But they do indicate the passions leading them to endorse him. Their concerns, which are typical of members of extremist organizations, reveal a continuity between support for David Duke, the extremist, and David Duke, the candidate.

One theme of the letters is that things are falling apart:

I am 66 years old and I have seen our United States become 2nd rate since WW2. I believe Mr. Duke and more like him can turn us around.[29]

The liberal Democrats have gotten this country in such a mess that it will take generations to straighten it out [a senior citizen].[30]

This country is falling apart around us. Someone has to address the issues that concern the average hard working middle class people in this country. I will vote for David Duke knowing he cannot win, but I hope to send a message that politicians will see. David Duke says a lot of things that the average person feels.[31]

Another theme is that of falling away from traditional values:

Shame on you! Get on your knees and ask for forgiveness. Matthew 7:1.[32]

Is David Duke the cause of the drug problem and the illegitimacy that's rampant in this welfare-burdened state? No![33]

Read the Bible. David Duke does. . . . David Duke is the future. He is Louisiana's solution; the white world's solution![34]

A different focus, explicitly racial, is on being taken over:

You see on TV black Miss America, black history week, black this, black that. But you get on TV here and say let's have White Miss America, that's totally out of the question.[35]

My son went to Jesuit High and held a CPA at the time he sart [sic] to go to Loyola Law School. But they pushed him aside to make room for Negroes and the bad taste in my mouth is still there.[36]

LA needs a solution that is not a problem. How about Gas Chambers. Jew Money, Race Mixers, Inc., Go Back to Africa.[37]

I believe there's a climate in this country that has become anti-Euro-American. . . . I'm not putting anyone else down, but we have to put a stop to this idea that we can't stand tall and say the European white man is one of the great races in the world.[38]

I am fed up with every program going to blacks only. If you are poor and white, you do not have a place to go to complain. Colin Powell with Cs and Ds in College was just promoted to the head of the Joint Chiefs of Staff only because he is black. Elevated over 37 whites. I am fed up just like millions of other whites. . . . I am against racial prejudice but the white people are getting the short end of the stick.[39]

David Duke will prevent, according to still another theme, a further winding down:

If nothing else is accomplished, David Duke has at least gotten Bennett Johnston out of "bed" with Teddy Kennedy, Joe Biden and the other eastern liberals.[40]

This categorization of themes follows Wilkinson's four fears that are central to American culture.[41] The concerns of Duke supporters are core concerns of Americans about their society. They are not atypical but typical. What makes them extreme are not the issues themselves but the lengths to which they are taken. Extremist movements in general often invoke the same cultural anxieties in overreaction to stress.

Extremist Supporters and the Duke Movement

In analyzing extremist movements, Seymour Lipset and Earl Raab point out that the critical ranks are not composed of evil-structured types recognizable as "extremists," but of ordinary people caught up in certain types of stress. The membership of American political movements typically has been related to a sense of power and status deprivation. In their theory of status politics, Lipset and Raab note that the strains giving rise to right-wing and left-wing political movements are different. "Never-hads," groups that have never gained their rightful share of power and status, tend to be attracted to left-wing movements, whereas groups that feel that they are losing their power and status—"once-hads"—are attracted to right-wing movements.[42]

Once-hads provide the base of support for David Duke and tend to see a falling apart of the society. Right-wing movements have appeared when economic and social changes have led to a perceived displacement or dislocation of some population groups. This results in decreased loyalty to social and political institutions and a pervasive sense that the society is winding down and losing vigor. Lipset and Raab observe that moral and religious dimensions are the remembered elements of culture. Customs, mores, sexual habits, religious habits, and styles of life are all viewed as the specific symbolic content of lost-status groups. Despite Duke's personal activities, his supporters perceive him to be a defender of these values, a barrier to the falling away from virtue.

Nativist bigotry is another critical element of right-wing extremism; however, it has sprung up out of a backlash against change that invented or reinvented nativist bigotry. Racism and anti-Semitism are two examples of this. David Duke's record in these areas is well known. His supporters echo his themes. In anti-Semitism, the notion of being controlled is a recurrent theme, and the image of black control over whites is prevalent among traditional racists. Both of these fears are symbolic. In fact, Edwin Edwards once stated: "I don't think there are 500 people in Louisiana that have either been adversely affected or benefited by affirmative action. But everyone who doesn't have a job or whose son cannot get into law school believes it's because of affirmative action."[43]

Just as the concerns of Duke's supporters parallel those of extremists, the emergence of Duke as a politician follows in part the pattern for the development of political movements. Neil J. Smelser suggests three initial requirements for the development of political movements:

1. The existence of a social strain of ambiguous proportions that creates widespread anxiety.

2. The designation of a specific course for that strain. (Without such a designation, there would be no movement, only hysteria.)

3. The designation of a specific solution. (Without such a designation, there would be no movement, only a kind of wish fulfillment.)[44]

In the case of David Duke, all three of these requirements are met. Desegregation and subsequent affirmative action programs are perceived by segments of the white population as having displaced or dislocated them. The resulting anxiety, coupled with the low democratic restraint that is characteristic of less privileged classes in American society, has given Duke an audience that is receptive to his message. The members of this audience feel that the loss of their power and status is related to governmental policies in the field of civil rights, that gains by blacks have been made at their expense. David Duke's solutions, whether they be the end of affirmative action or the return of traditional values, will restore their proven role in society. This position was affirmed by a thirty-year-old electrical engineering student, who told a *New York Times* reporter: "We don't want to go back to segregation, we just want equal rights for everyone."[45]

The limits on Duke's support are not clear. Whereas he is identified with Louisiana politics, his supporters are national. In fact, during the 1990 U.S. Senate campaign, he was supported by a 100,000-name mailing list that generated $2.2 million in contributions.[46] Although Duke has become the spokesperson for the once-hads in Louisiana, there are many more people throughout the United States who share the viewpoint of his Louisiana constituency. The question is whether he can mobilize these people on a national level. His ability to have an impact on the United States as an open neo-Nazi or Klansman is limited. The real danger lies in his ability to redefine himself as a mainstream politician who can both attract voters and influence government policy.

Many Duke supporters feel alienated because they believe establishment politicians and the Democratic party have not stood up for their interests and, instead, have supported special interests at their expense. These individuals are not neo-Nazis or Klansmen. But they do feel that they have lost power and status in contemporary America. As other chapters in this volume reveal, a significant minority in the United States shares the views of the Duke supporters in Louisiana. Despite Duke's success at the polls, it is unusual for backlash groups to achieve major electoral gains. More frequently, some extremist proposals are incorporated into the platform of a major party.

Conclusion

At first glance, David Duke appears to have come from extremist roots but now has a more mainstream appeal. Indeed, this is how Duke presents himself when he dismisses his past as youthful indiscretion. His opponents claim that he has not changed, pointing to continuities such as his enthusiastic core of supporters from extremist groups—once a Nazi, always a Nazi. My analysis of his personal history, organizational involvements, and electoral efforts supports the emphasis on continuity, but with a twist.

Duke continues to operate at the intersection of mainstream and extreme. He mainstreams extremism. His focus on gaining widespread acceptance for extremist views harkens back to his high school and college days. His broadening of an organizational base characterized his Klan leadership. Duke became a leader precisely because he could articulate an acceptable image for extremist groups—that is his forte. Duke was able to attract supporters who might otherwise have remained on the political sideline. His electoral efforts extended the mainstreaming to new levels of success.

To analysts of extremism, ordinary members of extremist groups are ordinary people, albeit under stress. Louisiana's once-hads perceive themselves as under pressure. Duke is experienced at bringing out the stressful elements of everyday life that extremism addresses. Thus, his mainstreaming of extremism involves a scapegoating appeal to frustration. What makes mainstreaming possible is that the concerns of extremists are not so different from the concerns of ordinary citizens. The fears of falling apart, falling away, being controlled, and winding down are characteristic of both groups. In extremist movements, these fears are taken to extremes. The boundary between extreme and mainstream, ordinary people and unusual stress, is not a hard and fixed one, and David Duke has made a career out of crossing it.

NOTES

1. Sims, *The Klan*, 179; Zatarain, *Evolution of a Klansman*, 60–61, 87.
2. Zatarain, *Evolution of a Klansman*, 75.
3. Sims, *The Klan*, 179.
4. Zatarain, *Evolution of a Klansman*, 100–101.
5. Ibid., 109–10; Lipset and Raab, *Politics of Unreason*, 282.
6. Anderson, "Jews, Blacks Lambasted," 1 (first quotation); Snyder, "The 'Nazi' of LSU," A4 (second quotation).
7. Quoted in Zatarain, *Evolution of a Klansman*, 125–26.
8. Sims, *The Klan*, 181.
9. Ibid., 182–83.
10. Bridges, "David Duke Tries to Bury Nazi Past, A1."
11. Zatarain, *Evolution of a Klansman*, 129–31.
12. Duke, *The Racialist*.
13. Duke, Letter to fellow members and supporters of the White Youth Alliance.
14. Sims, *The Klan*, 182.
15. Duke, "We Must Build a White Political Machine."
16. Chalmers, *Hooded Americanism*, 414; Anti-Defamation League, *Hate Groups*, 22.
17. Quoted in Anti-Defamation League, *Hate Groups*, 22.
18. Zatarain, *Evolution of a Klansman*, 187–88, 192 (quotation).
19. Sims, *The Klan*, chap. 15.
20. Anti-Defamation League, "Ku Klux Klan Tries for a Comeback," 264.
21. Duke quoted in Zatarain, *Evolution of a Klansman*, 254, and Anti-Defamation League, *Extremism*, 84–85, respectively.
22. Anti-Defamation League, *Extremism*, 84–85.

23. Zatarain, *Evolution of a Klansman*, 213, 215.
24. Sims, *The Klan*, 221–23.
25. Zatarain, *Evolution of a Klansman*, 248, 271 (quotation); Anti-Defamation League, *Extremism*, 85, 97.
26. Anti-Defamation League, *Extremism*, 35.
27. Applebome, "Ex-Klansman Puts New Racial Politics to Test," A1.
28. Hill, "Group Says Truth Weapon against Duke," 1. Detailed analysis of Duke supporters may be found in other chapters of this volume.
29. LCARN Collection.
30. Ibid.
31. Ibid.
32. Ibid.
33. Ibid.
34. Ibid.
35. O'Byrne, "Anatomy of an Upset," A1.
36. LCARN Collection.
37. Ibid.
38. Applebome, "Ex-Klansman Puts New Racial Politics to Test," A1.
39. LCARN Collection.
40. Ibid.
41. Wilkinson, *Pursuit of American Character*.
42. Lipset and Raab, *Politics of Unreason*, 484, 23–24. For a detailed discussion of their model of right-wing extremism, see chap. 12, 484–516.
43. Ibid., 23–24.
44. Smelser, *Theory of Collective Action*, quoted in Lipset and Raab, *Politics of Unreason*, 23.
45. Applebome, "Louisiana Tally," A1.
46. Stovall and Thorne-Thomsen to author.

REFERENCES

Anderson, Bob. "Jews, Blacks Lambasted at Heated Alley." *The Daily Reveille* (LSU campus newspaper), November 13, 1969.
Anti-Defamation League of B'nai B'rith. "The Ku Klux Klan Tries for a Comeback." *Facts* 25 (November 1979).
———. *Extremism on the Right*. Rev. ed. New York: Anti-Defamation League of B'nai B'rith, 1988.
———. *Hate Groups in America*. Rev. ed. New York: Anti-Defamation League of B'nai B'rith, 1988.
Applebome, Peter. "Ex-Klansman Puts New Racial Politics to Test." *New York Times*, June 18, 1990.

————. "Louisiana Tally Is Seen as a Sign of Voter Unrest." *New York Times*, October 8, 1990.

Bridges, Tyler. "David Duke Tries to Bury Nazi Past." New Orleans *Times-Picayune*, June 25, 1990.

Chalmers, David M. *Hooded Americanism: The History of the Ku Klux Klan.* 3d ed. Durham: Duke University Press, 1987.

Duke, David Ernest. Letter to fellow members and supporters of the White Youth Alliance, January 1972. In author's possession.

————. *The Racialist*, vol. 2, no. 4, April ed., n.d.

————. "We Must Build a White Political Machine." *Nationalist Magazine*, April 1972, 34–37.

Gannett News Service. "Duke Supporter." *Monroe* (La.) *News Star*, August 26, 1990.

Hill, John. "Group Says Truth Weapon against Duke." *Shreveport Times*, August 26, 1990.

Lipset, Seymour Martin, and Earl Raab. *The Politics of Unreason: Right Wing Extremism in America, 1790–1970.* New York: Harper and Row, 1970.

Louisiana Coalition against Racism and Nazism (LCARN). Collection, Amistad Research Center, Tulane University, New Orleans. The collection includes materials donated by LCARN relating to the coalition's activities during the 1990 U.S. Senate campaign in Louisiana.

O'Byrne, James. "Duke: Anatomy of an Upset." New Orleans *Times-Picayune*, March 5, 1989.

Sims, Patsy. *The Klan*. New York: Stein and Day, 1978.

Smelser, Neil J. *The Theory of Collective Action*. New York: The Free Press, 1963.

Snyder, David. "The 'Nazi' of LSU . . . Head of the Klan." New Orleans *States-Item*, May 26, 1975.

Stovall, Rev. James L., and Fletcher Thorne-Thomsen. Letter to author, November 26, 1990.

Wilkinson, Rupert. *The Pursuit of American Character*. New York: Harper and Row, 1988.

Zatarain, Michael. *David Duke: Evolution of a Klansman*. Gretna, La.: Pelican Publishing Company, 1990.

Elizabeth A. Rickey

4 | The Nazi and the Republicans

An Insider View of the Response of the Louisiana Republican Party to David Duke

David Duke is a man of many faces. He has been a state legislator from the Eighty-first District in Metairie, a recent candidate for the high offices of president, U.S. Senate, and governor, and a professional racist. His emergence on the political scene as a Republican has thrown the Louisiana Republican party into confused immobility. The hesitant response of Republican party leaders to Duke has helped to gain him precisely what he wants: mainstream respectability. In so doing, David Duke does damage to the conservative agenda by redefining it in his own image, an image that defines issues in a racial context.

I have gained a certain notoriety by trying to put the pieces of Duke's life—or lives—together. I did so hoping that my Republican colleagues in Louisiana would blanch when they learned what this man is all about. Instead, their response to the candidacy of this Nazi sympathizer has been curious at best and morally irresponsible at worst. They turned their heads or said "So what?" The moral crisis facing the Louisiana Republican party and its national parent is indeed a struggle for the soul of our party. This crisis began when the state leadership chose to ignore Duke's neo-Nazi philosophy. This chapter is the story of my unsuccessful attempt to have the leadership repudiate it.

In December 1988, I was pursuing a doctoral degree in political science at Tulane University in New Orleans and had been recently elected to the Louisiana Republican State Central Committee. One of my colleagues on the State Central Committee, John Treen, was running for a legislative seat in Metairie. A special election had been called for January 1989 to fill the vacancy, and John was one of many persons seeking the position. His major opponent was Jefferson Parish School Board member Delton Charles. David Duke's last-minute entrance into the race as a Republican was viewed more as a curiosity than a threat. However, Treen asked me to look into Duke's background so that he could be prepared in case the former Klansman became a serious contender.

Tulane University has one of the few collections in the nation of left- and right-wing political information, with an extensive collection on David Duke and his writings. I immersed myself in Klan and Nazi literature, and the more I read, the more appalled I was. Duke had left a paper trail that was twenty years long; there was no doubt that he was a professional racist and Nazi sympathizer. His claim that this was all in his "past" was blatantly untrue.

As a native Louisianian, I had heard of David Duke for years and dismissed him as a kook. No one took him seriously, at least in my circle of friends, and his frequent publicity stunts were just another sideshow attraction in the circus of Louisiana politics. Without knowing of his Nazi leanings, I was repelled by his leadership in the Knights of the Ku Klux Klan. In my family, the Klan was regarded as a terrorist organization, not as an upholder of southern tradition. My great-grandfather, John Henry Womack, for twelve years around the turn of the century was sheriff of St. Helena Parish, a Klan stronghold in the late 1800s. A story that deeply impressed me was that he once held off a Klan lynch mob gathered at the parish jail in Greensburg, Louisiana. My grandfather, only twelve years old at the time, recalled that his father, John Henry, directed him to bring a wagon to the back of the jail, to hide the black man under a bale of hay, and to take him to Clinton in the next parish. It was the dead of night, and roads were treacherous back then, especially at night, but my grandfather transported the man to safety. The black man had been wrongly accused of raping a white woman, and my great-grandfather was keeping him in the jail for his own protection. This bravery on the part of my great-grandfather and grandfather stuck with me, and I viewed Klansmen with contempt, as cowards who liked to terrorize and denigrate people.

As I read *The Crusader*, Duke's Klan newspaper, I saw racist cartoons, racist jokes, and articles on the superiority of the white race. My overwhelming impression of Duke from his writings was of a mean-spirited, unkind man, contemptuous of his fellow human beings, and deceitful. He was not a person to be considered a serious candidate for anything except a mental institution.

However, what really stopped me cold was Duke's obvious fascination with Adolf Hitler and Nazism. My father had served as a lieutenant colonel in the Third Army under General George S. Patton. He landed at Normandy and was a part of the Battle of the Bulge. Papa was very proud of his service to his country and used to tell me stories about the war. More than once, he told me of the camps where innocent civilians had been starved to death or left to die of typhus and other diseases by the Nazis. He spoke of how people were killed in the extermination camps just because they were of a particular religion. My father died when I was ten, but I never forgot how important it was to him that he had helped to liberate Europe. The lessons he had taught me of those evils and horrors left an indelible imprint.

So when it dawned on me that Duke was not only a white supremacist but also a devotee of Hitler and National Socialism, I was affronted. What particularly incensed me was Duke's continual denial, over a twenty-year period, that the Holocaust ever happened. I resolved to expose this man for the hatemonger that he is. I was sure that once my colleagues on the Republican State Central Committee heard that a Nazi was in their midst, they would all rise in collective indignation and denounce him.

David Duke won the state legislative seat in February 1989, if only by some two hundred votes. He prevailed in spite of endorsements for his opponent, John Treen, by President George Bush and former president Ronald Reagan. Billy Nungesser, as chairman of the Louisiana Republican party, had issued a lukewarm denunciation of "opportunists" and reaffirmed the party's support of Treen as the endorsed candidate. Chairman Lee Atwater had sent resources from the Republican National Committee (RNC) to assist the Treen campaign. All of these efforts helped to slow Duke down but did not prevent his narrow win over John Treen.

Within a week of Duke's victory, at the end of February, Lee Atwater polled the members of the RNC's executive committee, and they voted unanimously to censure Duke. Although widely approved outside of Louisiana, this action was roundly denounced by many Republicans in the state. Mail started flooding the party's state headquarters on North Sixth Street in Baton Rouge. Among the letters received are these two examples:

Because of the despicable attack upon Mr. Duke by Lee Atwater and other national Republican leaders, I have decided to withhold my support of the Republican Party until such time as this position is reconsidered and reversed. [Bogalusa]

I would like to see J. Bennett Johnston defeated at any cost, but Lee Atwater must apologize to David Duke for his past action on national television. After the apology I will forward a check for $100.00. [Pineville]

March 1989

On March 4, 1989, I was sitting in a jammed meeting room at the Bismarck Hotel in Chicago. I was a registered guest of the Populist Party National Convention, an amalgam of former Klansmen, neo-Nazis, and other right-wing extremists who had organized in 1984. The leader of the Populist party was Willis Carto, the shadowy head of the Liberty Lobby, a virulently anti-Semitic organization in Washington, D.C., and the Institute for Historical Review, whose sole purpose is to argue that the Holocaust never happened. Carto was a longtime associate of David Duke's, beginning in 1968 with the National Youth Alliance, a neo-Nazi organization. The Populist party had, for all intents and purposes, funded Duke's successful bid for the Louisiana legislature just two weeks before. Only 18 percent of Duke's contributions came from within Louisiana, and he received contributions from all fifty states. Carto's personal assistant, Patricia Katson, was now employed in Louisiana as Duke's legislative assistant.

Duke had run as the Populist party candidate for president the year before. He was on the ballot in twelve states, finishing fifth. He switched to the Republican party just weeks after his defeat in the presidential race and had tried to cover up his associations with right-wing extremists during his campaign for the state legislature. Yet here he was, the newly elected Republican representative from Louisiana, "coming home" to thank the Populists for their support.

What am I doing here? I thought to myself. To my right was a group of skinheads—neo-Nazi youths with shaved heads and wearing heavy jackboots. On my left was a man who appeared to be in a brownshirt uniform. At the podium the speaker was ranting about the Japanese. Suddenly, he announced that he had just received information that infiltrators from the B'nai B'rith were in the room. He suspiciously looked my way as if to warn me and said that there were people in the room to take care of people like them—and pointed at the skinheads sitting next to me. This was not your typical political convention.

Of course, I had had an inkling that things were amiss when I discovered that the Chicago chapter of the American Nazi party had provided security for the convention. In fact, my friend Linda and I had had to get through a security phalanx to be admitted into the closed meeting where Duke was going to speak. The press was forced to stay one floor below, so I felt rather vulnerable as I ascended the staircase to the meeting room. We were stopped on the stairway and I flashed my convention badge. The Nazi guard asked me if I was from the press, and I responded indignantly, "Of course not, I'm a Populist!" The next guard was eyeing us suspiciously so I went up to him and pretended that I knew him: "How are you—haven't seen you in awhile! How's your family?" The man looked confused; he was too embarrassed to tell me he did not know who I was and ushered us in.

I had a tape recorder under my coat, stuck in my skirt. The device kept working its way down. I had a vision of it falling to the floor so I grabbed the nearest chair and sat down. Breathing a sigh of relief, I turned my attention to the speaker. All of a sudden I heard a loud "CLICK." Linda started coughing to cover up the sound as people turned to see what the noise was. I had forgotten to turn the tape over. I got up, walking sort of bent over so the tape recorder would not drop out of my skirt, and scuttled into the nearest bathroom. I managed to fix the tape recorder and secure it better, then returned to the meeting.

The mood in the room was tense. The speakers were all angry—angry about minorities, angry about the media, just plain angry. As much as Linda and I tried to keep our sense of humor, we later admitted how frightened we were. We also knew we were there without benefit of the media as protection, so we tried to look as inconspicuous as possible. However, Linda is Asian-American and we did not blend in. It seemed funny later, but at the time we might as well have been blacks at a Klan meeting.

As David Duke was being introduced, I got up and went to the back of the room in case he recognized me. He stood before the group and said, "We did it!" The room erupted in applause and shouting. "My victory in Louisiana was a victory for the white majority movement in this country." I stood transfixed. Duke's bodyguards, members of the American Nazi party, surveyed the crowd like members of the Secret Service—they wore dark glasses and three-piece polyester suits. One of them stared at me during the Duke speech and I felt obliged to clap and yell, "Duke! Duke! Duke!" At the end of his speech, Duke said, "Listen, the Republican Party of Louisiana is in our camp, ladies and gentlemen. I had to run within that process, because, well, that's where our people are." I looked at the crowd, mostly male—

skinheads, Klansmen, T-shirted. It seemed incredible that I was listening to a man who had run as a Republican just two weeks ago and was now telling these bigots that his victory was a victory for them. It was like I was in on a dirty little secret.

When Duke had finished, Linda jumped up and said rather loudly, "I've had enough of this!" I tried to hustle her out, muttering under my breath, "Be quiet, they're watching us," while I smiled and spoke to people as we left. It was a nerve-wracking experience. We were both so rattled that we skipped the press conference afterward. This is when Duke was photographed shaking hands with Art Jones, chairman of the American Nazi party. Jones got into a scuffle with a reporter, pushing him and calling him a "low-life scumbag."

Duke returned to Louisiana and apologized to the legislature for the incident in Chicago. In a letter addressed to all the representatives he explained that Jones was some "Nazi kook" whom he had never seen before and that the Populist party meeting was a "conservative anti-tax" rally. Moreover, he continued:

Because of my controversial Klan background and my dabbling in far-right politics as a teenager, the media saw this as a great opportunity to suggest that I have connections with the politics of extremism. I reject categorically racial or religious intolerance. Furthermore, I am diametrically opposed to the totalitarian policies of both Communism and Nazism. Both those ideologies I find personally abhorrent.

. . . I also repudiate any efforts of extremist groups to capitalize on my election victory. My victory was a victory for true equal rights and greater understanding and not intolerance and discrimination.

One of my friends in the legislature sent me a copy of Duke's letter. It was unbelievable audacity for the darling of the Populist party to tell the Louisiana legislature that he repudiated "any efforts of extremist groups to capitalize on my election victory." That was the whole purpose of his talk in Chicago—to present his victory in Louisiana as a blueprint for other extremists to use in their campaigns.

I immediately went to see the state Republican party chairman, Billy Nungesser. He was troubled by Duke's visit to Chicago. I believe that he was genuinely turned off by the Nazi incident but wanted to keep a lid on things. Nungesser's approach to leadership is to control and contain, and he feared that publicizing this event might give Duke the attention he craved. I must say, though, that while his arguments seemed tactically sound, I was disturbed that he did not seem to share my visceral distaste for David Duke.

April 1989

I gave one interview to WWL-TV on the Chicago convention and this aired at 10:30 P.M. on Sunday, April 1. In that time slot it was not widely seen and only contained a brief statement of mine on the subject. This program, however, was sent to the Republican National Committee, and I was contacted by Dan Beck, a former southern field coordinator who had been in Louisiana for the Treen race. He told me that Lee Atwater was deeply concerned about David Duke, and that the RNC wanted to send a field person to meet with me and look at the research I had on Duke. I agreed to help them out, and the staff person called me and arranged a day and time to fly to New Orleans. Meanwhile, I thought that it would be appropriate to notify the state chairman that an RNC representative was coming to meet with me, so I called Billy Nungesser to inform him of this. He became agitated and told me he did not want any of "those national people" down here messing around. He thought that it would backfire if Duke found out that the national party was involved again. Nungesser's ears were still ringing from the calls he received from irate Republicans who were angry over the national party's censure of Duke.

Nungesser told me that he was going to call Atwater and tell him to call off the dogs, that he intended to handle the situation. I agreed that it was reasonable to try and work things out ourselves. Billy talked about raising money to research the issue, and I was assured that he wanted to address this problem. The visit by the RNC staffer was canceled.

Meanwhile, my friend and Tulane University colleague, Lance Hill, suggested that we try and see if Duke was still selling Nazi books now that he was a state legislator. Many people had argued with us that Duke had changed, that his Nazi "stuff" was in the past. Hill, a student of the far right for ten years, was curious to find out whether Duke was using his legislative office as a vehicle to promote his book business.

Lance phoned the number listed under National Association for the Advancement of White People (NAAWP) in the directory. The phone was answered, "David Duke, District 81." Lance then asked the receptionist if they had a copy of *The Turner Diaries* for sale. *The Turner Diaries*, written by William Pierce, a longtime Nazi activist and one of Duke's mentors, is a novel about guerrilla warfare and violence against Jews and blacks. According to the Anti-Defamation League of B'nai B'rith, *The Turner Diaries* was the blueprint for the Order, an underground terrorist group founded by members of Pierce's National Alliance. The Order was responsible for a series of criminal and terrorist activities in 1983–84; it is most notorious for its assassination of Alan Berg, a Denver talk-show host, in 1984.

The NAAWP receptionist asked Lance to hold for a minute and returned to say that, yes, they did have a copy of the book. He asked for the price and thanked her.

Lance and I decided that I would go over to Duke's office and buy *The Turner Diaries*. A colleague of mine at Tulane, David Hagy, went along with me because I was not comfortable going by myself. We entered the basement office at 500 North Arnoult. The reception area was empty except for a desk and a broken chair. There were wires hanging down from the ceiling, and people kept walking through the reception area without acknowledging our presence. Finally, David stopped one of the people and said we were interested in purchasing a book. The receptionist looked a little suspicious, so I said that we wanted to buy *The Turner Diaries*. She got the book and gave me a receipt from Americana Books. Then we left.

May 1989

On May 24 and 26 we purchased more books and some tapes from Duke's legislative/NAAWP offices. I sent another researcher so that suspicion would not be aroused. I instructed the buyers to ask for *Imperium* by Francis Parker Yockey, *Hitler Was My Friend*, *The Myth of the Six Million*, *The New Mythology of Equality*, *Hate Nanny* by Odis Cochran, and two cassette tapes: the *Three Bigots* and *George Lincoln Rockwell v. NAACP*.

The researcher who went on May 24 said that she was greeted in the reception area by a woman in her late twenties. The researcher said that she wanted to buy some books and the receptionist told her to wait. She disappeared into a storage area. The researcher observed that the office was "shabby." There was a small, well-worn desk and a single telephone on the desk. On one side of the desk were stacks of newspapers and on the other side were cardboard boxes. At the rear of the office were a washing machine and clothes dryer. In a back room one wall was lined with shelves containing stacks of David Duke and NAAWP T-shirts. The floor was littered with debris.

After about five minutes, a man entered from the storage room. He introduced himself saying, "My name is Chris Winter, like the season." The researcher asked for *Hitler Was My Friend* under the pretext that the book was for her boyfriend. Winter went back into the storage room.

A few minutes later he returned with Hitler's *Mein Kampf* (published by Angriff Press in Los Angeles, California, and distributed by Americana Books, P.O. Box 10453, New Orleans, Louisiana 70181), stating that he was out of *Hitler Was My Friend*. Winter was animated as he explained that *Mein*

Tapes of Duke discussing race and "The Jewish Question" advertised for sale in December 1988. (From NAAWP News 54)

RACE: A TIME FOR TRUTH Discussion of the race issue by David Duke, considered by most to be the most articulate spokesman on race and race-related issues in the Western world today. He has appeared on the Tomorrow Show, Today Show, Donahue and many other programs in other nations such as the largest watched talk-show in Britain, the BBC Tonight Program. In this video cassette, Duke discusses the race issue. He thoroughly discusses the true nature of, affirmative action, the effects of integration and forced busing, the coming crisis of massive non-White immigration and high non-White birthrates, and he offers a vision for the future for White racialists. It is an excellent introduction to the race issue that is edifying for those who know the truth and enlightening for those yet to learn it. 45 minutes color   **$30**

David Duke on Race An excellent discussion of integration, minority violence, welfare, birth-rates, immigration, and racial differences.   **$8**

The Jewish Question (Part 1) In depth discussion of anti-American, pro-Israel Mideast policy, Zionist domination of the mass media and the U.S. Government, Jewish involvement in integration and the establishment of Communism.   **$8**

The Jewish Question (Part II) The ADL, Christianity, the Talmud, Khazars, Holocaust myth, Jewish finance, Kosher food tax, Jewish organized crime, summary.

DUKE SPEAKS AT U OF MONTANA (PART 1) In the face of well-organized opposition, David Duke, through the power of his presence and his eloquence, wins the audience over to a basic racial understanding.

DUKE SPEAKS AT U OF MONTANA (PART 2) The second hour of this great speech with a masterful question and answer period. Terrific.
                          SOLD AS A SET $15

ALL VIDEO TAPES $30 or 3 for $75
ALL Audio tapes $8 or 5 for $30

Kampf was the "one book" about Hitler everyone should read. The researcher bought the book for seven dollars. When Winter returned with her change, he gave her several NAAWP pamphlets and copies of *NAAWP News*, urging her to pass the literature around to her friends.

When she asked to browse through the books in stock, Winter declined. He then accompanied her out to her car. As she was leaving she noticed in her rear-view mirror that he was copying down her license plate number.

Two days later the researcher returned for another buy. Chris Winter greeted her warmly. He asked her to wait because he had something for her. He returned with a copy of *Imperium* and a cassette tape entitled *Rockwell v. NAACP*. The researcher bought both at fifteen dollars each. She and Winter then struck up a conversation. She commented on books lying on the desk and began to browse through them. Winter gave all of them to her for free. The titles included *Zoological Subspecies of Man, Racial Difference in Mental Growth and School Achievement, Ethnic Group Differences, The Control of Evolution in Man, Race Differences—20 Years Later, Did Six Million Really Die? The Truth at Last, The Racial History of Scandinavia, Heredity and Environment: Major Findings from Twin Studies of Ability, Personality and Interests,* and *The American Melting Pot: Its Meaning to Us.*

Now we had the evidence that Duke was (1) still selling Nazi books and (2) doing so under the auspices of his legislative office. Lance and I pondered what to do at this point. We consulted with the Reverend James Stovall, of Baton Rouge, the executive director of the Louisiana Interchurch Conference. I had first spoken with Stovall by telephone after Duke's election, and he was very supportive of our efforts. Stovall set up a meeting in Baton Rouge with state representatives Kip Holden, Randy Roach, and Mitch Landrieu to discuss the situation. Also present was Leonard Zeskind, research director of the Center for Democratic Renewal in Atlanta (formerly known as the Anti-Klan Network). We discussed how best to release the materials—whether it should be done by political leaders, religious leaders, or a combination of both. We did not reach any definitive conclusions, except an agreement that Duke's involvement with them should be publicized.

It was my opinion that I should bring this up at the upcoming Republican State Central Committee meeting on June 3. I also wanted to propose a motion of either censure or investigation into the charges that Duke was using his legislative office to distribute Nazi books. I had submitted a motion of investigation to Billy Nungesser on May 22, 1989. He phoned me right away, very concerned. He told me that I was going to stir up a hornet's nest and help Duke by giving him publicity. He did not want me to raise the matter at the meeting and inferred that my motion would never make it out of committee. I agreed to find another way to bring it up.

June 1989

On June 3, the Louisiana Republican State Central Committee met in the chamber of the House of Representatives at the state capitol in Baton Rouge. Although word was not officially out about the books, a few people did know of them. I had the books with me in my bag and showed them to interested persons. David Duke was at the meeting, wandering around the floor of the House chamber, shaking hands. I had yet to meet him. I was sitting with John Treen when Duke approached John with his hand outstretched. John refused to shake his hand and proceeded to lambast Duke for spreading rumors that he (Treen) had been arrested. Treen also let him have it for spreading the false rumor that he was a child molester and let Duke know that he was facing a lawsuit on that one. Duke denied ever making those comments. John said, "You are a lying, character-assassinating son of a bitch." I decided that Treen did not need any help; he was handling Duke quite nicely. I left them in heated discussion.

A few minutes later, however, Duke followed me across the chamber. He held out his hand and said, "Hi, I'm David Duke." Then he said, "You know, I never had seen Art Jones before in my life." Obviously, he was aware that I had attended the Chicago convention where Nazi party chairman Art Jones was photographed shaking his hand. I replied, "Oh, come on. He was one of your bodyguards."

"I swear, Beth, I had never seen the guy before in my life."

"Then what were you doing at a convention where Nazis were hanging out?"

At this point, the meeting was called to order and I had to take my seat.

Duke was behind the railing of the chamber holding hands with a Nordic-looking blonde. He stared at me throughout much of the session. Finally, toward the end of the meeting, I got up to get coffee. The sergeant at arms informed me that I could not bring coffee on the floor of the House, so I sat on a couch behind the railing. The next thing I knew this voice says "Beth." I turned to my right and there was Duke, seated next to me on the couch. He had his arm around the back of the couch and was leaning toward me.

He wanted to talk about the books I had bought from his legislative office. I said I thought it was awful that he sold propaganda claiming the Holocaust never happened. He told me that I just misunderstood him, that he meant no harm to Jewish people. He also told me that it was his belief that race was the defining element for civilizations, and that race mixing had caused the downfall of many civilizations. As he talked about race, his face took on an eerie glow and he became more animated. I sat there sort of fascinated, and I finally said, "You really believe all this, don't you?" And he replied, "Oh, yes, it's a religion for me." Then I asked him about his mentor, Jim Lindsay, who was murdered in 1975. Lindsay was a Nazi and Klan activist in the New Orleans area and a surrogate father to Duke. Lindsay's estranged wife was charged with the murder but was acquitted. I said, "David, I find it a strange coincidence that Lindsay was murdered and you became grand wizard of the Klan."

"Yes, some people think I killed him," Duke said. I told him that I did not think so, but that I did not believe Lindsay's wife was guilty either. Duke responded, rather bitterly, that of course she was. (Later, I thought that it was an odd conversation to have with a legislator in the state capitol.)

At this point we had been talking for about twenty minutes. I looked up and, much to my amusement, noticed that about half of the members of the State Central Committee had swiveled in their chairs to watch Duke and me instead of the speaker at the podium. The sergeant at arms, Tommy Gaudet, was signaling to me asking me if I was okay. I nodded affirmatively. Gaudet would have been glad to muscle Duke away if necessary, I gathered.

The meeting closed and Duke said that he wanted to introduce me to his girlfriend. He brought me up to her and said, "This is Ginger Swenson. She has a degree from Loyola." I was a little startled by this strange introduction.

Afterward, Jason Berry, a local writer who is an expert on hate groups, suggested that we take advantage of the Simon Wiesenthal exhibit that was being set up in the rotunda of the state capitol. The Wiesenthal Center of Los Angeles, California, was taking an exhibit of photographs of the Holocaust around the country. Jason said it would provide an excellent backdrop for a press conference. On June 6, when the exhibit opened to the public, the media reported that a Holocaust survivor confronted Duke, who was lingering in the rotunda looking at the photographs.

That night in New Orleans, people who were concerned about the election of David Duke met at Loyola University. This group later evolved into the Louisiana Coalition against Racism and Nazism. After the meeting, where we discussed the Nazi books, I decided to strike quickly. Lance prepared a press release, and the next morning David Hagy and I drove to Baton Rouge to present our case to the media.

Hagy and I met the press in the hallway outside of the House committee rooms where, coincidentally, Duke himself was in a meeting that day. As we distributed our packets Duke appeared and began signing autographs for admirers. He was oblivious to us until Robyn Eckings of WVUE-8 in New Orleans grabbed my copy of *Did Six Million Really Die? The Truth at Last* and waved the book in his face on camera. When Eckings asked, "Are you selling this out of your legislative office?" Duke's face reddened, and he asked her excitedly who had brought her that book. Eckings pointed at me. Duke, with obvious agitation, turned and asked me why I was doing this.

"You're treating me like Salman Rushdie!" he said to me, then turned on his heel and hurried away from us, pursued up the stairs by camera crews and reporters until he reached the sanctity of the floor of the legislature, where the press is not allowed. This bizarre reference to the author of *The Satanic Verses*, hiding from Muslim assassins, was vintage Duke, always the martyr. Reporters told me later that Duke called his office in Metairie from the House floor and warned his staff not to sell any more books.

The "Nazi books" incident was considered a successful hit at Duke's claims that he had changed. Chairman Nungesser called to congratulate me after he saw the media coverage. However, he said that the State Central Committee should not say anything about Duke. Nungesser still clung to the idea that Duke was not a racist but just an opportunist.

I began to suspect that there was more agreement with Duke on the race issue than I had heretofore believed. (An example of Nungesser's position on Duke later surfaced in the *New Republic* of September 18-29, 1989, when he was quoted as saying that Duke was "an opportunist, rotten to the core" but argued that censuring him would only give him publicity and only stoke the antiestablishment fire. Nungesser further claimed that only a small core of Duke's supporters was racist, and that the rest of the people were drawn to Duke because of his position on taxes, affirmative action, and so forth.)

On June 22, the still-unnamed Louisiana Coalition against Racism and Nazism held a meeting at my apartment. Present were Lance Hill, the Reverend James Stovall, Professor Lawrence Powell of Tulane, Professor Paul Sanzenbach of Louisiana State University, and myself. We were discussing strategies for dealing with David Duke.

About ten o'clock the phone rang and a voice said, "Beth, this is David Duke." At first I thought it was a joke, but the voice was unmistakable. It was a strange coincidence. I told him that I had company and asked if he could call later. He called back in thirty minutes and we talked for three hours. In the background he kept playing a song by Mike and the Mechanics entitled "Can You Hear Me Running?"; he said it was one of his favorites. Ever the media creature, he was providing his own incidental music.

We talked about Franklin D. Roosevelt's "treason" at Pearl Harbor, a man named Dr. Schweiler who claims that there is no equality between the races, India and its caste system, Greek culture, blondes in India, how Iceland is a superior culture, sperm banks, Duke's love of nature, hiking in Vientiane (Laos) during the Vietnam conflict, and on and on. When I got off the phone, I was very tired and a bit disoriented. Duke was now no longer an abstract entity but a real person.

July–August 1989

Over the next few weeks I spent a good bit of time in Baton Rouge observing Duke and his working relationship with members of the legislature. He and I got together several times to talk, and now and then he would sit with me in the back of the chamber. It was difficult at times to maintain a psychological distance from him, because he is a master of political courtship. He would call me occasionally at home and talk about Jews and blacks.

I asked him one day what he wanted from me and he said, "I want you to hold a press conference and say you were wrong about me." I replied that that was an unlikely prospect considering the fact that I totally disagreed with his racial theories. Suddenly, his demeanor changed from affable to a bit menacing. "Well, Beth, remember, I haven't attacked you—yet."

On August 4, Duke invited me to a lunch meeting at the Ming Palace restaurant in Metairie. He brought with him two books, *The Six Million Reconsidered* and *The Grand Dragon*—the former is about how the Holocaust did not happen, and the latter is a novel about a Jewish reporter who has an overnight fling with a grand dragon of the Ku Klux Klan. *The Grand Dragon* is supposed to be based on a real-life incident. Its author—a woman —was a writer for *The Times* of London. Duke claimed that it is based on him but denied ever sleeping with the writer. In any case, he was very proud of the book and seemed oblivious to the unflattering portrait it paints of him. Any kind of publicity makes him happy, apparently.

On the way to the restaurant our conversation turned to the "Nazi books" episode. Duke told me that whenever I "pulled a stunt like that," I would "stir up the Jews." He complained about receiving death threats and said that incidents such as publicizing the fact that he sold Nazi books were "going to get me killed." I told him I would not feel responsible if he were assassinated, and he said, "I hope you'll feel a little guilty if I get killed." I told him that I would feel a little guilty if that would make him happy. That is the patented Duke charm for you—guilt.

As we ate, he propped up the *Six Million* book on the table in front of his plate and pointed out passages from the Talmud that he claimed prove the Satanic qualities of the Jewish people. Talking about Nazi Germany, he said: "Rudolf Hess was a great man, because of his loyalty to Hitler and because of his attempts at peacemaking. He should have received the Nobel Peace Prize for his flight to England." He especially admired Hess's skill as a pilot and observed what a feat it was to make that flight successfully. He concluded somberly, "One of the greatest travesties of justice was his imprisonment in Spandau Prison." I remembered that the *NAAWP News* and other right-wing publications often featured the campaign to have Hess released. Hess, who stunned the world in 1940 by flying to England solo to offer terms personally to Winston Churchill, had been Hitler's closest deputy since the 1920s, but by 1940 he was losing favor in Hitler's inner circle.

Then came the bone chiller. "And Dr. Mengele," Duke said.

"Oh, you like him, too?" I asked. Josef Mengele was the monsters' monster among the Nazi death camp sadists, the surgeon who treated prisoners, even children, like laboratory rats.

Duke leaned over on his elbow with a confiding look and said, "Beth, he had a Ph.D.! Do you think he would have jeopardized his career by performing experiments on people with so many witnesses around? Come on!"

"It would seem illogical," I replied, feeling a little queasy. Duke's seeming naiveté can be stomach turning. His calm sincerity gives one the sense of dining with an ax murderer.

He talked some about Mengele's research on twins and how interesting it was. Then he began to rail about the injustices done to Adolf Eichmann, the death camp superintendent captured in South America in the 1960s and executed after his trial in Israel in 1961. Now my head was spinning. Here I was, seated at a normal restaurant in the heart of suburban New Orleans, and this normal-looking man was arguing like a personal injury lawyer for Nazis. It was surreal.

Duke was on a roll now. Auschwitz, he said, was never an extermination camp, merely a labor camp. The stench in the air, he said, was from the manufacture of rubber, not from bodies. On a napkin he drew a map of the Mauthausen "labor" camp, explained that he had visited the place, and assured me that there was no such thing as "gas showers." Zyklon-B, the killer gas, he said was only a pesticide used to kill lice and was used only for delousing. If Zyklon-B had been used to kill people, it would have required massive doses of the stuff, which would leave a residue known as "Prussian Blue." He said he had personally examined the walls of the camp and there was no evidence of Prussian Blue.

"What about all of the bodies?" I asked. His answer was that most of the people had died of typhus, some of starvation—as if cruelty were natural. Besides, he claimed, a lot of the photographs of bodies were "doctored" and fakes. As he got deeper into the story, his eyes lit up and he became more and more animated.

"You see, Beth, the extermination camps were a myth concocted by Hollywood to help create the state of Israel." When I asked him why Hollywood would invent such a story, he replied, "Because [it is] controlled by the Jews!"

Duke also talked about how there was no "Final Solution" as history tells us. There is no record of Hitler ordering the extermination of the Jews, he said. The Final Solution was merely a plan to segregate the Jews from the rest of society, much like we segregated the Japanese during World War II. He used Hitler's own reasoning that Jews were enemies of the state who supported communism.

"Oh, come on, David. You don't believe all of this?" I said.

"Beth, don't you think that transporting the Jews to Poland and other far away locales would be stupid if Hitler wanted to kill them? Why would he transport these people all over the place, make a big deal out of it if they were going to be killed? They were just going to labor camps." He said this as if human slavery were a reasonable alternative and as if the bones of millions and the testimony of both victims and ex-Nazis had not convinced a generation of Hitler's guilt.

At this point I had had enough. He invited me to continue the discussion at his office but I declined, wanting to get away from him. During our meeting Duke had informed me that he would be making his annual pilgrimage to Bavaria that month (August). I laughed and told him I thought that was pretty funny—he did not see the humor in this. Duke does not have a sense of irony.

September 1989

He disappeared for the next four weeks and we were out of touch. When he returned, he looked somewhat different. His face seemed redder and tighter. I knew that Duke was a fan of cosmetic surgery (he lauds it in his sex manual, *Finders Keepers*), and he told me that he had had a nose job a long time ago. He said it was because he had fallen asleep at the wheel while delivering newspapers in New Orleans as a teenager—his car ran into a tree and he broke his nose. He insisted that it wasn't cosmetic surgery but a necessary medical procedure to fix his nose.

Anyway, Duke had a new face. (I later heard that he had had a chemical peel and needed to be out of sight for a while. When ABC's "Prime Time Live" came to town in October, he said that he had gone to Brazil to look at rain forests and write articles on ecology.)

The next Republican State Central Committee meeting was scheduled for September 23, 1989. There was a lot of speculation as to whether a motion to censure Duke would be introduced. At first, I had no plans to do so, but my colleague Neil Curran, a member of the evangelical wing of the party, said that he intended to introduce a censure motion. Neil had worked in John Treen's legislative race against Duke and shared my distress over Duke's anti-Semitism and bigotry. He felt strongly that Duke's agenda was opposed to the Judeo-Christian ethic, and he had openly denounced Duke since the election.

Curran was unfairly characterized as a man with a vendetta because of Treen's loss to Duke. Actually, his revulsion was based on an entirely different reason. After sifting through research on Duke for hours on end, he came to a realization that this man was trying to build a white power movement under the nose of the Republican party.

The week preceding the State Central Committee meeting, Curran was featured in several articles about the pending censure. One in particular, written by Jason Berry for *Gambit*, a New Orleans weekly, received a lot of attention. Curran was taking a lot of heat for his decision, and I felt that it was important that I publicly sign on and support him. On Wednesday, September 20, Curran and I met and drafted a resolution condemning Duke's politics of racism and bigotry, spelling out detailed examples of his recent ties to neo-Nazi groups. The resolution called for censure by the state Republican leadership. We realized that censure carried little weight but felt that it was important that a moral statement be made. It was, after all, a decision our national leadership had reached without flinching.

The chairman of the Resolutions Committee was state representative Charles Lancaster of Metairie, an apparent Duke sympathizer. Since Lancaster was not very likely to be pleased at the prospect of moving a Duke censure vote through his committee, particularly with national TV cameras focused on him, Curran assumed that Lancaster would try and derail the resolution on a procedural move. He checked with the parliamentarian for the committee, Robert Edgeworth, to make sure the resolution was being submitted in a timely and correct manner.

Edgeworth assured Curran that as long as the resolution was delivered into the hands of Chairman Lancaster in advance, then it was properly submitted. Assuming the worst, Curran also got a ruling from the parliamentarian that if Lancaster tabled the resolution in committee, Curran—as a member of the Resolutions Committee—could still bring it up for discussion in the form of a minority report.

The night before the vote, I arrived at the Ramada Inn in Baton Rouge, where out-of-town members were staying. Stopping by secretary of state Fox McKeithen's hospitality suite, I encountered Billy Nungesser. He was very displeased with the censure move and said that he wanted to speak privately with Curran and me. Later that evening, we met with him and the Reverend Billy McCormack in the hospitality suite of state senator Ben Bagert. The meeting was tense and lengthy.

The presence of McCormack was particularly significant, since he represented the powerful evangelical bloc of the GOP central committee, the so-called born-agains. The born-agains had been elected, district by district, across the state during the March 1988 Super Tuesday presidential primary in Louisiana to support televangelist Pat Robertson's bid for the Republican presidential nomination.

The nickname of the evangelical members denoted a certain naiveté about politics, since most of them were freshmen members of the committee as well as newly registered Republicans who switched parties so they could run for the central committee. Though it was new to politics, there was nothing amateurish about the numbers the Robertson flock had rolled up across the state the year before. At least 60 of the 140 members of the GOP State Central Committee were now born-agains who voted as a bloc, and they were becoming sophisticated in finding the dozen or so votes necessary to achieve a majority.

McCormack, their leader, a Baptist minister who insisted on being called "Dr.," planted himself in the only available chair in the room. Nungesser sat on one of two beds, while Curran and I sat together on the other facing him. Chain-smoking and talking in a voice like Marlon Brando in *The Godfather*, Nungesser browbeat Curran and me for two hours. He always calls me "Baby" when he is not mad at me and "Beth" when he is. Tonight, I was Beth.

"You have no right to do this!" he said repeatedly. How dare people like Curran and myself assume the role of declaring David Duke a moral disgrace to the state party? That was the gist of the interrogation, which Curran and I had expected. McCormack just watched this performance, for the most part, from his "throne" as Nungesser did his damnedest to overpower us. We could have left, of course, but felt it was important to hear them out.

It was important, too, not to be argumentative, so we kept the response simple: "We just want to follow in the footsteps of the national Republican Party and censure David Duke."

After a while, Nungesser lost his patience and declared that, in fact, the national party had never censured Duke at all. He was quite insistent about this. I was reminded of Duke himself, pressing me to apologize for exposing his racist activities. Only Nungesser was anything but charming in his demeanor to Curran and me.

As you go down the Duke food chain, things get less and less charming. I discovered this at the Chicago Populist party convention, where the delegates resembled nothing so much as a casting call for extras in another Mad Max sequel.

"Billy," I told the party chairman, under the eye of the born-agains' leader, "he was censured by the national party a week after the election. It was all over the newspapers."

He maintained that I was imagining things.

This was ridiculous. I was getting angrier and angrier. Curran, thank God, kept his composure, even when Nungesser implied that the censure vote was just a publicity stunt for those of us proposing it.

Finally, I blew up.

"Listen, Billy, yesterday I received a phone call that said if I get up in front of the committee tomorrow and move to censure Duke, the caller will put a bullet in my head."

Suddenly, McCormack, who had been listening impassively to all this, sat up and relieved the nonplussed Nungesser. It was your classic bad cop/good cop routine—first the rubber hose and then the prayers.

The reverend doctor said something to the effect that I had gone through a lot. Duke, he said, convincingly, was evil. That much we should all agree with. Nungesser was silent for the first time since we had entered the room.

I felt that McCormack was genuinely distressed over the situation and wanted to address it, so we discussed a compromise. What we worked out was that Nungesser would recognize Curran, have him read the motion of censure, and then offer a motion to form a committee to investigate the charges for purposes of censure at the next meeting. This way, we would go around the Resolutions Committee and its reluctant chairman, Charles Lancaster. We shook hands all around, and then McCormack asked us to join hands and pray over our decision. It was a strange moment—Nungesser, Curran, McCormack, and I huddled together holding hands, praying for God's blessing.

I went to bed that night believing that we had reached an agreement and that at least McCormack, if not Nungesser, was aware of the problems Duke posed for the party. But unbeknownst to me, the next morning Nungesser and Lancaster had figured out their own compromise, pulling McCormack in on the deal. "Tag" Livingston, a New Orleans central committee member and retired rear admiral, was selected to derail our resolution by moving to have it tabled. McCormack's people, a near-majority of the State Central Committee, were instructed to vote to table it. I was sitting in my seat thinking that everything was still in order. I noticed Lancaster huddled in the back of the House chamber with Duke, which disturbed me, but I shook it off. Then, someone came up to me and said that Nungesser and McCormack were double-crossing me. I was told that Curran and I would be allowed to read the resolution but that it would be tabled.

I was furious. McCormack was sitting two seats in front of me, and, resisting the urge to grab him by his hairpiece, I grasped his chair and spun it around. "You deceived me," I said in a low voice. "Then you prayed with me, and I believed that you wanted to help."

"Beth, I swear, I have nothing to do with the motion to table," McCormack replied, looking a little shaken.

"Don't hand me that, reverend, you control the votes in that caucus," I replied. "What bothers me more than anything is that you are a minister, and you lied to me. I will never forget this," I said and went back to my seat. I then sent a message up to Chairman Nungesser by courier. It read:

Dear Billy,

You double-crossed me. I will never ever let you forget this.

Sincerely yours,
Beth Rickey

At this point messages started flying between the podium and the area where Neil and I were seated. The thing that really floored me was that in the very act of the double-cross, Nungesser and McCormack were denying any responsibility. Sometimes I thought they were as nervy as Duke, denying in the face of hard evidence.

Neil and I were recognized by the chairman. Knowing that we had been shanghaied, I just stood next to Neil. The moment Neil finished reading our resolution, Tag Livingston jumped up and moved that it be tabled. It was seconded. Nungesser called for a voice vote and declared that the ayes had it. A division of the House was called and I asked that the committee be polled so that the members could go on record. Nungesser ruled me out of order. We proceeded to a secret ballot and the results were never published. I later learned that only about 25 out of the 140 members voted with Neil and me.

After the meeting, Livingston was asked why he moved to table the motion. He said that although Duke was a "charlatan," further investigation of his record would keep him in the eye of the media, thereby enhancing his celebrity. I told the press that I was very disappointed in the party's inability to confront a racist in their midst.

As I left the chamber I was nearly assaulted by angry people. I have gone head-to-head with Duke supporters on radio talk shows, and I have interviewed Klansmen and neo-Nazis, but nothing compares to the insulting behavior I encountered from fellow Republicans on the State Central Committee. You would have thought that I had just made a motion to censure Ronald Reagan. I thought one little old lady was going to hit me, she was so mad.

An irate member of the evangelical caucus followed me down the steps of the capitol. I tried to ignore his shouts but he pursued me all the way to my

RESPONSE OF THE LOUISIANA REPUBLICAN PARTY 79

car. The man accused me of staging all of this to make money and get publicity for myself. At this point I stopped in my tracks, turned around, and said, "I don't like Nazis. I especially don't like them running around in the Republican party. If you have a problem with that, then I suggest that there is something seriously wrong with you and the other 114 members of the State Central Committee who voted to ignore this matter." The last thing I remember hearing as I got into my car was, "Now wait a minute, I never said I liked Nazis!"

What a twilight zone, I thought. I had been standing in front of the state capitol in 1989 arguing with someone over condemning an open racist and Nazi sympathizer. I just did not understand how anyone could look at David Duke, listen to him for any length of time, know of his background, and not want to put garlic around their neck.

Susan E. Howell and
Sylvia Warren

5 | Public Opinion and David Duke

The civil rights revolution and the accompanying Great Society programs of the sixties left an aftershock, a depth and centrality of racial attitudes, that researchers are just beginning to analyze. Racial attitudes have fueled the 1980s' realignment, especially in the South. Racial attitudes have also been demonstrated to be at the center of ideological belief systems.[1]

The candidacy of David Duke for the U.S. Senate was a highly visible symbol of white aftershock to the civil rights movement. From the moment Duke astonished observers by receiving 33 percent of the vote in his primary election to the Louisiana House of Representatives, he has been a focal point for discussions of white racism. In this chapter, using survey data from the greater New Orleans area, we will examine the racial beliefs distinguishing Duke supporters. Because the racial attitude questions used in these surveys are identical to questions asked in national surveys, we will also be able to make explicit comparisons between New Orleans and national public opinion.

Kinder and Sears (1981) identified a new form of racism, symbolic racism, which includes both a general antiblack feeling and a belief among whites that many blacks fall short of the American ideals of individualism and the work ethic. Symbolic racism is heavily infused with the notion of individual responsibility; it holds that every person is responsible for his or her own well-being and rejects treating individuals as members of a group. In that way it differs from "old-fashioned racism," which is expressed in beliefs about the innate inferiority of blacks. Old-fashioned racism, which is now socially unacceptable, has been replaced with symbolic racism, and it is the new attitude that has the strongest political effect.[2]

Symbolic racism has predictive power in a number of models. It is an important influence on attitudes toward racial policies as well as voting and candidate preferences.[3] Furthermore, some of the literature demonstrates an effect that is independent of and stronger than the usual political variables, ideology and party identification.

To discover whether the concept of symbolic racism can help us to understand the phenomenon of David Duke, we address three questions: (1) How do whites in the greater New Orleans area compare to whites nationally on measures of symbolic racism? (2) What are the dimensions of symbolic racism? and (3) Which dimensions are most useful in predicting Duke support?

In political science the term *dimensions* refers to the few, largely independent aspects or facets of a concept that, when put together, capture most of what is meant by the concept. Symbolic racism has several facets or dimensions. These include individualism, a belief in the work ethic, beliefs about how the environment has not disadvantaged blacks, and plain fear of and anger toward blacks. A number of indicators have been used to construct a symbolic racism scale.[4] As yet, we know of no attempt to evaluate the dimensionality of the items or their comparative usefulness. It is possible that some items or dimensions are much more central to the theoretical notion than others. It is also possible that certain dimensions of symbolic racism are more theoretically useful, that is, they are better predictors of candidate preferences. David Duke is an excellent test case because his campaigns have voiced most of the values contained in symbolic racism.

The Data

The national survey data used in this chapter were produced by the University of Michigan's Inter-University Consortium for Political and Social Research (ICPSR), which conducts national election surveys every even-numbered year. Our analysis is based on the responses of registered white voters from the 1986 and 1988 surveys. The questions used to measure symbolic racism were first asked nationally by the ICPSR.

The local New Orleans surveys were conducted by the Survey Research Center at the University of New Orleans. Through telephone interviews, the center surveyed systematic random samples of registered voters in the metropolitan area (Orleans and Jefferson parishes). The research includes only the white respondents from these surveys: 625 in 1989 and 594 in 1990. In both local surveys, the Michigan measures of symbolic racism were exactly replicated. The first local survey occurred immediately after David Duke's election to the state House of Representatives in March 1989, and the second survey took place at the beginning of Duke's U.S. Senate campaign in March 1990.

Symbolic Racism in New Orleans and the United States

The question of the uniqueness of David Duke has often been raised. Could he have run successfully for public office in some other state or city? To address this question we can directly compare the racial attitudes of whites in metropolitan New Orleans to whites in the United States as a whole (see Table 5.1).

Most of the survey questions measuring symbolic racism tap the notion that blacks do, or do not, live up to the ideal of the work ethic. For example, respondents were asked to agree or disagree with these two statements: "It's really just a matter of some people not trying hard enough; if blacks would only try harder they could be just as well off as whites" and "Over the past few years blacks have gotten less than they deserve." Other statements referred to beliefs about the extent of white discrimination, such as "Generations of slavery and discrimination have created conditions that make it difficult for blacks to work their way out of the lower class."

There was remarkable similarity in the direction of preferences in New Orleans and the United States generally. That is, about the same percentages agreed and disagreed with the various statements. A majority of whites in New Orleans and in the nation took a "conservative" position on nearly all of the questions. White voters tended to deny that whites control things and believed that blacks just need to try harder. The difference between public opinion in New Orleans and the nation was that whites in New Orleans were more likely to hold these views "strongly"; they were more intense about their preferences. The "intensity gap" was about ten percentage points. The

Table 5.1

Symbolic Racism Measures among Whites in New Orleans and the United States

"Over the past few years blacks have gotten less than they deserve."

	New Orleans 1990	U.S. 1988*
Strongly agree	6%	3%
Somewhat agree	19	20
Neither	10	21
Somewhat disagree	30	34
Strongly disagree	29	20
Don't know	6	2
Number of responses	595	1,249

"Irish, Italians, Jewish and many other minorities overcame prejudice and worked their way up. Blacks should do the same without any special favors."

	New Orleans 1990	U.S. 1988*
Strongly agree	39%	40%
Somewhat agree	33	33
Neither	5	9
Somewhat disagree	12	14
Strongly disagree	6	3
Don't know	5	1
Number of responses	595	1,249

"It's really just a matter of some people not trying hard enough; if blacks would only try harder they could be just as well off as whites."

	New Orleans 1990	U.S. 1988*
Strongly agree	33%	22%
Somewhat agree	31	36

Table 5.1 *(continued)*

	New Orleans 1990	U.S. 1988*
Neither	5	13
Somewhat disagree	19	21
Strongly disagree	9	7
Don't know	3	1
Number of responses	595	1,249

"Generations of slavery and discrimination have created conditions that make it difficult for blacks to work their way out of the lower class."

	New Orleans 1990	U.S. 1988*
Strongly agree	13%	12%
Somewhat agree	30	36
Neither	4	11
Somewhat disagree	24	25
Strongly disagree	25	15
Don't know	4	1
Number of responses	595	1,249

"Some say that the civil rights people have been trying to push too fast. Others feel they haven't pushed fast enough. Do you think that civil rights leaders are trying to push too fast, are going too slowly, or are they moving at about the right speed?"

	New Orleans 1989	U.S. 1988*
Too fast	36%	27%
About right	44	58
Too slowly	7	11
Don't know	13	4
Number of responses	595	1,249

Source: National Election Study, Inter-University Consortium for Political and Social Research, University of Michigan, 1988.

presence of David Duke may have helped account for this intensity. His candidacy has tapped latent racial antagonisms among white voters.

Based on these findings, David Duke, as he presents himself today, will have electoral appeal in other areas of the country. The antiwelfare, antiaffirmative action themes in the Duke campaigns are popular with many white voters across the country. However, we suspect that Duke's own extremist past is preventing him from achieving his potential support based on the views he expresses currently.

The Dimensions of Racism

Definitions of symbolic racism include several facets or dimensions— individualism, work ethic values, antiblack feelings, and a belief that circumstances do not contribute to the relative disadvantage of blacks. Does one of these attitudes best describe people's thinking on this matter? Which of the subconcepts is most crucial in identifying Duke supporters?

Many specific indicators have been used to construct symbolic racism scales.[5] We have selected seven of these items, which appear with a few exceptions in both the national election studies and the local New Orleans surveys. The seven items are questions about the speed of the civil rights movement and whether blacks try hard enough, whether blacks receive less than they deserve, whether blacks should work their way up like other minorities, whether years of discrimination have kept blacks down, and whether the government pays less attention to blacks. The exact wording of these questions is identical in all four surveys (see Appendix).

A statistical technique, called principal components analysis, is used to identify the important dimensions or facets of symbolic racism. The first dimension discovered by this technique is the most important in that it captures much of the meaning of the concept as it applies to these voters. The second dimension identified is the second most important facet and so on.[6]

The results of this analysis of the symbolic racism items are presented in Table 5.2. The most important dimension in all four surveys is what we call the *black work ethic factor*. This dimension considers questions such as whether blacks try harder, whether they should work their way up, whether they receive less than they deserve, and whether slavery created conditions that make it difficult for them to succeed. All of these items have something to do with blacks working hard or blacks succeeding.

The second dimension in three of the four surveys is what we call the *white discrimination factor*. It contains questions relating to whether whites control things and act to keep blacks down and whether government pays less atten-

Table 5.2

Factor Analysis of Symbolic Racism among Whites

National Election Study, 1986

	Black Work Ethic	White Discrimination
Blacks try harder	.85	−.25
Others overcame prejudice	.84	−.12
Slavery created conditions	.60	.19
Blacks receive less	.59	.36
Civil rights	.57	.12
Whites control	−.12	.82
Gov't gives less attention	.20	.67
Percent of total variation	39.7	16.6
Factor correlation	.216	

National Election Study, 1988

	Black Work Ethic
Others overcame prejudice	.75
Blacks receive less	.74
Blacks try harder	.73
Slavery created conditions	.68
Civil rights	.62
Percent of total variation	49.8

New Orleans Survey, 1989

	Black Work Ethic	White Discrimination
Others overcame prejudice	.81	−.12
Blacks try harder	.81	
Civil rights	.63	
Blacks receive less	.62	
Slavery created conditions	.61	.20
Whites control		.78
Gov't gives less attention		.78
Percent of total variation	38.9	14.8
Factor correlation	.319	

Table 5.2 *(continued)*

New Orleans Survey, 1990

	Black Work Ethic	White Discrimination
Blacks try harder	.88	−.16
Others overcame prejudice	.78	
Slavery created conditions	.46	.44
Whites control	−.27	.87
Gov't gives less attention	.26	.60
Blacks receive less	.42	.43
Percent of total variation	40.7	18.1
Factor correlation	.217	

*Entries are principal components analysis factor loadings, derived from an oblique rotation.

tion to blacks. This dimension reflects the belief that circumstances, as opposed to individual behavior, are the cause of blacks' economic disadvantages. The white discrimination dimension is clearly secondary to the black work ethic dimension.

The black work ethic facet of symbolic racism was the most important dimension in two national surveys and in the racially charged environment of New Orleans during 1989 and 1990. Apparently the notion that symbolic racism captures best is that blacks do not live up to the American ideals of hard work and discipline.

Predicting Candidate Preference

Prior research has demonstrated that symbolic racism influences candidate preferences in a variety of contexts ranging from mayoral elections to presidential elections.[7] Election data for New Orleans in 1990 present a unique opportunity to observe symbolic racism with a candidate, David Duke, who is frequently (if not exclusively) evaluated in terms of racial politics. Because symbolic racism has been shown to be an important predictor of Jesse Jackson evaluation among whites,[8] it seems probable that similar findings will hold for a polar opposite candidate.

Table 5.3 presents simple cross-tabulations of several of the racial questions with candidate preference. Duke's support is concentrated at the ex-

Table 5.3

Racial Attitudes and Duke Support among Whites

"Irish, Italians, Jewish and many other minorities overcame prejudice and worked their way up. Blacks should do the same without any special favors."

	Strongly Agree	Somewhat Agree	Neither	Somewhat Disagree	Strongly Disagree
Johnston	34%	37%	21%	47%	42%
Duke	28	13	11	3	10
Bagert	12	17	17	20	13
Undecided	26	33	51	30	35
Number of responses	227	194	32	72	33

"It's really just a matter of some people not trying hard enough; if blacks would only try harder they could be just as well off as whites."

	Strongly Agree	Somewhat Agree	Neither	Somewhat Disagree	Strongly Disagree
Johnston	29%	43%	8%	43%	42%
Duke	32	15	5	5	4
Bagert	9	14	22	22	23
Undecided	30	28	65	30	31
Number of responses	196	184	26	111	54

"Generations of slavery and discrimination have created conditions that make it difficult for blacks to work their way out of the lower class."

	Strongly Agree	Somewhat Agree	Neither	Somewhat Disagree	Strongly Disagree
Johnston	49%	38%	42%	34%	30%
Duke	8	7	24	18	31
Bagert	18	18	4	13	14
Undecided	25	37	30	35	25
Number of responses	78	173	25	139	149

treme ends of the symbolic racism scales. For example, among those respondents who said they "strongly agree" that blacks should try harder, 32 percent supported Duke, 29 percent supported J. Bennett Johnston, and 9 supported Ben Bagert. But Duke's support drops off sharply after the most conservative response. Among respondents who were less intense and replied simply, "agree" (that blacks should try harder), Duke received only 15 percent of the support. Thus, Duke support is related to intense racial attitudes more than to simple racial conservatism.

We can compare the influences of racial attitudes on Duke support to their influence on other Republicans through the use of multiple regression. Table 5.4 displays the results of three regression equations using support for various Republicans as the dependent variables. From the 1986 National Election Study (NES) we used approval of Ronald Reagan, from the 1988 NES we used presidential preference for George Bush, and from the 1990 New Orleans survey we used U.S. Senate preference for David Duke.

The black work ethic dimension of symbolic racism was a significant predictor of voter preference for Reagan, Bush, and Duke. As expected, its impact on Duke support was much greater than its impact on Reagan approval or Bush support. The second dimension, white discrimination, was much less important than the black work ethic in predicting both Reagan approval and Duke support.

Also as expected, party identification had more influence over Reagan and Bush support than over Duke support. Although he was a Republican, David Duke drew support from Democrats, Independents, and Republicans alike. In contrast, education was more important as a predictor of Duke support than of either Reagan or Bush. Educated white voters were less likely to support Duke, regardless of their racial views. We suspect that educated white voters who agreed with Duke's current positions on issues were at the same time alienated by his past.

The overall predictive power of the model of Duke support is low ($R^2 = .20$). We believe this is due to both the absence of a normal partisan contest, like the 1988 election, and measurement error in the vote intention variable. David Duke is so associated with racism that there are strong prohibitions against publicly stating a preference for him, even to a telephone interviewer. Such a pattern is consistent with Elisabeth Noelle-Neumann's (1984) "spiral of silence" theory. If people perceive their opinions to be unpopular, they will be less willing to express them. This measurement error reduces the validity of the dependent variable, thus reducing the predictive power of explanatory factors. When people's responses become "noisy" with error, even explanations that ought to ring true get confused with static.

Table 5.4

Predicting Candidate Preference among Whites

	Candidate Preference or Evaluation Unstandardized Regression Coefficients		
Independent Variables	NES 1986 Reagan	NES 1988 Bush	N.O. 1990 Duke
Black work ethic factor	.37	.22	.52
	(.05)	(.05)	(.09)
White discrimination factor	.21	NA*	.18
	(.05)		(.09)
Education	**	**	−.28
			(.11)
Party identification	.29	.75	.14
	(.03)	(.04)	(.05)
Ideology	NA*	.19	**
		(.04)	
Intercept	3.41	.53	2.62
R^2	.20	.46	.20
Adjusted R^2	.20	.46	.18
Significance	.000	.000	.000
Number of responses	793	710	265

*Items were not asked in that survey or in the required form of the survey.
**Indicates that the coefficient was insignificant at the .05 alpha level.

Conclusion

Duke's early support in the New Orleans area can be explained in part by the simple fact that about one-third of the white voters hold very intense racial feelings. They believe that blacks do not live up to the work ethic ideal and thereby do not deserve special favors. They do not believe that discrimination by whites keeps blacks down. They think that if blacks only tried harder, they would be as successful as whites. They not only agree with these statements, but also they agree "strongly."

These opinions are not unique to New Orleans. National surveys reveal much the same attitudes, albeit less intense, among whites in the United States as a whole. The strength of feelings in New Orleans is probably a result of the pervasive racial political conflict in that city. We suspect that voters in other locations where race is a dominant issue will exhibit intense racial feelings as well.

Appendix

National Election Study Questions to Indicate Racial Attitudes

Others Overcame Prejudice: "Irish, Italians, Jewish and many other minorities overcame prejudice and worked their way up. Blacks should do the same without any special favors."

Blacks Try Harder: "It's really a matter of some people not trying hard enough; if blacks would only try harder they could be just as well off as whites."

Blacks Receive Less: "Over the past few years blacks have gotten less than they deserve."

Slavery Created Conditions: "Generations of slavery and discrimination have created conditions that make it difficult for blacks to work their way out of the lower class."

Civil Rights: "Some say that the civil rights people have been trying to push too fast. Others feel they haven't pushed fast enough. How about you: Do you think that civil rights leaders are trying to push too fast, are going too slowly, or are they moving at about the right speed?"

Whites Control: "A small group of powerful and wealthy white people control things and act to keep blacks down."

Government Gives Less Attention: "Government officials usually pay less attention to a request or complaint from a black person than from a white person."

Hiring Preference: "Some people say that because of past discrimination, blacks should be given preference in hiring and promotion. Others say that such preference in hiring and promotion of blacks is wrong because it discriminates against whites. What about your opinion—are you for or against preferential hiring and promotion of blacks?"

College Quotas: "Some people say that because of past discrimination it is sometimes necessary for colleges and universities to reserve openings for black students. Others oppose quotas because they say quotas discriminate against whites. What about your opinion—are you for or against quotas to admit black students?"

Government Should Integrate Schools: "Some people say that the government in Washington should see to it that white and black children go to the same schools. Others claim that this is not the government's business. Do you think the government in Washington should see to it that white and black children go to the same schools, or stay out of this area as it is not the government's business?"

NOTES

1. Markus 1979; Carmines and Stimson 1984; Stanley 1988; Petrocik 1987; Carmines and Stimson 1982.
2. Sears 1988, 62.
3. Sears and Allen 1984; Jessor and Sears 1986a; Sears 1988, 61; Kinder and Sears 1981; Sears, Citrin, and Kosterman 1985; Sears and Citrin 1985.
4. Jessor and Sears 1986a.
5. See ibid.
6. Kim and Mueller 1978.
7. Kinder and Sears 1981.
8. Sears, Citrin, and Kosterman 1985.

REFERENCES

Axelrod, R. 1983. "Schema Theory: An Information Processing Model of Perception and Cognition." *American Political Science Review* 67:1248–66.
Bobo, L., and F. Licari. 1990. "Societal Obligations, Individualism, and Re-Distributive Policies II: Prejudice and Politics." Paper presented at the annual conference of the American Association for Public Opinion Research, Lancaster, Pa., May 17–20.
Carmines, E. G., and J. A. Stimson. 1982. "Racial Attitudes and the Structure of Mass Belief Systems." *Journal of Politics* 44:2–20.
Carmines, E. G., and J. A. Stimson. 1984. "The Dynamics of Issue Evolution: The United States." In *Electoral Change in Advanced Industrial Democracies*, edited by R. J. Dalton, S. C. Flanagan, and P. A. Beck, 134–53. Princeton, N.J.: Princeton University Press.
Fiske, S. T., and P. W. Linville. 1980. "What Does the Schema Concept Buy Us?" *Personality and Social Psychology Bulletin* 6:543–57.
Hughes, M. 1990. "White Opposition to Affirmative Action: Symbolic Racism, Perceived Interests, and Antipathy toward Government Coercion." Paper presented at the annual conference of the American Association for Public Opinion Research, Lancaster, Pa., May 17–20.
Jessor, T., and D. O. Sears. 1986a. "Racial Conflict in the 1985 NES Pilot Study." NES Report, May.

———. 1986b. "Realistic and Symbolic Explanations for Racial Conflict." Paper presented at the annual meeting of the Midwest Political Science Association, Chicago.

Kim, J. O., and C. W. Mueller. 1978. *Introduction to Factor Analysis.* Sage Quantitative Applications Series. Beverly Hills: Sage Publications.

Kinder, D. R., and D. O. Sears. 1981. "Prejudice and Politics: Symbolic Racism versus Racial Threats to the Good Life." *Journal of Personality and Social Psychology* 40:414–31.

Markus, G. E. 1979. "The Political Environment and the Dynamics of Public Attitudes: A Panel Study." *American Journal of Political Science* 23:338–59.

Noelle-Neumann, Elisabeth. 1984. *The Spiral of Silence: Public Opinion—Our Social Skin.* Chicago: University of Chicago.

Petrocik, J. R. 1987. "Realignment: New Party Coalitions and the Nationalization of the South." *Journal of Politics* 49:347–75.

Rumelhart, D. E., and A. Ortony. 1977. "The Representation of Knowledge in Memory." In *Schooling and the Acquisition of Knowledge,* edited by R. C. Anderson, R. J. Spiro, and W. E. Montague, 99–135. Hillsdale, N.J.: Lawrence Erlbaum.

Sears, D. O. 1988. "Symbolic Racism." In *Eliminating Racism: Profiles in Controversy,* edited by P. A. Katz and D. A. Taylor, 53–84. New York: Plenum Press.

Sears, D. O., and H. M. Allen. 1984. "The Trajectory of Local Desegregation Controversies and Whites' Opposition to Busing." In *Groups in Contact: The Psychology of Desegregation,* edited by N. Miller and M. B. Brewer, 123–51. New York: Academic Press.

Sears, D. O., and J. Citrin. 1985. *Tax Revolt: Something for Nothing in California.* Cambridge: Harvard University Press.

Sears, D. O., J. Citrin, and R. Kosterman. 1985. "The White Response to Jesse Jackson in 1984." Paper presented at the annual meetings of the American Psychological Association, Los Angeles, and the American Political Science Association, New Orleans.

Sears, D. O., L. Huddy, and L. G. Schaffer. 1986. "A Schematic Variant of Symbolic Politics Theory as Applied to Racial and Gender Equality." In *Political Cognition,* edited by R. Lau and D. O. Sears, 159–202. Hillsdale, N.J.: Lawrence Erlbaum.

Sniderman, P. M., and M. G. Hagen. 1985. *Race and Inequality: A Study in American Values.* Chatham, N.J.: Chatham House.

Stanley, H. 1988. "Southern Partisan Change: Dealignment, Realignment, or Both?" *Journal of Politics* 50:64–88.

Taylor, S. E. 1981. "The Interface of Cognitive and Social Psychology." In *Cognition, Social Behavior, and the Environment,* edited by J. H. Harvey, 189–211. Hillsdale, N.J.: Lawrence Erlbaum.

Taylor, S. E., and J. Crocker. 1981. "Schematic Bases of Social Information Processing." In *Social Cognition: The Ontario Symposium,* edited by E. T. Higgins, C. P. Hermand, and M. P. Zanna, 1:89–134. Hillsdale, N.J.: Lawrence Erlbaum.

6 | Nazi Race Doctrine in the Political Thought of David Duke

Locating David Duke's position on the political spectrum involves analyzing his public message as well as his underlying ideology. Duke identifies himself as a populist and a racialist, while his critics assign him labels ranging from white supremacist to Nazi. This chapter will examine one aspect of Duke's mature political thought, his race doctrine, and analyze the manner in which his thinking remains permeated with National Socialism (Nazism).

The election of David Duke to the Louisiana legislature in 1989 drew international media attention. During the campaign, most of the controversy surrounding Duke derived from his association with the Knights of the Ku Klux Klan—in which he was active from 1973 to 1980. That emphasis on Duke's Klan phase tended to obscure the crucial ideological thread that continues to connect and define his political activity over the past twenty-one years. That common thread is National Socialism.

In recent years Duke has tried to dismiss his associations with Nazism as little more than a youthful indiscretion. He refuses to admit any direct involvement in the Nazi movement. In truth, Duke entered the far-right movement as an avowed National Socialist. Since then, like his Nazi forebears, Duke's politics have been marked by opportunism. For twenty years he has searched for a way to popularize his racial views. His newfound conservatism provides a politically acceptable language for his race doctrine.

Duke's journey across the political spectrum parallels that of Adolf Hitler, who also began as a revolutionist but acquired power constitutionally as a "jobs and bread" conservative. As did Hitler, Duke has adapted Nazism to the fears, aspirations, prejudices, and political culture of the nation, thus representing himself as part of the national political tradition. This process has culminated in his new political image in which his positions are clothed in the rhetoric of equality and democracy.

Duke's official biography paints a portrait of a young man drawn to the simple segregationist views of the Ku Klux Klan. In fact, Duke was initiated into the extremist right as a National Socialist. Evidence indicates that the first organization Duke joined was the neo-Nazi National Socialist Liberation Front (NSLF).[1] The NSLF was the college-youth organizing section of America's largest neo-Nazi organization, the National Socialist White People's party, commonly known as the American Nazi party. In the ensuing years Duke attempted to conceal his early Nazi party affiliation. But in 1969 a younger and unabashed Duke told a crowd at Louisiana State University (LSU), "I am a National Socialist. You can call me a Nazi if you want to."[2]

In November 1969 the LSU student newspaper, *The Daily Reveille*, opened up its editorial page to the intrepid young Nazi, who wrote:

> The NSLF has different views from the run-of-the-mill political groups on campus, whether they support the right or the left. Their approach to the problems confronting our civilization is completely mechanical, economic, and materialistic. National Socialism, on the other hand, is unique! . . . We believe that race plays a primary part in our civilization and our culture, and that a particular culture is a product of the realization of a race's inner soul and spirit.[3]

More than a defense of his college Nazi group, Duke's editorial is a succinct restatement of Nazi doctrine, particularly as expressed in Hitler's *Mein Kampf*. Indeed, while at LSU Duke once rebuked a professor for criticizing *Mein Kampf*, which Duke said "was the greatest piece of literature of the twentieth century."[4] As we shall see, twenty years later Duke remained faithful to these Nazi principles, though expressing them through a new political vocabulary purged of classic Nazi language.

To compare Duke's contemporary politics to National Socialism, it is first necessary to outline the broad features of Nazi ideology. National Socialism was a historically evolving system of ideas that changed from the founding of the German Workers' Party in 1919 to the collapse of the Third Reich in 1945. Its antecedents date back to the nineteenth century. From its beginning,

National Socialism was shaped by the contending influences of party ideologues, especially Dietrich Eckart, Gottfried Feder, Alfred K. Rosenberg,
Otto and Gregor Strasser, and Richard Walther Darre.[5]

Even after the demise of the Third Reich, National Socialism continued
to evolve. Post–World War II neo-Nazi ideologues such as Francis Parker
Yockey adapted National Socialist doctrine to contemporary American politics, stripping it of its German national trappings. The product was an Amer-
icanized Nazism with new terms for old concepts—"founding majority"
substitutes for "Aryan," "nonproductives" for "inferior races" (*untermensch*).
For the most part, American neo-Nazis like David Duke acquired their understanding of National Socialism either from contemporary derivative works
such as Yockey's *Imperium* or from the pre-1933 Nazi classic *Mein Kampf*
and Alfred K. Rosenberg's *Myth of the Twentieth Century*.[6] As late as 1989
Duke was offering the latter two books through his Nazi book mail-order
business, touting Rosenberg as a "leading philosopher of Europe" and describing his Nazi magnum opus as "inspiring."[7]

German Nazi Race Doctrine

Nazi politics went through three distinct stages after its founding in 1919.
From 1919 to 1923 Nazism put forth a revolutionary, illegal image. It openly
advocated the overthrow of the fragile German democracy. In 1923 this is
precisely what Hitler attempted in the infamous Beerhall Putsch. The revolt
failed and Hitler and other Nazi leaders were imprisoned. On his release in
1924, Hitler revamped the Nazi party image. In its second stage—from 1924
through Hitler's ascent to power in January 1933—the Nazi party represented
itself as a legal body that pursued power through constitutional means. The
shift toward legality was entirely for the sake of political expediency: Nazi
goals remained the same while the rhetoric shifted toward the middle of the
political spectrum.

Moreover, the Nazi party de-emphasized its antidemocratic goals. Nothing
in its program suggested that free elections and civil liberties would be
suspended. Nor did the Nazi party offer any hint of its designs to exterminate
the Jews. It was not until the third stage—commencing with its consolidation
of power in 1933—that the full horror of Nazi doctrine came to light. David
Duke's racial doctrines, for the most part, have been drawn from Hitler's
writings in the second stage of Nazism—the period of opportunism during
which the party attempted to legitimize itself through a law-abiding, conservative image, counterbalancing its extremist reputation.

Throughout the three periods, National Socialism retained a few common principles. These included exaggerated nationalism; racial Social Darwinism —marked by virulent anti-Semitism; expansionistic social imperialism; exaltation of action over intellect; and glorification of individual, authoritarian leadership. While National Socialism is fundamentally revolutionary in that it seeks to overthrow the old social order, it thrives primarily on negativity: it is antidemocracy, antiliberalism, and anti-Marxist, and it holds a profound disdain for human and moral values. Of all of these elements, it is National Socialism's racial theories that distinguish it from all other revolutionary movements. History has been plagued with totalitarian governments and ethnic atrocities. Yet only Nazism strove to reorganize the world racially and exterminate entire races in the process. And it is this aspect of National Socialism, its most dangerous dimension, that survives most clearly in the thought of David Duke.[8]

At the core of National Socialism's racial theories are the related notions of biological determinism and Aryan supremacy. National Socialists view the world as a patchwork of distinct racial nations, each nation imbued with a particular "spiritual unity," with specific moral, physical, and intellectual qualities. (In contemporary National Socialist vernacular, the pseudoscientific term *genetic homogeneity* takes the place of the older, mystical concept of spiritual unity.) Rising above these contentious, "inferior races" is the Aryan—German-Nordic northern Europeans who constitute the master race.

For National Socialists, nation and race are identical; nations are defined by race rather than by shared values and political principles. National qualities such as culture and intelligence are not the product of environment nor can they be absorbed by mere contact between nations. National qualities are immutable, embedded in race, thus making it impossible for "inferior" nations to rise to the same cultural level as the Aryans. National Socialists argue that the existence of the superior Aryans is threatened by lesser races, including Slavs, Czechs, Poles, Jews, and blacks. In its final, developed stage, National Socialism proposes to elevate the Aryans to their rightful ascendant position by purifying the Aryan race, while subjugating or exterminating the inferior races.[9]

National Socialist racial theory did not develop as an aberration of the 1920s. Its distinctive features—racist biological determinism, Aryan supremacy, and anti-Semitism—all find well-developed antecedents in the nineteenth-century *volkisch* and Pan-German movements. Tracing the development of these ideas can provide insight into the ideological roots of David Duke's political philosophy.

Volkisch has no direct English equivalent, translating literally as "of the people." Unlike the American notion of a heterogeneous "melting pot" nationality, volkisch nationalism suggests that race and nation are identical.

Only members of the "superior" German race are members of the German nationality. This German nation is imbued with a distinctive greatness, intelligence, and creativity. Volkisch nationalism emerged as a nineteenth-century German ideological movement based on racism and anti-Semitism. It glorified Germans as a millenarian people entrusted with an imperial mission to rule over non-Germans. Its worldview was antimodernist and antiliberal, positing itself as the last redoubt to industrialization and capitalism. Volkisch nationalism found its most fervent proponents in Habsburg Austria, where "pure Germans" resented the "dark races" of the empire, including Slavs, Jews, and Czechs.

By the end of the nineteenth century, advocates of volkisch nationalism were combining Darwinism with their doctrine of national racial purity, giving rise to an even more racist worldview.[10] Volkisch nationalists twisted Darwinist theories of natural selection, adapting them to the human world. They proposed that, just as in the world of animals, the demise of inferior people was natural and beneficial. The volkisch movement extended Darwin's theories to nations, arguing that competition and elimination of nations were natural processes in international relations. In the twentieth century Hitler would express these ideas with detached cogency: "Those who want to live, let them fight," he advised, "and those who do not want to fight in this world of eternal struggle do not deserve to live."[11]

The volkisch movement also adapted Darwinism to the Jewish question. Jews were perceived as agents of destruction of traditional German values. They were held responsible for industrialism (as manipulators of finance capital), liberalism, and Marxism. Volkisch nationalist racial theories were invoked to characterize Jews as an unassimilable biological entity.[12] Relegating Jews to a subhuman biological species would later serve to rationalize their extermination under the Third Reich.

The Pan-German movement of Georg von Schönerer absorbed elements of these volkisch views. This movement strove for a Pan-German Empire that united all German-speaking people to rule over non-German nationalities. By the beginning of the twentieth century this racist volkisch movement had gained considerable strength; it had even elected some of its members to the Reichstag (German parliament).[13]

There were many other influences in National Socialist thinking, including the nineteenth-century writings of Richard Wagner, Joseph-Arthur de Gobineau, Friedrich Nietzsche, and Houston Stewart Chamberlain. However, Hitler's initial exposure to these ideas came during his stay in Vienna beginning in 1908. In the heart of the multinational Habsburg Empire, Hitler found himself surrounded by the impoverished members of what the volkisch adherents perceived as the "dark races." He was soon attracted to the occult wing of the volkisch nationalist movement and became an avid reader of the teachings of Adolf Josef Lanz, also known as Lanz von Liebenfels.[14]

An occult practitioner of an intensely racist volkisch worldview, Lanz was infatuated with medieval Teutonic mythology, replete with gods and knights and holy grails. The former monk was the author of a book curiously titled *Theo-Zoology or the Lore of the Sodom-Apelings and the Electron of the Gods*. Lanz believed that the blond-haired, blue-eyed Aryans belonged to the Adamic biblical race of Genesis. The heroic Aryans debased themselves by interbreeding with beasts, thus creating the "lower races."[15] This act of miscegenation signaled the Aryans' fall from grace; from that moment forward, they were haunted and terrorized by the "dark-people" who threatened destruction.

The conflict between the Aryans and non-Aryans was a battle between good and evil, between civilization and barbarism. For Lanz, the only solution to this conflict was extermination. The blond-blue Aryan solution would include "humane extermination of the inferior races through an enforced program of sterilization and castration." At the same time the Aryan race would be purified through a eugenic program in which racially superior children would be bred in convents by brood mothers and Aryan stud males.[16]

Hitler absorbed much of this thinking through Lanz's publication, *Ostara*, which he collected in 1909. On one occasion he even met personally with Lanz. Twenty-five years later Hitler had his first opportunity to realize Lanz's eugenic schemes through the government-ordered sterilization of the physically and mentally handicapped. By 1941 the führer had expanded Lanz's plans to encompass euthanasia for the handicapped. Similar eugenic theories inspired Heinrich Himmler's designs to breed an Aryan master race through the Lebensborn program and his proposed polygamy for the "pure Aryan" SS soldiers. The attempted extermination of Jews was the clearest example of Lanz's volkisch madness infecting the Nazi state.[17]

Hitler incorporated Lanz's ideas and other volkisch notions into *Mein Kampf*, which he penned during his imprisonment at Landsburg am Lech in 1924. Hitler intended the volume to be a coherent presentation of his political worldview. Superficial and occasionally impenetrable, however, *Mein Kampf* was a jumble of political prejudices and extremist nostrums that circulated in Germany and Austria during the Weimar Republic period. At times the book revealed the influences of Nazi ideologues such as Alfred K. Rosenberg and Dietrich Eckart. But Hitler's only acknowledged mentor in *Mein Kampf* was Gottfried Feder. For Feder, finance capital—rather than the Jews—was responsible for the social problems of industrialization. Traditional populist economic panaceas such as the abolition of interest figured prominently in Feder's thinking.[18]

Hitler grafted these socialist principles onto his racist volkisch nationalism, hence the term *national socialism*. In this sense, *Mein Kampf* reflected traditional German sensibilities, refining them into a complete worldview. *Mein Kampf*'s National Socialist principles were clear: biological determinism, equation of race with nation, Aryan supremacy in culture and biology, "sub-race" inferiority, Jewish conspiracy and domination, and eugenics. It was a world in which the lordly Aryans were encumbered by Jews, the lower races, liberal democracy, and Marxism.

Duke's Racial Thought

National Socialist race doctrine remained the foundation for David Duke's political thought throughout the 1980s. During his legislative bid in 1989, Duke insisted that he had abandoned his racist views when he left the Ku Klux Klan in 1980 and created the National Association for the Advancement of White People (NAAWP). Despite these claims of apostasy, his public embrace of conservatism owes more to political expediency than to moral conversion. Indeed, on several occasions from 1989 through 1990 he made statements that indicated an enduring faithfulness to Nazi race doctrine. As late as November 1989, Duke reaffirmed his extremist racial beliefs when he told an interviewer that he still believed in "racial science":

> I do believe in racial science. I believe we should be able to study that, and learn about that, and see if race does make an impact on civilization and culture. I tend to believe it does. . . .[19]

Compare Duke's wording:

> I believe that in fact nationality comes from genes . . . [20]

with Hitler's:

> . . . nationality or rather race does not happen to lie in language but in blood. . . .[21]

Here Duke echoes the National Socialist precept of the identity of nation and race: that nationality is genetically embedded, and that culture and civilization are controlled by nationality. Both Hitler and Duke argue against the notion that people of different ethnic backgrounds can be assimilated into a national culture. And both argue that genetic inferiority limits the ability of

Duke picketing at Tulane University in 1970, wearing a Nazi armband.
(Courtesy of Michael P. Smith)

ethnic groups to absorb "superior culture." For Duke, America is not a melting pot in which new immigrants assimilate American culture and make their own contribution. Instead, Africans, Hispanics, Jews, and even some Europeans (southern Italians) pollute the gene pool and destroy American culture (Duke even retains this concept in several of his campaign speeches, albeit in sanitized form).[22]

In the same interview Duke was queried on the relationship of his racial science to the theories of Adolf Hitler. He was asked about a 1985 interview in which he declared that he thought Hitler was "right on race." Duke responded:

> You know, so many quotes [are] out of context. . . . I wouldn't say Hitler was right on race, but I do believe that there are genetic differences between the races and that they profoundly affect culture.[23]

In this comment Duke repeats a familiar pattern. First he denies his belief in the principle but then follows with a statement that virtually reaffirms the principle. These contradictory comments are a product of the conflict between his Nazi worldview and his attempts to feign conservatism. He is, quite simply, falling out of character.

In the interview Duke went on to argue that races differ in physical ability, musical talent, and intelligence. Whites, he said, are "inherently" superior in the latter category:

> There's some things that give whites advantages in certain areas . . . and I.Q. is a reflection of western culture—or western civilization. . . . And I think whites score better in that particular category, that particular talent.[24]

This statement mirrors the National Socialist belief that whites (the term *Aryan* is interchangeable in Duke's usage) possess a unique, genetic superiority in the spheres of culture and intelligence. Prior to his election in 1989, Duke was even more candid about his racial views.

In December 1988, while publicly denying charges of extremism, he continued to express fundamental agreement with biological determinism, the heart of National Socialist race theory. Duke told the neo-Fascist publication *Instauration*:

> I realized that the white species of humanity, that segment responsible for most of the world's great civilizations, was in grave danger of extinction. And I came to understand that the most crucial element in the well-being of any society was, ultimately, the biological quality of the

people who compose it. I learned that once the gene pool was damaged[,] all hope and promise for the future would be lost irretrievably.[25]

In this instance, Duke restates three essential premises of Nazi race doctrine. First, people of northern European descent are the sole producers of great culture. Second, this cultural superiority is the product of biology. Natural resources, climate, geography, technology, politics, and economics are all minor influences in the development of a people. Race determines history. Civilization derives from the genetic composition of a people. Race sets absolute limits on the advance of some people. Racial distinctions are so influential that they can lead "one people to go to the moon while another lives in the mud."[26] Finally, Duke repeats the millenarian National Socialist theme that civilization will perish without whites. When one compares Duke's 1988 phraseology with that of Hitler's, the similarity is striking. In *Mein Kampf* Hitler observed:

Everything we admire on this earth today—science and art, technology and inventions—is only the creative product of a few peoples and originally perhaps one race [Aryans]. On them depends the existence of this whole culture. If they perish, the beauty of this earth will sink into the grave with them.[27]

These two quotations reveal parallel themes. Duke has taken Hitler's concepts and adapted them to contemporary American scientific jargon and political concepts. But the meaning remains the same. Elsewhere Duke is more specific about the unique racial characteristics of whites. The brains of white people are literally "wired" differently than those of others:

The truth is that our brains are like magnificent computers with billions of circuits and architecture that varies from person to person and race to race.[28]

At times Duke finds it awkward to remain faithful to Hitler's Aryan mythology. National Socialists regarded the Aryan as a physically superior being, a myth Jesse Owens left in the dust. But Duke is undaunted by history. He argues that whites are superior to blacks in "strength, endurance, and finesse sports." For evidence Duke notes that whites dominate the athletic field in polo, bobsledding, ice sailing, and curling. Blacks' genetic defects, rather than income or geography, supposedly account for their poor performance in these sports.[29]

Having established the National Socialist premise of racial superiority, Duke then embraces the concept of racial inferiority. During the 1980s he attempted to deflect criticism of his racism by arguing that races are not superior or inferior but simply have different traits. Through this device, he has attempted to impart an egalitarian and modern air to his nineteenth-century thinking. Yet the idea that races are genetically "separate but equal" is still consistent with the Nazi tenet that nationalities are biologically distinct species. And although races merely possess different "traits," Duke carefully assigns these traits different values on a hierarchical scale. Predictably, his white "genetic" traits are those indispensable to contemporary civilization: intellect, technological expertise, and the capacity to govern. In 1983 he told *Hustler* magazine, "If you ask me whether blacks are as well suited as whites in a modern technological society of the Western variety, the answer is no."[30]

For Duke, even crime is genetically ingrained in blacks:

> I do think that there are certain tendencies, certain behavioral tendencies, that are inherited, and I think that Blacks generally, in terms of our society, have more of a tendency to act in anti-social ways.[31]

As is often the case, in this statement Duke employs sociological language to give a scientific cast to his crude biological determinism. The "tendency to act in anti-social ways" is a euphemism for "criminal." Viewed through Duke's prism of race, crime is not the product of poverty or environment but rather the result of racial defects. Eliminate the defective race and you will eliminate crime. During the Senate campaign he defended his criminal theories by returning to his "separate but equal" ploy. Whites, too, are victims of biology when it comes to crime, he confessed:

> White people, for example, have a tremendous tendency towards car theft. There is something in white people that makes them steal cars a lot more than black people. Genetics are reflected in various aspects of society—music, art, singing . . .[32]

Hitler's influence on Duke's thinking regarding Jews is also evident. Duke portrays them as a powerful, manipulative, alien elite bent on corrupting white civilization. "A small, alien minority [Jews] has control over the airwaves, and it is costing us our freedoms, our cultural integrity, our money, and even our lives," warns Duke in a 1983 article entitled, "Who Runs the Media?"[33] Though Jews have inhabited America for nearly 365 years, they are forever condemned to "alien" status in the National Socialist worldview of David Duke. Because of their unique genetic composition, they remain eternally outside and destructive to "Western culture" (read: "white" culture):

> The media is dominated by Jews. . . . As a result, the media—and by media I mean movies, TV, newspapers and magazines—is more a re-

flection of Jewish values than Western values. These Jews are not good Americans.[34]

Duke's anti-Semitic portrait of Jews closely resembles Hitler's description of Jews as manipulative aliens. In *Mein Kampf* Hitler tell us:

> The fact that nine tenths of all literary filth, artistic trash, and theatrical idiocy can be set to the account of a people [Jews], constituting hardly one hundredth of all the country's inhabitants, could simply not be talked away; it was the plain truth.[35]

Duke's theories of "race mixing" reveal an adherence to National Socialism extending to the most minute detail. For instance, Hitler dedicates a special section of *Mein Kampf* to refuting Gregor Johann Mendel's "hybrid vigor" theory. Mendel believed that crossing species tended to promote the best traits of both species. The notion was anathema to Nazis given their opposition to race mixing. The hybrid vigor theory threatened to discredit Hitler's tightly crafted racial cosmos, and he attempted to refute Mendel in *Mein Kampf*:

> If, for example, an individual specimen of a certain race were to enter into a union with a racially lower specimen, the result would at first be a lowering of the standard itself; but in addition, there would be a weakening of the offspring as compared to the environment that had remained racially unmixed.[36]

Duke makes the same argument in a 1986 signed editorial entitled, "Why I Oppose Race Mixing":

> What the public is not told is that Hybrid Vigor only exists for one generation, and then if certain traits are to be sustained there must be very controlled breeding of subsequent generations. If general mixing is allowed, there is always degeneration in the population.[37]

His fear of miscegenation goes well beyond conventional Klan hostility against the mixing of blacks and whites, for Duke even applies the policy to European "sub-races" (English, French, and so forth). As late as 1986 he ardently defended Hitler's opposition to European intermixing:

> The media also didn't tell the public that racial mixture leads to many physiological anomalies that can be very damaging. As an example, one can cite the fact that differences between European sub-races are nominal compared to those between the major races, yet even in mixing between them, we find severe physiological problems. For instance, braces and orthodontic work are needed much more commonly in the

United States than in Europe because there is much more mixing here of different European sub-races . . . but the dentition problems may be minor compared to say the physiology of the brain and the vital organs.[38]

In this remarkable passage Duke is suggesting that European nationalities are so genetically dissimilar that intermarriage could cause damage to "vital organs." Given the melting-pot demographics of America, his theory leads one to conclude that America is producing a generation of handicapped whites with orthodontic problems. His basic racial cosmology precludes the possibility of miscegenation. From his perspective, interracial marriage would always be to the disadvantage of the superior white race.

Duke's racial logic leads him to several ominous solutions. Foremost is "racial integrity"—the physical, genetic, and geographic separation of whites. "I embrace racial integrity because I know that genetic advances can better be identified and promoted in racially homogeneous populations, and I am interested in the improvement of my people with each generation." To accomplish this racial separation, Duke draws inspiration from Nazi relocation schemes. Between 1984 and 1989 Duke repeatedly proposed dividing America into separate racial nations and ending immigration from the Third World. As late as 1986 he explicitly advanced a scheme to remove Jews from the United States, reminiscent of Hitler's plan to relocate Jews to Madagascar: "I think probably, in a moral sense, the Jewish people have been a blight. . . . And they probably deserve to go into the ashbin of history. . . . I think the best thing is to resettle them some place where they can't exploit others."[39]

Duke's panacea of racial separation is complemented by National Socialist–inspired dreams of government eugenic programs. Duke advocates many of the Nazi eugenic programs promoted by Hitler in the 1924–33 period, attempting to legitimize them by suggesting that they would be voluntary. In 1984 he published an NAAWP editorial calling for a government loan program to encourage white couples to have more children. One-fourth of the loan would be forgiven for each child produced. Duke's proposal was not an original idea. The plan was first conceived in 1933 by the Nazi government. As recently as 1989 Duke continued to espouse similar government-sponsored race-purification projects.[40] In November 1989 he explained his views on the desirability of government control of reproduction:

I see nothing wrong with encouraging unproductive people to have fewer children, economically, and encouraging the most productive people to have children. And I think that adds beauty to the whole society, and quality and excellence to all society.[41]

Hitler had articulated the same philosophy sixty-four years before:

> It [the Nazi state] must see to it that only the healthy beget children; that
> there is only one disgrace; despite one's own sickness and deficiencies,
> to bring children into the world . . . and conversely it must be con-
> sidered reprehensible; to withhold children from the state.[42]

Duke specifically proposed that the government provide low-interest loans to
college graduates in the top 10 percent of their class to encourage them to
produce elite children.[43] The program—a modernized version of Lanz's
brood convents—is identical in philosophy and objectives to the Nazi
Lebensborn program. Its explicit assumption is that intellectual achievement
is genetically determined and that the state must influence procreation.

Of course, Nazi ideologues were not satisfied with simply propagating the
superior elements in society. They aggressively sought to eliminate those
whose maladaptive genes allegedly impeded Aryan development. As early as
1924 Hitler advocated sterilizing the "incurably ill" and "defective people."
Duke has also advanced similar voluntary sterilization programs for welfare
recipients, criminals, and "mentally defectives."[44] In his attacks on the U.S.
welfare system, he has proposed reducing the number of welfare recipients
by reducing the number of black people. Similar to Hitler, Duke frankly
argues that the government has both the right and the obligation to control
who shall reproduce:

> The choice is clear. You and your actions over the next few decades will
> decide who will propagate and who will not, who will control and who
> will be controlled.[45]

Duke adamantly denies that he is a Nazi because, as he points out, he is not
a totalitarian, nor does he advocate government force in his racial programs.
His premise is that totalitarianism and coercion are essential features of
National Socialism. This was true of Nazism once Hitler seized state power in
1933, but it is not an accurate description of Nazi political theory in its
formative period (1924–32). National Socialists seldom advocated dictatorial
policies during their ascent to power. After the abortive Beerhall Putsch,
Nazis represented themselves as advocates of "German democracy" and as
opposed to "democratic parliamentarianism." German democracy denoted a
form of government in which a leader would be elected democratically but
then left to rule without the interference of a contentious parliament. In
fact, in the first edition of *Mein Kampf* Hitler called for a central parliament
as the highest body of the Nazi state, though he eliminated the demand in
subsequent editions. Nevertheless, the initial inclusion of the parliamentary

demand reflects the willingness of Nazis to maintain a democratic pretense.[46]

David Duke's newfound democratic and egalitarian rhetoric is entirely consistent with early Nazi practice. It would be difficult for any authoritarian and racist movement to win support in the United States if it openly articulated a racist and elitist creed. Indeed, authoritarian movements seldom portray themselves as such in their early stages. Yet the logic of Duke's racial doctrine inevitably leads to authoritarian policies. Massive relocation and eugenic plans, even if legislated by the majority, would violate basic civil liberties and meet widespread resistance by minorities. It would be impossible to implement these draconian policies without resorting to authoritarian coercion.

But there is a deeper authoritarian strain to Duke's thinking. He projects a vision of the world in which "white civilization" is under assault by genetically defective people who are incapable of self-government. In Duke's worldview, the only solution to crime and poverty is biological: reduce the number of people of color. It is doubtful that minorities would submit willingly to such a policy. Their only defense is political equality. Yet political equality contradicts Duke's "natural" principle of biological inequality. For Duke, to share political power with people of color is to commit racial suicide for the "white race." The contradiction between political equality and Nazi doctrine is reflected in an epigram that appeared on the masthead of one of Duke's favorite publications in the 1970s: "Free men are not equal, and equal men are not free." The concept is at the heart of his Nazism: that political equality prevents the true racial elite from realizing its potential.

Throughout the 1980s David Duke continued to embrace the Nazi tenets of biological determinism, white supremacy, anti-Semitism, and government-sponsored relocation and eugenic programs. Duke's racism is Nazism, rather than an eclectic mixture of indigenous American racism. David Duke is not merely a bigot, he is a Nazi. He began his career as a self-proclaimed Nazi intellectual and continues to espouse Nazi race doctrine, albeit through a new language.

As he matured Duke grasped the key to Nazism's success: that it adapted to the specific fears, aspirations, prejudices, and political traditions of the nation. National Socialism represented itself as the embodiment of German political tradition. It did not clothe itself in the garb of foreign ideology. For American fascism to succeed, it must pretend to be squarely in the mainstream of American political life. It must abandon the foreign garb of Nazism. Ironically, the less Duke appears to be a Nazi, the more he fits the historical uniform.

NOTES

1. Louisiana Coalition against Racism and Nazism, "Politics and Background of . . . Duke."
2. Anderson, "Jews, Blacks Lambasted," 1.
3. Duke, "Duke on Nazism."
4. Snyder, "The 'Nazi' of LSU," A4.
5. Lane and Rupp, *Nazi Ideology before 1933*. See p. xvi and Introduction for a discussion of these competing influences.
6. Anti-Defamation League, *Extremism*, 56–57.
7. "Americana Books" advertisement, *NAAWP News*, no. 50, [1988].
8. Bracher, *German Dictatorship*, 47, 128; Hitler, *Mein Kampf*, passim.
9. For a thorough discussion of Nazi ideology, see Nolte, *Three Faces of Fascism*.
10. Bracher, *German Dictatorship*, 3–4.
11. Hitler, *Mein Kampf*, 289.
12. Goodrick-Clark, *Occult Roots*, 5.
13. Bracher, *German Dictatorship*, 40–44.
14. Goodrick-Clark, *Occult Roots*, 197.
15. Ibid., 93–94.
16. Ibid., 197, 96–97.
17. Ibid., 195, 97.
18. Hitler, *Mein Kampf*, xv–xvi.
19. Kaplan, "Interview Transcript," 4.
20. Ibid.
21. Hitler, *Mein Kampf*, 389.
22. For Duke on race and culture, see his extensive comments in "Videotape Interview," 1984.
23. Kaplan, "Interview Transcript," 2.
24. Ibid.
25. Robertson, *Instauration*.
26. Duke, "Letter of the Month," 3.
27. Hitler, *Mein Kampf*, 288.
28. Duke, "Letter of the Month," 3.
29. Duke, "Are Whites Inferior Athletes?," 5.
30. Bane, "Duke," 5.
31. Kaplan, "Interview Transcript," 3.
32. "Duke Interview Focuses on Present."
33. Duke, "Who Runs the Media?," 1.
34. Bane, "Duke," 5.
35. Hitler, *Mein Kampf*, 58. For Hitler on Jews as plunderers, see ibid., 310.
36. Ibid., 400.
37. Duke, editorial, *NAAWP News*, no. 42, 10.
38. Ibid.

39. Ibid. (first quotation); Kaplan, "Interview Transcript," 5; Duke, "Stop Immigration," 1; Evelyn Rich Interview with Joe Fields and David Duke, Culver City,
Calif., 1986, Political Ephemera Collection, Howard-Tilton Library, Tulane University (second quotation).
40. Duke, "Issues and Answers"; Kaplan, "Interview Transcript," 4.
41. Ibid.
42. Hitler, *Mein Kampf*, 403–4.
43. Kaplan, "Interview Transcript," 4.
44. Hitler, *Mein Kampf*, 255; Duke, "Letter of the Month," 1.
45. Duke, "Black Population Bomb Ticks," 1.
46. Hitler, *Mein Kampf*, 87–91, xviii.

BIBLIOGRAPHICAL NOTE

The most significant recorded interviews with David Duke include a 1984 video
interview by Burwell Ware, Xavier University Archives, Xavier University, New
Orleans; a series of audiotaped interviews conducted in 1985–86 by Evelyn Rich,
Political Ephemera Collection, Howard-Tilton Library, Tulane University, New Orleans; and a November 1989 taped interview by Abby Kaplan (cited in Louisiana
Coalition against Racism and Nazism [LCARN], "Media Resource Packet"), copy of
tape and transcribed excerpts in the Amistad Research Center, Tulane University,
New Orleans. LCARN has donated to the Amistad Research Center its collection of
Duke's radio and television interviews and commercials, taped speeches, and mis-
cellaneous articles. LCARN also has its own collection, including newspaper clippings from all state and major national publications (1988–present), Duke campaign
promotional materials, anti-Duke organizational materials, and extensive background
documents. The Howard-Tilton Library has a collection of Duke materials from the
1970s. The Amistad Research Center and the Louisiana Collection of the University
of New Orleans both have nearly complete runs of the *NAAWP News* (published by
the National Association for the Advancement of White People) between 1982 and
1991. Duke is the publisher and a frequent editor of the *NAAWP News*. Its issues are
numbered but not dated, creating some difficulty in determining the month of publication.

REFERENCES

Anderson, Bob. "Jews, Blacks Lambasted at Heated Alley." *The Daily Reveille* (LSU
campus newspaper), November 13, 1969.
Anti-Defamation League of B'nai B'rith. *Extremism on the Right*. Rev. ed. New
York: Anti-Defamation League of B'nai B'rith, 1988.

Bane, Michael. "David Duke: Is the White Race Doomed?" *Hustler*. Reprinted in *NAAWP News*, no. 24, [1983].

Bracher, Karl Dietrich. *The German Dictatorship: The Origins, Structure, and Effects of National Socialism*. New York: Holt, Rinehart, and Winston, 1970.

Duke, David. "Duke on Nazism—His Superior System." *The Daily Reveille*, November 16, 1969.

————. "Are Whites Inferior Athletes?" *NAAWP News*, no. 23, [1983].

————. "Who Runs the Media?" *NAAWP News*, no. 18, [1983].

————. "Issues and Answers." *NAAWP News*, no. 31, [1984].

————. "Videotape Interview." 1984. Xavier Archives, Xavier University, New Orleans. Filed under "Duke Campaign Television Program," Amistad Research Center, Tulane University, New Orleans.

————. Editorial. *NAAWP News*, no. 42, [1986].

————. "Letter of the Month." *NAAWP News*, no. 39, [1986].

————. "Stop Immigration." *NAAWP News*, no. 40, [1986].

————. "Black Population Bomb Ticks." *NAAWP News*, no. 48, [1987].

"Duke Interview Focuses on Present." *Xavier Herald* (Xavier University, New Orleans), September 27, 1990.

Goodrick-Clark, Nicholas. *The Occult Roots of Nazism: The Ariosophists of Austria and Germany, 1890–1935*. With a foreword by Rohan Butler. Wellingborough, Northamptonshire: Aquarium Press, 1985.

Hitler, Adolf. *Mein Kampf*. Translated by Ralph Manheim. Boston: Houghton Mifflin Company, 1971.

Kaplan, Abby. "Interview Transcript." Taped interview with David Duke at his legislative headquarters, November 21, 1989. LCARN collection, Amistad Research Center, Tulane University, New Orleans.

Lane, Barbara Miller, and Leila J. Rupp. *Nazi Ideology before 1933: A Documentation*. Austin: University of Texas Press, 1978.

Louisiana Coalition against Racism and Nazism. "The Politics and Background of State Representative David Duke," edited by Lance Hill. 1990. Biography section, LCARN collection, Amistad Research Center, Tulane University, New Orleans.

Nolte, Ernst. *Three Faces of Fascism: Action Française, Italian Fascism, National Socialism*. Translated by Leila Vennewitz. London: Weidenfeld and Nicolson, 1965.

Robertson, Wilmot. *Instauration*. Cape Canaveral, Fla. December 1988.

Rosenberg, Alfred. *The Myth of the Twentieth Century: An Evaluation of the Spiritual-Intellectual Confrontations of Our Age*. 1st English ed. Torrance, Calif.: Noontide Press, 1982.

Snyder, David. "The 'Nazi' of LSU . . . Head of the Klan." New Orleans *States-Item*, May 26, 1975.

Varange, Ulick [Francis Parker Yockey]. *Imperium: The Philosophy of History*. 1948. Reprint. Torrance, Calif.: Noontide Press, 1983.

William B. McMahon

7 | David Duke and the Legislature

"A Mouth That's Different"

Until his election to the Louisiana House of Representatives, David Duke, thirty-nine when sworn into office, had spent his adult life at the edge. Election gave him status and legitimacy. It also gave him a new forum for presenting his views. As former grand wizard of the Knights of the Ku Klux Klan, guest on talk-show television, and president of the National Association for the Advancement of White People, Duke was a public figure. As state representative from District 81 in suburban New Orleans, he became a legitimate public figure.

But gaining his new position as an elected public official made him no less contentious. As a state representative, Duke brought his racialist brand of controversy to the lower house. This chapter examines Duke as a lawmaker carrying a racial agenda, beginning with disagreement over his being seated. Once sworn in, the new legislator continued his associations with white supremacist groups, particularly during a trip in early March 1989 to Chicago to speak before the Populist party, causing a flap just several days after the seating debate. Although censured by the national Republican party, he built friendly relations with Republicans and other conservatives in the state House. Duke opposed the governor over revisions in state tax policy, stumping the state to carry his message. And as a freshman legislator he filed bills that in committee and floor debate pitted black against white, bringing more disorder to the often-confusing process of making law in the Louisiana legislature. This chapter looks at Duke's activities in the legislature as viewed by a newspaper reporter who watched him almost daily.

Seating a Klansman

Even before he was sworn into office as a Louisiana state representative, the question of Duke's qualifications—specifically whether he met residency requirements—stirred the House of Representatives. The House was preparing to go into special session on Wednesday, February 22, 1989, to consider a tax reform package proposed by Governor Buddy Roemer. Duke had been elected the Saturday before. In those several days, lawmakers questioned whether the former Klansman should be seated. Positions were taken. Lines were drawn. In emotional intensity and racial division the fight showed a pattern that Duke's presence in the House would produce many times.

Debate in the immediate days preceding the vote was argued on two levels. Most of the argument was on the legal, constitutional question of whether Duke met residency and domicile requirements, but heightened emotions were also roused by those who feared that Duke's racist views would spill over into the legislature.

Representative Joseph Accardo, a Democrat from LaPlace, a respected member and vice chairman of the House and Governmental Affairs Committee, pointed to the quandary facing lawmakers on the seating issue. "If you challenge his election, do you make him a martyr, immensely more powerful? Or do you sit back and say the people have spoken and don't do anything?" Do you conclude that "he is perhaps an aberration on the horizon, that his views will not spread and that others will not espouse his views?" asked Accardo. "Or do you take an activist position and say his views are dangerous to our community and, therefore, it's best to oppose him?"[1]

When it came to a vote two days later, Accardo would be in that minority of representatives who voted against the motion to table. The motion was made by Representative Odon Bacque that the House investigate Duke's qualifications to serve. As the only state representative without a Democratic or Republican party label, Bacque, a Vietnam veteran, was a good choice to carry the seating issue. The attempt to investigate Duke's qualifications would not be seen as a partisan fight.

"Some things are right and some things are wrong," said Representative Bacque. "I have no problem with him being elected if he did it the right way. I am going to challenge him based on the law that before you can run, you need to be a resident of the district. We in the Legislature can challenge. We are really the court of last resort. I have thought about it. I am firm in my resolve to do what is right, even if I stand alone."[2]

The possibility of the seating challenge had been broached at a news conference on the Sunday after Duke's election. Duke said allegations that he had not lived in the district for the required year were "frivolous. The political process must remain inviolate. The men and women of good will in the legislature will not tolerate any challenge of this nature."[3]

Bacque's fellow Lafayette representative, Ron Gomez, a Democrat and a floor leader for Governor Roemer, in effect followed Duke's lead: "If anyone wanted to challenge Duke, they should have done so when he qualified as a candidate. They chose not to do that. Now they want to come back and take another bite of the apple and make the House do what they should have done back then. That creates a lot of problems for people [in the House]."[4]

The governor took a similar position. "In a democracy, that fact [that the voters had elected Duke] must be respected regardless of what one might think personally about David Duke's philosophical principles," Roemer said. "While I don't agree with him philosophically, he is only one member of a 144-member legislative body and has the obligation to his constituents to act responsibly in that body."[5]

ONE OF THE 144?

If Roemer was suggesting that Duke's future as a legislator would be measured merely as 1 among 144, he misjudged. He particularly missed the divisiveness that Duke would bring to a fairly disorganized legislative body, where caucuses and delegations were growing in power. House interest groups had splintered further, as disagreements among them grew. During the 1980s the House had formed rural, Acadiana, and black caucuses. There were also Republican, New Orleans, and Baton Rouge delegations. Political action committees—representing big business, chemical industries, trial lawyers, home builders, teachers, pharmacists, medical doctors, and others—were powerful influences in the legislature, spending tens of thousands of dollars in legislative election campaigns.

Representative Avery Alexander, a black minister from New Orleans who had joined with Dr. Martin Luther King in the 1950s in founding the civil rights movement, disagreed with Roemer's assessment. "He's only one man, that's true, but Hitler was only one man," said the Reverend Mr. Alexander, who was nearing eighty at the time. "We know that one man can make an impact. Martin Luther King was only one man."

Alexander saw more deeply into the differences between what Duke said and what he meant than others did. "He's made some racist statements that he is opposed to minority set asides and he wants to get rid of welfare and welfare babies and that sounds like genocide to me," said Alexander. "The late Dr. Martin Luther King warned us that once we won the struggle there would be, to some extent, a violent reaction. Now we find the run-of-the-mill white citizen supporting a racist. They are not Klansmen. Those are just regular white folks who voted for Duke."[6]

When the special legislative session began that Wednesday at 10 A.M., Representative Jimmy Dimos, of Monroe, the Speaker of the House, was prepared. Dimos, a fourteen-year member of the House and in his second year as Speaker, having researched the issue and found no precedent, said a motion would be needed to give Duke a hearing: the former Klansman could not be denied his seat without due process. Lawmakers found on their desks copies of the applicable section of the Louisiana Constitution that dealt with residency and domicile qualifications. According to Article III, Section 4(A): "An elector who at the time of qualification as a candidate has attained the age of eighteen years, resided in the state for the preceding two years, and been actually domiciled for the preceding year in the legislative district from which he seeks election is eligible for membership in the legislature."

Representatives Bacque and Mitch Landrieu of New Orleans, a first-term Democrat and the son of former New Orleans mayor Moon Landrieu, distributed documents showing that Duke's residence was not in House District 81 but nearby at 3603 Cypress Street, Metairie. They cited three instances in which during the preceding year Duke had listed his residence at the Cypress Street address, rather than what he showed on his House qualifying papers: (1) when he sought to have his name on the ballot as a candidate for president in the presidential primary, January 15, 1988, (2) when he declared his intent to run as an Independent (Populist party) candidate for president, July 28, 1988, and (3) when he voted, November 11, 1987.

Before making his motion, Representative Bacque explained that the issue was not one of whether Duke had been elected but whether he was qualified to serve. And in Bacque's eyes, Duke had not fulfilled the basic requirement of residency. His brief speech to the House showed, however, what seemed to be a broader concern, one grounded more in morality than in law. Fundamentally, Bacque seemed uncomfortable with the notion of a former grand wizard of the Klan sitting as a member of the Louisiana House of Representatives. "I took an oath, and I hold that oath to be sacred," Bacque said. "I believe that men of principle must stand when principles are in jeopardy. I believe that laws without enforcement are only words and empty promises. And I can never let that happen. We today have the opportunity to stand up for what's right and just and sacred. Edmund Burke once said that the only thing necessary for evil to triumph is for good men to do nothing."[7]

Defending the seating of Duke was Representative John Alario of West-wego, Speaker of the House for the previous administration of Edwin W. Edwards (1984–88). Alario is the rare Democrat in the Jefferson Parish delegation and stands to the left of his mostly Republican colleagues. He was chairman of the Ways and Means Committee (the tax-writing panel in the House) during the 1980–84 administration of Republican David C. Treen, and while House Speaker supported Edwards's 1984 tax package. During the Roemer administration Alario led a cadre of anti-Roemer lawmakers on some issues, anticipating the fourth coming of Edwards. Edwards was first elected in 1972 and again in 1975. Because of constitutional prohibition against serving a third consecutive term, he sat out for four years and then was reelected for a third term in 1983—and to a fourth in 1991. Roemer's election in 1987 sidetracked Edwards's attempt at back-to-back terms in the 1980s.

In opposing Bacque's motion, Alario argued that House members should be more concerned about the tax reform package facing them than with Duke. The state's election code says that any candidacy can be challenged within ten days of filing for office, said Alario. "That was not done in this case. Whether Mr. Duke resides or does not reside, the people of that district have now elected Mr. Duke by majority vote." Alario then sought to reinforce his liberal credentials and address the discussion's emotional side. "My parents didn't teach me bigotry." America is great, he said, because its political system "will allow anyone from any walk of life to be elected to public office. . . . I stand today not to defend Mr. Duke but to defend American democracy. Neither Louisiana nor America can survive in hatred and bigotry and prejudice. This has to be a state of equality and justice for all. . . . [But] the question before us today is whether Mr. Duke is a duly elected representative."[8]

Alario then made the motion to table the Bacque motion. The House voted 69–33 for the Alario motion. Duke was sworn in.

NEVER SAID STERILIZATION

After the vote was cast, blacks charged they had not had an opportunity to speak. Alario's motion had cut off debate. Black representative Naomi White Warren of New Orleans charged that the process had been "railroaded" through by not allowing her and others to talk before the vote. "I was in a state of shock witnessing what the members of this House did by way of not allowing me as a member and not allowing other members of this House to be a part of the democratic process and express our views," said Warren in a personal privilege speech after the vote. She also said she was "disappointed with Alario, our friend." Other blacks chose to warn Duke they would be watching him. "I'm here to put you on notice that not only black folks in Louisiana but black folks all over the country will be watching you," said Representative Diana Bajoie of New Orleans.[9]

Duke got zero support from the House's fifteen blacks, who voted unanimously against killing an investigation into Duke's residency qualifications. The maverick Republican did much better with his fellow GOP members, with fifteen of the eighteen voting to table Bacque's motion. Given the political makeup of the House membership—many of them were rural Democrats and suburban Republican conservatives—the refusal to pursue an investigation into Duke's election was not surprising.

"I want to allay fears that I will be divisive or a problem in this great body," Duke observed at his swearing in. What he next told representatives became a repetitive theme. It included his call for equal opportunity: "And I believe that discrimination is wrong and reprehensible when it is waged against anyone, black or white, in this country," Duke said. He denied that he had ever spoken of sterilization for anybody. He warned of a "rising welfare underclass that's sown so much of the crime in our state." And he called for a slowdown in the illegitimate welfare birthrate—with no suggestion of how that might be done. "If we have fewer children being born, we'll have more money available for housing and training and education for these people," he said.[10]

Later in the day, a petition was filed in Lafayette Parish seeking to recall Representative Bacque. Although nothing further developed, it was another sign of the tension arising from Duke's election.

This was the first instance where Duke's presence in the legislature was a source of racial conflict, and it was not the last. In less than a year and a half as a member of the Louisiana House, Duke continued to be a major cause of disagreement among the members. Combined with his campaigning for the U.S. Senate—at a peak in mid-1990—he broadcast his racial message throughout the halls of the skyscraper state capitol building that Huey P. Long had built. He maintained his ties with white supremacist groups and continued to sell his anti-Semitic and racist tracts and to publish the newsletter of the National Association for the Advancement of White People, which he headed. He rarely spoke in legislative debate on other than those old issues that were the foundation of his racist philosophy.

Duke Revisits His Extremist Past

Within two weeks of his being sworn in, the sincerity of Duke's campaign claims that he had recanted his white supremacist past was brought into question. On March 5, the Baton Rouge *Sunday Advocate* published an article and picture on Duke's trip to Chicago to address a meeting of the Populist party; the picture showed him shaking hands with American Nazi party official Art Jones. The Associated Press story said Duke, following a news conference, "posed with American Nazi Party vice chairman Art Jones, who shouted anti-Semitic, racial slurs at reporters and got into a shoving match with a television reporter who asked Duke about his connection to Jones."[11]

Duke's handling of assertions that he is mixed up with extremists—whether Liberty Lobby's Ralph Forbes, Identity Church leader Jim Warner, National Alliance leader William Pierce, Klansman Don Black, or whomever—is denial: he denies knowing them or else claims he once knew them a little. In the Chicago incident, Duke responded with a letter to members of the House in which he wrote that he did not know this "person identified as an officer of the American Nazi Party." He calls the article a "media smear" caused by his speaking to a "conservative, anti-tax group called the Populist Party." In the letter Duke described Jones as "a kook mayoral candidate who is also in a tiny Nazi Party. I had no knowledge of this when I shook hands with this individual." Jones identified himself, said Duke, "and caused a commotion with one of the television reporters, becoming belligerent and abusive. My heart sunk [*sic*] at that moment because I realized how the press would use this incident to discredit me." "Because of my controversial Klan background and my dabbling in far-right politics as a teenager," Duke continued, "the media saw this as a great opportunity to suggest that I have connections with the politics of extremism."[12]

Duke Is Welcomed by Republicans

Aside from the Chicago incident, Duke accommodated to the legislative routine as well as most entering freshmen. He was generally accepted by the other 104 members: it was commonplace to see Duke moving about the floor of the House, shaking hands and chatting with his hand on the shoulder of a fellow representative. He did particularly well with the 18 House Republicans. Most voted with the former Klansman on his bills.

Republicans on the national level held a different point of view. The executive council of the Republican National Committee (RNC) denounced

Duke and declared that it would give him no financial or technical assistance. National party spokesman Leslie Goodman said the decision, made by the twenty-eight-member party council, was unanimous. Before the vote, Joan McKinney reported in an interview with national party communications director Mark Goodin that censure was an unusual step. "I don't know if it's ever been done before," Goodin said.[13]

Goodin, described by McKinney as a southerner and a former aide to conservative U.S. senator Strom Thurmond (R-S.C.), early on understood who David Duke was. "It's all code words. What does doing away with the welfare underclass really mean? That could smack of something pretty outrageous," said Goodin. Further, Goodin commented: "You can't parade around in a bedsheet and wear a swastika on your arm, and then later try to convince people you aren't what you said you were."[14]

After the censure vote was taken, RNC spokesman Goodman said that national committee chairman Lee Atwater had talked to Louisiana party chairman William ("Billy") Nungesser of New Orleans and that Nungesser agreed with the national party's decision. Duke, however, was not bothered by the RNC's action. He had not gotten any help when running for the District 81 seat, he said, and there was no reason for him to expect any once elected. And, contrary to Nungesser's claims of state disavowal of Duke, the new House member pointed out that he had not been rejected on his new turf. "We not only agree on most of the issues," said Duke of the Louisiana House Republican delegation, but also "we've come to the point of friendship. They've accepted me. The voters have accepted me. The Legislature has accepted me."[15]

The Republicans and conservative Democrats in the state House who chose to befriend Duke apparently ignored or did not care that their choosing Duke and his mainstream conservative views, which they favored, also carried with it Duke's more extremist beliefs, which they may or may not have favored. That message, however, was out for them to read. "Duke maintains he has severed ties with the Klan and the neo-Nazis, and his political dialogue today could be lifted straight from the Republican Party platform: no new taxes, limits on the welfare state and an end to affirmative action," wrote Knight-Ridder reporter Teresa Watanabe. But also, Watanabe noted, quoting Leonard Zeskind, research director for the Center for Democratic Renewal, the issues for Duke and other politicians like him "are racism and scapegoating with a veneer of populism."[16]

Writing similarly within days after Duke's election was *Chicago Tribune* columnist Clarence Page, who cited Atwater's claims that Duke is no Republican and concluded that Atwater had made a "nice try" in attempting to disown Duke. But Atwater's argument would not work, said Page, for "the

Republicans have no one but themselves to blame for Duke's victory. The GOP has flirted for years with the bigot vote, through racial code words and racially loaded messages like that of Willie Horton, the black rapist and murderer featured in some of President Bush's campaign commercials. It was inevitable that someday an articulate Klansman would put on a nice suit and plow that fertile field from another direction." Pointing out that Duke's District 81 opponent John Treen and his brother, former governor David Treen, were attached to the segregationist States' Rights party in the 1960s, Page concluded: "Yes, Duke had good reason to join the Republican Party. He felt welcome."[17]

In judging Duke's new legislative friends, the not-so-easily-answered question is how much of their attraction to him came from issues founded in Republican party strategy and how much came from good old-fashioned racism.

MACHIAVELLIAN EMBRACE

Representative Emile ("Peppi") Bruneau, Jr., of New Orleans, chairman of the Republican delegation in the House, was Duke's leading supporter. "Peppi's been his mentor," said Representative Bacque.[18] After several days of interviews and observations during the 1989 summer legislative sessions, Larry Cohler concluded:

> To many observers, Bruneau leads a coterie of ultra-conservative senior Republicans who are locked in a Machiavellian embrace with Duke. Through association with them, Duke gains legitimization statewide as a mainstream conservative Republican. The most recent issue of the delegation's official newsletter, for example, featured a brief profile of Duke as the party's most recently elected lawmaker. The profile made no mention of his Klan background, saying only, "He ran on a conservative platform."
>
> Meanwhile, the Republican conservatives gain a high-profile point man for the controversial issues they have long pushed to little effect and much criticism. "He helps them," said Bacque. "He's kind of taken the heat."[19]

In Baton Rouge, one who saw the danger of this Republican-Duke embrace was Yigal Bander, a member of the Republican party's parish (county) executive committee. Bander wrote fellow Baton Rouge Jewish leaders from his position as executive director of the Jewish Federation of Greater Baton Rouge. He, too, noted the "sympathetic article" in the Republican legislative delegation's newsletter, and he did not like what he saw:

What is going on here? What has become of Lee Atwater's unequivocal declaration that there is no place in the Republican Party for David Duke? Do we really think that the Delegation is stronger with 24 members including Duke than it would be with 23 members excluding Duke?

The time has come for us here in Louisiana to follow Lee Atwater's lead and decide, once and for all, that David Duke is not one of us. If we don't act now, we may wake up one day to find that this insignificant little hatemonger has succeeded in destroying our party.[20]

The Governor's Tax Plan Gives Duke a Forum

Once comfortably welcomed by Republicans in the legislature, Duke found a stage on which to perform when he decided to attack Governor Roemer's tax reform package. It was an issue most Republicans could relate to, for, after all, had not President George Bush been elected on a no-new-taxes platform? Not so much a tax-raising proposition as a shifting of taxes, Roemer's tax revision package plan would have lowered the state property tax, removed the three-dollar limit on automobile license tags, and rewritten the personal and corporate income tax schedule. A constitutional amendment would have established a transportation trust fund by increasing and earmarking state gasoline taxes.

Roemer was elected as a fiscal conservative. But as a member of Congress and in most of his personal life, the Harvard-educated governor saw himself as a liberal on social issues. Earlier in his administration, he had established a sometimes-fragile rapport with black lawmakers. Now he was supporting a proposal by the Black Legislative Caucus, H.B. 18, instructing the administration to investigate racial discrimination in the awarding of past state construction projects. Following the study, the administration was to create a set-aside program guaranteeing some of the contracts in the transportation construction program to minorities. It was in the minority set-aside discussion that Duke became active.

Representative Charles D. Jones, a black lawmaker from Monroe, was the lead author of the measure. Speaking before a House committee, Roemer, who needed black support to get his tax package through the legislature, said that it was in the "common interest for the entire population to have access to economic growth and development." Only Duke spoke against the bill in the committee hearing, calling it "racial discrimination against white contractors."[21]

When H.B. 18 came before the entire House, Duke again opposed the measure, claiming that to provide special treatment for minorities would be an affront to "equal rights." He offered a floor amendment, coauthored by other Republicans, to prohibit set-aside programs. "Set-asides do in fact discriminate," Representative Duke argued. "They don't allow the contract to go to the low bidder. They specifically discriminate against lower-bidding white contractors."[22]

Steven Watsky reported that the debate on Duke's amendment broke down into a discussion over past injustices against minorities, instead of the bill's provisions. "I would like to welcome some members of this house to the fight for equal rights for everyone," said Raymond Jetson, a black representative of Baton Rouge. "Where have you been so long? Where were you when black folks couldn't walk into an office and get a job? Where have you been?" Jetson asked. "Now all of a sudden you want to jump on this band-wagon of equal rights for everyone. Now all of a sudden we're having selective righteousness, after years and years of abusing folks."[23]

Representative Sherman Copelin, a black political leader from New Orleans, charged that Duke and the Republicans were trying to kill the bill. He stopped just short of calling them racists: "I want to remind you of something. You take what I'm saying in a good light. This is the Louisiana Legislature. This is not a Klan meeting. This might be harsh words, and if I offended anybody, I apologize now. But I feel it, you feel it."[24]

The debacle continued for more than two hours. Duke later responded, not very clearly: "It has never been my intention to divide this body. I know I have a colorful past, if I can use that word. I think it's time to end the divisions and go on merit." The amendment failed by a 34–55 vote. The bill passed the House by a 58–34 vote with 13 not voting. Duke and all but one of the eighteen Republicans in the House—V. J. Bella of Berwick, who was close to Roemer—voted against the bill.[25]

DUKE AND BRUNEAU REMAIN TOGETHER

During the special session, Duke voted against both parts of Roemer's tax package—H.B. 1, a proposed constitutional amendment revising the state's tax laws (which passed by a 80–25 vote), and H.B. 2, the statutory measure, calling for a sales tax decrease, business tax breaks, and increases in income, motor vehicle, cigarette, and wine taxes (which passed by a 76–25 vote). The Republicans were split. The half with close ties to Roemer voted for both measures. Anti-Roemer Republicans—Duke and Bruneau among them—voted against the package. Only two blacks voted against the bills —Representatives Wilford Carter of Lake Charles and Jetson of Baton Rouge.[26] Only Duke and Bruneau among the Republicans voted against the transportation trust fund program. The vote was 75–16 with 14 not voting.

Two of the eighteen Republican House members were among those not voting.

The tax reform program was almost revenue neutral for the state treasury but would have provided potential for growth, Roemer argued, through an expanding economy. Although the package offered a reduction in regressive sales taxes, it was opposed by some black lawmakers whose constituents would have benefited. One black state senator in particular, William Jefferson of New Orleans, "organized black ministers in New Orleans and over the state to oppose Roemer's tax reform program. . . . Jefferson was a major factor in the program's [ultimate] defeat," said *Times-Picayune* reporter Iris Kelso.[27] One source of the disagreement between Roemer and Jefferson lay in Roemer's backing of a single board to govern higher education, which Jefferson, as lawyer for the mostly black Southern University Board of Supervisors, opposed. A merging of the state's four higher education boards would lessen the power black administrators and the black establishment had in the majority-black higher education institutions. The shared opposition of Duke and Jefferson to the Roemer tax reform package was one of those rare moments when similar political interests had the white supremacist Duke and the black power broker Jefferson fishing out of the same boat.

Roemer stumped the state in support of the program. Duke pledged to stump against it. "This is a massive tax increase," he declared, "and it needs some truth in packaging." The effectiveness of Duke's opposition got mixed reviews. One rural lawmaker, Representative James David Cain of Dry Creek, said the constitutional amendment would pass "if David Duke travels around the state opposing it. A lot of blacks will vote for it just because he's opposing it. He will play right into Gov. Roemer's hands." Tanya Barrientos, writing for the Knight-Ridder news service, concluded in an analysis on Duke: "In slightly more than 60 days since he took office, Rep. Duke, R-Metairie, has emerged as a popular political leader here, using a recent statewide campaign against an unpopular tax-restructuring plan as his step to legitimacy, political analysts say."[28]

Duke Uses the Legislative Session to Air His Issues

Returning to Baton Rouge for the 1989 regular session, Duke introduced a series of bills that followed a pattern from the past. The racial message was there, for he had used them in his previous failed legislative campaigns. When running against Senator Kenneth Osterberger of Baton Rouge for the Sixteenth Senate District seat in 1975, for instance, one of his fliers read: "David Duke is staunchly opposed to forced busing for racial integration and all plans to force the merger of mostly white LSU and all-black Southern University. He is also opposed to the reverse discrimination going on against White people in employment, promotions, and scholarships."[29]

Now Duke laid out a similar platform in a letter to *Gambit*, a New Orleans news magazine, in response to an article by Jason Berry. He said that when he ran for the House District 81 seat his program was "clear," his platform "different," and that he "spoke about issues no one has dared to address—the pervasive racial discrimination against whites called affirmative action and minority set-asides, the educational disaster of forced integration and busing in public education, the need to get the abuse out of the welfare system by mandating that the able-bodied work for their welfare benefits, and incentives to lower the high illegitimate welfare birthrate."[30] (Even in his 1990 U.S. Senate campaign, the message would be similar. The subjects of his direct mail solicitation letters included "Stop Welfare Abuse"; "Workfare instead of Welfare"; "Reduce the Illegitimate Welfare Birthrate"; "Eliminate Wasteful and Unfair Minority Set-Asides"; "Freedom of Choice and Tax Credits in Education"; "Stop Illegal Immigration.")

Bills that Duke introduced in his first regular session of the Louisiana legislature followed much the same issues. During the session, he introduced eight bills and one resolution. The bills sought to raise penalties on drug offenders in public housing projects, repeal affirmative action programs, repeal minority set-aside programs, require drug testing of young, first-time applicants for drivers' licenses, require drug testing for public assistance, and provide loss of entitlements for drug offenders.

Debate on the bills—none passed—generally produced arguments grounded in race. On the surface Duke's presentations were couched in mainstream Republicanisms. "There is massive institutional racial discrimination going on in this state and nation now. And it's against whites," Duke told a House committee in arguing for a bill to abolish affirmative action and minority set-asides. "I believe in equal rights for everybody—special privilege for no one," Duke said. The black member of the panel, Representative Joe Delpit of Baton Rouge, responded when asked if he objected to the bill, "I'm objecting to the author." The bill was approved by the committee on a 5–1 vote, with three of the five yes votes from Republicans. Delpit voted no and walked out in protest.[31]

WHAT ABOUT THE INNOCENT?

Blacks in the House were almost alone in opposing a Duke measure that would have prohibited persons convicted on a drug charge from receiving

Aid to Families with Dependent Children, food stamps, and Medicaid. Black representative Naomi White Warren of New Orleans asked about the effect on children, "who are totally innocent," when their mothers are denied public assistance for a drug offense. Representative Charles D. Jones of Monroe said the bill would mean that a family could be denied assistance when a young person in a family is found guilty of smoking a marijuana cigarette, "while somebody who murders somebody, who rapes somebody or who robs somebody still gets benefits. That's totally crazy."[32]

The House vote on the bill, however, was 78–16, with fourteen black and two white representatives voting against. It was eventually killed in the Senate. Senators, elected from larger districts than representatives, often have larger percentages of black constituents than do those House members living in suburban districts where there are few blacks. A senator elected with black support and dependent on those blacks for reelection is going to be more responsive to black voter interests.

In other instances, opposition to the Duke agenda showed more sophistication. Several white lawmakers took lead positions in killing Duke bills, either through parliamentary maneuvers or amendments that diluted the original intent. Duke's bill to abolish affirmative action and set-aside programs was killed on the House floor on a motion to table by Representative Landrieu. The motion, which is nondebatable, was approved by a 44–40 vote. Sixteen of the eighteen Republicans opposed the tabling motion. Two did not vote. Twelve of the black representatives voted with Landrieu. Three did not vote.[33]

The black and white coalition also dismantled a Duke bill to require mandatory one-year sentences for felony drug offenders in public housing projects. Representative Bajoie authored the first successful amendment, making the extra penalty applicable for drug offenders living on "any residential property." "Don't be hypocritical," urged Representative Melvin ("Kip") Holden, a black lawmaker from Baton Rouge. "Make it apply to everyone."[34]

Two moderate white Democrats, Representative Randy Roach of Lake Charles in southwestern Louisiana and Representative Edward Deano of Mandeville in the southeast, then neutered Duke's bill with an amendment to make the additional, one-year sentence applicable to all felony drug sentences, no matter where the crime was committed. Arguing against the amendment, Duke asked, "Is it racist to try to help people who are poor?" Roach replied, "Mr. Duke, I'm not going to stand up here and judge your motives." Deano followed by telling Duke that his focus on housing projects "is without a doubt . . . a matter of discrimination in the grossest sense." The amendment passed by a 77–14 vote, with 11 of the votes against coming from Republicans. The bill passed the House by a 94–2 vote and was sent to the Senate, where it died.[35]

Duke's bills were most often killed by the skill of his adversaries—referral to unsympathetic committees, tabling motions before debate could commence on the House floor, and outright rejection in the rare instances when one of his bills got as far as the Senate for floor debate. During the 1989 regular session, UPI intern Jill Fernandez revealed in an analytical piece that the state would have lost as much as $2 billion if Duke's bill had become law. "The onetime Ku Klux Klan leader presented his legislation as ways to save the state money and get tough on drugs," Fernandez wrote. "But the effect of most of the bills would have been to stop or reduce aid to minorities. Some would have cost the state money. All were of dubious constitutional merit."[36]

The Difference a Year Makes

In 1990 Duke tried his anti–affirmative action bill again and again brought about heightened racial division. In an article in the *Christian Science Monitor*, reporter Garry Boulard described "black and white legislators . . . engaging in increasingly rancorous debate, with many blaming Rep. David Duke." As Representative Holden, a black lawmaker, saw it, "The agenda of this man [Duke] is to divide people in this body and divide the people of this state along racial lines. That's his whole agenda. . . . We're dealing with this man and with legislation that is racially divisive. That's all we're dealing with."[37]

This time the bill succeeded. After a 66–28 vote in the House that sent it to the Senate, Duke claimed that he had won through popular vindication: "What a difference a year makes. . . . The difference is that the representatives are hearing the footsteps of their constituents around the state on this issue."[38]

A CRAZY SESSION

Duke won his victory on affirmative action during a session that included debate on several bills that were both emotionally charged and guaranteed to cause conflict. The bills would have allowed a flag burner to be assaulted at a penalty of only twenty-five dollars (failed to pass), prohibited abortion (twice vetoed), required labeling of "dirty" records and tapes (vetoed), and legalized a state lottery, which had been sent to voters as a proposed constitutional amendment. Debate on each of these issues was covered by the national press and, excepting the abortion issue, illustrated just how crazy a session of the Louisiana legislature can get.

The fate of Duke's bill got tangled in a racial split that occurred during voting on a lottery bill by Representative Raymond ("La La") Lalonde of Sunset. Lalonde is a member of the Acadiana delegation of lawmakers, who represent southern Louisiana, much of it inhabited by settlers driven from French-speaking Nova Scotia years ago. Seventy votes were needed to pass his bill, but when the vote was called, three black lawmakers who had earlier voted for a similar bill failed to respond. Lalonde had promises from two or three representatives—among them, Speaker Dimos—that if the vote got close to 70, they would vote yes. Because of the switch by the blacks, the vote, 65–36, fell short.

Minutes later, when Duke's anti–affirmative action bill came up for action, the Acadiana delegation provided votes ensuring passage of Duke's bill. Acadiana members represent blacks and hold similar interests with the black representatives; as Associated Press reporter Guy Coates pointed out, they had generally opposed the Duke bill in 1989. Now more members apparently supported it. Coates asked the delegation chairman, Representative Elias ("Bo") Ackal of New Iberia, if the vote was in reaction to the lottery vote by the black lawmakers. "It certainly played a part in the vote," said Ackal. Representative Raymond Jetson of Baton Rouge, a member of the Black Legislative Caucus, said "absolutely," that the support of the Duke bill was retaliation at black lawmakers for their nonvote.[39] Seventeen of the eighteen Republicans in the House also voted for the Duke bill.

JONES CHARGES RACISM

At a news conference the next morning, Black Caucus chairman Charles D. Jones of Monroe charged that Duke's bill had passed through racism. Jones said the result of the vote on the Duke bill was that it "negatively impacted on blacks and poor people in this state. It divides the races. It attempts to set us back." Duke responded that the blacks "are the real racists in this matter."[40]

Be it vindication, political payback, or racism, the bill's passage furthered Duke's divisive effect. Quoted in a column the following Sunday, Representative Holden described Duke as the "vocal conscience" of some legislators. Holden said that Duke magnified racial division in the House because what he said was "simply put in a black-white context. By and large, I think what he's doing—and I hope now some of these guys will see it—that he's tending to put people against one another who were friends before I came to this body."[41]

Duke's bill was not successful in the Senate. It was sent to the Finance Committee, where members argued that the bill would either cost the state money or would have no effect. Senator Don Kelly of Natchitoches, a Roemer floor leader, reported that the state highway department was under a federal court consent judgment on hiring and promotion practices. The state highways chief, Kelly said, had told him that "it makes no difference what we do with this bill or anything else. He's sitting there with a federal court order staring him in the face." And Senator Jefferson pointed out that the state was receiving $2.7 billion in federal funds. "We place a lot of that in jeopardy with a bill like this," Jefferson said.[42] After the committee deferred the bill, effectively killing it, Duke blamed the report on partisan, not racial, politics. His opponents, he said, had "pulled a dirty political trick by sending my bill to the Finance Committee. There are no Republicans on this committee."[43]

Duke passed none of the five bills he introduced in the 1990 session. As in the 1989 session, the topics of the bills were drugs and welfare benefits, affirmative action, drug testing for first-time drivers, minority set-asides, and drugs in public housing projects. Except for the affirmative action bill, they were either killed in committee, tabled on the House floor, or defeated in Senate committees.

GETTING VOTES VERSUS BEING HEARD

Assessing the relationship between former Klansman Duke and the Louisiana legislature (mostly the House of Representatives), there is an argument on one side that he was a failure because, as the New Orleans *Times-Picayune* pointed out at the end of the 1989 session, "none of his bills had passed and little had changed in the programs he took on."[44] The other side, the side Duke takes, is that he was a success because he brought his issues to the legislature. He also believes that members of the House responded to his agenda and that candidates in future races will "start vocalizing" his ideas.[45]

Duke: "A Mouth That's Different"

Conclusions drawn about Duke's significance are muddled, reflecting the ambivalence of those dealing with him, who often are torn between responding to the issues he promotes and reacting to what he personally represents to them. Governor Roemer expressed some of that in mid-summer of 1990, as the legislative session neared an end. Duke, in the middle of his U.S. Senate race, was continuing to draw attention to his special agenda. Interviewed by the *New York Times*, Roemer said, "I find an almost universal dislike for set-

asides. I don't share that. But you can't come down here and say that
Louisiana has a problem that's different than anyone else's. We have a mouth
that's different, but not a problem."[46]

Former senator Birch Bayh, writing shortly after Duke's election, saw
Duke's success as a clear warning: "Perhaps some good can come from the
Duke election if we stop treating David Duke as an isolated example, an
aberration of our political process. Let us recognize that Duke is one of a
large and growing number of Americans who espouse prejudice and bigotry
and who, if left uncontested, will divide and destroy our nation. The David
Dukes of America do not live only in Louisiana. They exist in every region of
our republic."[47]

Yet the vote on Duke in the media is still muddled. The *New York Times*
reporter, claiming Duke "had little impact on the Legislature before the vote
on his bill on affirmative action," also deduced that "the vote was a sign that
legislators believe he speaks for a powerful constituency."[48] Following the
1989 session, *USA Today* noted in the lead paragraph that Duke "hasn't made
many waves in the Louisiana Capitol. 'He hasn't changed anybody's voting
pattern,' says House Speaker Jim Dimos. 'We really haven't heard from him
at all. Y'all (the media) ought to ignore him.'" But in the last two paragraphs, state capitol correspondent John Hill quotes Senator Dennis Bagneris, a black from New Orleans, drawing a different conclusion. Duke, said
Bagneris, "did have an impact, but it's not the impact portrayed by the
media. He set up a comfort zone for those already in the House who already
voted the way he votes. They didn't switch the way they vote, but they feel
more comfortable with his taking the lead."[49]

A DISCOMFORT ZONE

Another black lawmaker described Duke's effect in terms of discomfort.
Speaking to the Press Club of Baton Rouge in 1989, at the close of the
legislative session, Representative Jetson said that Duke brought about a
"polarization" of the races: "Duke has caused issues that may have otherwise
been able to be discussed based on their merit to now be discussed on racial
connotations. . . . He has caused a very tense feeling on the floor of the
Legislature. Where affirmative action or minority set-aside issues would
come up previously where you could talk to other members about them
whether they were opposed or a proponent of them, now there is this air of
tension that is obviously race based."[50]

Jetson said that a new minority now is being heard from by legislators, a
minority that agrees with Duke and lets their representatives know how they
feel. "Now those legislators are hearing from segments of their district," said

Jetson, "that they never heard from before—the very, very vocal minority, if you will, regardless of [the fact] that Mr. Duke would like to label them the majority. . . . Legislators are now conscious they have a few folks in their district who share views like Mr. Duke. So, it makes for a rather uncomfortable situation."[51]

Two white representatives, who, according to *Times-Picayune* columnist Iris Kelso, had acted as "point men in the effort to blunt Duke's race-based legislation," were straightforward about their feelings toward Representative Duke. Fundamentally, they said, Duke was a fraud. Representative Landrieu did not buy Duke's claims that he favored "equal rights for all," Kelso said, nor did Landrieu believe Duke had broken his ties with a neo-Nazi past. Duke "doesn't care about equal rights for everybody," Landrieu said. "He cares about creating a white Christian nation, with no room for anybody else. He understands that if he said that stuff, he'd sound like the kook that he really is."[52]

Representative Roach, however, the other "point man," joined Landrieu in warning "fellow legislators to look beyond Duke's easy manner": "I think that packaging legislation in a somewhat benign manner to conceal your true interest is a very dangerous thing. . . . When I consider the activities Mr. Duke has been involved in in the past and when I look at his legislation, I'm very concerned about where that legislation is headed, what door he is trying to open and where he is trying to take us."[53]

A year later, Representative Duke made it clear at least what he intends as his effect. In a long interview in which Howell Farrell of Metairie, his campaign chairman for the U.S. Senate race, participated, Duke claimed that his effectiveness reached beyond any measurement tied to the passage (or nonpassage) of his bills.

For one thing, he said, his fellow Republican challenger in the Senate campaign, state senator Ben Bagert of New Orleans, would neither have offered nor have passed his "workfare" legislation in the 1990 legislative session had Duke not been in the legislature. Farrell agreed. Lawmakers "would not have spoken about it as openly and without reservation as they've been able to do now," Farrell said. "And David takes the heat for them. You see, they're able to say it without any heat, and when they say it, people get mad at David. [Farrell laughed.] So he absorbs all this animosity for them. So he's of benefit to them. He's of benefit to the whole Democratic process."[54]

THE DAVID DUKES

For another thing, Duke forecast in the Senate campaign interview that he would have an influence beyond his legislative election and senatorial successes. He dreamed of his ideas, his issues "spill[ing] over into the Legislative races, perhaps into the governor's race next year, . . . to have an impact on local races around the state, . . . to have an impact nationwide."[55] He envisioned a world of more David Dukes.

Some of that has come to pass. He correctly projected he would have an impact on the governor's race. Governor Roemer's switch from Democrat to Republican and the state Republican party's endorsement of U.S. Representative Clyde Holloway of Forest Hill (while the national party was backing Roemer) resulted in Republican Duke running second in Louisiana's open primary election. Roemer was squeezed out of a runoff position in the unique system that pits candidates against each other regardless of their party affiliation, leaving only the two front-runners as general election candidates if neither gets a majority in the primary. Duke was responsible for Roemer's defeat and Edwards's election.

While Bayh in his article asks that "each of us vow to stand up and speak out against these purveyors of hate and prejudice," Duke hopes that his election to membership in the Louisiana House of Representatives will become a guidepost for others. If Duke with his controversial background can be elected, said Duke in an interview, "it's going to make it possible and enable other people across this country to speak out as well." Duke would like others to adopt his legislative proposals wrapped in coded messages— obvious to some, dimly seen by others—and carry them elsewhere. "I hope to see a lot of mainstream candidates who privately think these things [who will] start vocalizing these ideas in political races. . . . I think I represent change."[56]

WILL THERE BE MORE OF DUKE IN THE FUTURE?

Duke's loss to three-term incumbent J. Bennett Johnston in the U.S. Senate race in 1990—by a 44–56 percent margin—was taken by some as a sign that the former Klan grand wizard would win no more, that his election in House District 81 was a fluke. After all, while he narrowly defeated a weak opponent, fellow Republican John Treen, in capturing a legislative seat in an almost all-white district, he did not defeat Johnston, a vulnerable incumbent who many voters believed had drifted too far from Louisiana and too close to Washington, D.C., literally and politically.

But just weeks after Duke's Senate campaign defeat, the former Klansman announced his intention to run for governor. Because he could not run for reelection to the Louisiana House and governor at the same time, he had to give up his seat in the legislature in 1992. After his defeat in the governor's race by former governor Edwards, Duke announced that he would run for president and days later began maneuvering to get on presidential primary ballots. Duke did not go away. Neither did his ideas.

NOTES

1. McMahon, "Duke's Win Could Spark Seating Fight," A1.
2. Coates, Associated Press dispatch, February 21, 1989.
3. Ashton, Associated Press dispatch, February 20, 1989.
4. Ibid.
5. Ibid.
6. Ibid., February 21, 1989.
7. Redman, Notes from floor debate, February 22, 1989.
8. Ibid.
9. Ibid.
10. Ibid.
11. Baton Rouge *Sunday Advocate*, March 5, 1989.
12. Duke letter to House members, March 5, 1989, in author's possession.
13. Redman and McKinney, "Duke Says Snubbing by National GOP Won't Hurt Him," A5; McKinney, "GOP Expected to Vote Disavowal," A1.
14. McKinney, "GOP Expected to Vote Disavowal," A1.
15. Ibid.
16. Watanabe, "Duke Sheds Robes and Swastika," A13.
17. Page, "GOP Caught What It Was Fishing For," B6.
18. Cohler, "Ex-Klan Wizard Duke Forges Links," 9.
19. Ibid.
20. Bander to Community Relations Committee of the Jewish Federation of Greater Baton Rouge, May 30, 1989, in author's possession.
21. Shuler and Pursnell, "House Rejects Move to Make Roemer's Tax Increase Temporary," A1.
22. Shuler, "House Vote on Highway Plan Stalls," A1; Watsky, Report filed for United Press International (quotation).
23. Watsky, Report filed for United Press International.
24. Ibid.
25. Ibid. (quotation); Shuler, "House Vote on Highway Plan Stalls," A1.
26. Capitol News Bureau, "Roemer Budget Now in Works," C17.
27. Kelso, "Roemer's Push for Jon Johnson," B11.
28. Pursnell, "Tax Plan Depends Partly on Roemer's Popularity," A1 (first two quotations); Barrientos, Knight-Ridder news service release.
29. Baton Rouge *Morning Advocate* and *State-Times* library files.
30. *Gambit*, September 1989.
31. Pursnell, "Delpit Walkout Protests Duke," B1.
32. Capitol News Bureau, "House Backs Welfare Cutoff Bill," A10.

33. McMahon, "House Kills Duke Measure," A12.
34. McMahon, "Legislators Dismantle Duke Bill," A10.
35. Ibid.
36. Fernandez, UPI.
37. Boulard, "Duke Exploits Fuss in Louisiana House," 7.
38. Applebome, "Stirring a Debate," A18.
39. Coates, Associated Press dispatch, May 30, 1990.
40. McMahon, "Black Lawmakers Term House OK," A1.
41. Redman, "Race-based Bickering in House," B7.
42. McMahon, "Senate Panel Kills Duke Bill," A5.
43. Coates, June 25, 1990.
44. Nauth, "Lawmakers," A1.
45. McMahon, Interview with Duke.
46. Applebome, "Ex-Klansman Puts New Racial Politics to Test," A1.
47. Bayh, "My Turn," 8.
48. Applebome, "Ex-Klansman Puts New Racial Politics to Test," A1.
49. Hill, *USA Today*, A2.
50. McMahon, Notes, Jetson Press Club speech.
51. Ibid.
52. Kelso, "Taking the Point," op-ed page.
53. Ibid.
54. McMahon, Interview with Duke.
55. Ibid.
56. Ibid.

REFERENCES

Applebome, Peter. "Stirring a Debate on Breaking Racism's Shackles." *New York Times*, May 30, 1990.
———. "Ex-Klansman Puts New Racial Politics to Test." *New York Times*, June 18, 1990.
Ashton, Linda. Associated Press dispatch, February 20, 1989.
———. Associated Press dispatch, February 21, 1989.
Barrientos, Tanya. Knight-Ridder news service release, May 10, 1989.
Baton Rouge *Morning Advocate* and *State-Times* library files.
Bayh, Birch (chairman, National Institute against Prejudice and Violence). "My Turn." *Newsweek*, April 17, 1989.
Boulard, Garry. "Duke Exploits Fuss in Louisiana House." *Christian Science Monitor*, June 14, 1990.
Capitol News Bureau. "Roemer Budget Now in Works Proposes $658 Million in Cuts." Baton Rouge *State-Times*, March 8, 1989.
———. "House Backs Welfare Cutoff Bill." Baton Rouge *Morning Advocate*, June 16, 1989.

Coates, Guy. Associated Press dispatch, February 21, 1989.

———. Notes from floor debate, Louisiana legislature, February 22, 1989. In Coates's possession.

———. Associated Press dispatch, May 30, 1990.

———. Associated Press dispatch, June 25, 1990.

Cohler, Larry. "Ex-Klan Wizard Duke Forges Links with Dixie Republicans." *Washington Jewish Week*, August 10, 1988

Fernandez, Jill. United Press International dispatch, June 29, 1989.

Hill, John. *USA Today*, July 7, 1989.

Kelso, Iris. "Taking the Point." New Orleans *Times-Picayune*, June 22, 1989.

———. "Roemer's Push for Jon Johnson." New Orleans *Times-Picayune*, September 16, 1990.

McKinney, Joan. "GOP Expected to Vote Disavowal of Duke." Baton Rouge *Morning Advocate*, February 21, 1989.

McMahon, Bill. "Duke's Win Could Spark Seating Fight." Baton Rouge *Morning Advocate*, February 20, 1989.

———. Notes from floor debate, Louisiana legislature, February 22, 1989. In author's possession.

———. "House Kills Duke Measure to Abolish Affirmative Action." Baton Rouge *Morning Advocate*, May 31, 1989.

———. "Legislators Dismantle Duke Bill, Criticize Author." Baton Rouge *Morning Advocate*, June 17, 1989.

———. Notes, Jetson Press Club speech, July 10, 1989. In author's possession.

———. "Black Lawmakers Term House OK of Duke Bill 'Racist.'" Baton Rouge *Morning Advocate*, May 30, 1990.

———. "Senate Panel Kills Duke Bill to End Affirmative Action." Baton Rouge *State-Times*, June 26, 1990.

———. Interview with Duke at his Senate campaign headquarters in Baton Rouge, July 12, 1990. Notes in author's possession.

Nauth, Zack. "Lawmakers: Duke Flunked Freshman Term." New Orleans *Times-Picayune*, July 16, 1989.

Page, Clarence. "GOP Caught What It Was Fishing For." Baton Rouge *State-Times*, February 24, 1989.

Pursnell, Allan. "Tax Plan Depends Partly on Roemer's Popularity." Baton Rouge *Sunday Advocate*, March 12, 1989.

———. "Delpit Walkout Protests Duke." Baton Rouge *Morning Advocate*, May 27, 1989.

Redman, Carl. Notes from floor debate, Louisiana legislature, February 22, 1989. In author's possession.

———. "Race-based Bickering in House Helps Duke's Candidacy Along." Baton Rouge *Sunday Advocate*, June 3, 1990.

Redman, Carl, and Joan McKinney. "Duke Says Snubbing by National GOP Won't Hurt Him." Baton Rouge *State-Times*, February 25, 1989.

Shuler, Marsha. "House Vote on Highway Plan Stalls." Baton Rouge *Morning Advocate*, March 3, 1989.

Shuler, Marsha, and Allan Pursnell. "House Rejects Move to Make Roemer's Tax Increase Temporary." Baton Rouge *Morning Advocate*, February 28, 1989.

Watanabe, Teresa. "Duke Sheds Robes and Swastika but Critics Say New Image Cloaks Real Views." Baton Rouge *State-Times*, April 5, 1989.

Watsky, Steven. Report filed for United Press International from the Baton Rouge bureau, March 2, 1989.

Gary Esolen

8 More than a Pretty Face

David Duke's Use of Television as a Political Tool

On the face of it, the most surprising thing about David Duke's successful bid for a seat in the Louisiana legislature, his run for the U.S. Senate seat held by J. Bennett Johnston, and his effort to become governor of Louisiana is that he was able to mount a serious candidacy at all. Given his lifetime record of deliberately outrageous behavior and extremist politics, how did Duke get so far into the mainstream?

In fact, it is worth noticing that Duke's electoral career would be singularly unimpressive for a normal politician. Duke narrowly won his House seat in 1989 from a small, suburban, blue-collar white ethnic district, where he moved his residence for the specific purpose of running for office. His opponent, John Treen, politically almost as far to the right as Duke, was an unpopular, weak campaigner who was distinguished only by his family name: his brother had been a congressman and governor. One elected Republican official from a nearby district remarked sardonically that Duke would have lost if the Republicans had picked a candidate at random from the telephone book.

In the U.S. Senate race Duke pulled 44 percent of the vote, which would normally be considered a landslide defeat. A similar outcome was enough to derail the political career of Henson Moore, a former Louisiana Republican candidate for the Senate. It is only because of Duke's extremism that the results were impressive.

Nevertheless, it was a remarkable performance. David Duke has worn a Nazi uniform, donned the white robes of the Knights of the Ku Klux Klan, burned crosses and saluted them with a Nazi stiff-arm salute, peddled the most extreme Nazi and racist literature, denied the existence of the Holocaust, suggested that the United States was on the wrong side in World War II, and pretended to a military record he does not have. He has posed as a black militant to write a book advising blacks on how to attack whites, and he has posed as a woman to write a book advising women on their sex lives, including how to pick up men and when to have one-night stands or affairs with married men. Moreover, he has done these things not in hiding but out in the open, seeking publicity.[1] For him to sustain any credibility as a candidate for public office baffles political analysts and frustrates his opponents. Any one of those actions would end the career of most politicians, yet Duke has survived all of them and much more. How does he do it?

There is no one answer to that question, and important answers are suggested throughout this book, but most observers would probably agree that one key to Duke's political success is his skill in handling the news media. He gets a lot of free media attention and uses it well to advance his cause.

Duke's Media Message

David Duke has built a political campaign out of coverage by the news media. Here is how: (1) he uses a simple, often-repeated, and persuasive message; (2) to get attention for himself and his message, he takes advantage of his notoriety, which he keeps alive by continuing to draw controversy; and (3) once the news media are paying attention, he delivers his message with unusual persistence and skill, making use of the structural characteristics of the news media, especially television, to get the most and best coverage he can.

Duke's political message has two parts, which feed into one another in a kind of endless cycle:

1. *Why do reporters and politicians pick on me and say hateful things about me when anyone can see I'm a nice guy and a reasonable fellow?*

Besides, even if I did say or do extreme things once or twice that's all long over with now.

2. *The real reason they pick on me is that they are afraid of my message on the issues, which is that affirmative action has gone too far and become racism in reverse, the black underclass is dragging us down, we can't afford welfare, and it's time white people had some rights again.*

Duke's message thus defines two issues and two issues only as the subjects of his political campaign. One is the Duke issue: where do you stand on David Duke and those who criticize him? The other is the issue of race-welfare-affirmative action-white people's rights.

A public opinion poll done by Susan Howell at the University of New Orleans indicates that a majority of white Louisiana voters seem to agree at least in part with Duke's criticism of affirmative action and minority set-aside programs, and to think that the rights of white job seekers have been compromised.[2] Their sympathy with half of Duke's message makes them more receptive to the other half: they may accept his characterization of himself as a nice guy and of his past as innocent because they tend to agree with him now. Clearly, the two halves of Duke's message are mutually reinforcing. People who sympathize with his views will be persuaded to ignore his past, while those who accept him as a nice guy may find his views less disturbing.

To enter and remain in the political mainstream, Duke has needed a steady stream of attention from television news. But television news producers do not ordinarily oblige by giving what political campaign managers call "free media"—news time to air a candidate's message. A major part of Duke's political strategy has been to exploit free media. Newspeople pay attention to Duke because of his extremism and his (deliberately) outrageous political persona. He was the media's favorite KKK wizard long before he was elected to office, and he has proved irresistible to TV cameras and reporters ever since.

Vintage Duke combines a targeted direct mail and personal appearance campaign, raises money, cements the loyalty of his followers, and keeps himself sufficiently controversial to foment continuing television coverage. This alternation of roles (the charming and polished Dr. Jekyll before the TV cameras, horrible Mr. Hyde in his publications and personal appearances, then back to Jekyll for the TV cameras again) is the engine that drives his unusual political campaigns.

The paradox is that although Duke's TV message is that he has cleaned up his act, he cannot in fact leave his original politics too far behind or he will fizzle out. A scoundrel who goes straight will soon lose the attention of the news media. At the same time, to the extent that Duke actually believes in his

TONIGHT ON TV!

DAVID DUKE

The Candidate for Governor
ALL of Louisiana is Talking
About!

WATCH TONIGHT!

CHANNEL 8, WVUE - TV
6:30 PM

For more information, call 831-5216

Paid for by David Duke Campaign. Paul Allen, Treasurer

To gain viewers for a televised commercial, Duke advertises himself as the controversial center of attention. (From Times-Picayune, *October 15, 1991, D9)*

extreme political positions, he will want to soften them as little as possible. Opportunism and ideology thus both drive him to maintain as much of his extremist position as possible, while to the greatest possible degree combining it with a role acceptable to the television news and through the news to mainstream voters.

It is a neat trick, and in part at least he does it by exploiting inherent, structural weaknesses in television news coverage. David Duke is not the only political candidate to exploit these weaknesses, but he has been unusually consistent and successful in doing so. Furthermore, his success may show the way to others who share his ideology or his ambitions.

An Extremist Strategy

Duke's strategy is appropriate to his role as an extremist seeking acceptance in the mainstream. He needs to hold his base of voters who like and support his extremist positions, while extending his reach to those who are uncomfortable with some of his extremist posturing but are sympathetic to his racially polarized message.

In fact, Duke's strategy resembles that of other latter-day extremists-turned-moderate. The formula—develop a message acceptable in the mainstream, remake your image accordingly, keep at least one foot planted in your original constituency, and capitalize on personal notoriety and controversy—resembles the path taken by Louis Farrakhan, Yasir Arafat, and many others, with varying degrees of sincerity in their conversions. Some have succeeded in gaining a broader audience; many have failed.

Based on the results of intensive statewide political polling conducted during Duke's race for the U.S. Senate, the strategy has worked for Duke. Analysts agree that Duke has two levels of support—his hard-core supporters, who are unconcerned with revelations about his past; and a second, potentially larger but softer group of supporters, who are more or less uneasy about his extremism. His core support has been estimated to be from 12 to as much as 25 percent of the statewide electorate, yet his total support in his race for the U.S. Senate climbed to over 40 percent.[3]

Obviously, Duke's room for growth is all in the soft category of supporters. He got some of them in his Senate race, but he needs a lot more to become a majority candidate. Thus, his ability to control the media's presentation and interpretation of his past behavior and of his political campaign remains critical to his future success. Skillful handling of television news is one element of that success.

Here are seven structural characteristics of television news coverage, why they exist, and how David Duke has used them to deliver his message and with what effect on voters.

The First Two Flaws in TV News Coverage

Two structural characteristics of television coverage severely limit the viewer's understanding of a news event:

1. *Television news has no memory.*

Television news is unable, because of time constraints, to review more of the history of an issue, a person, or a situation than can be contained in a few words or at most a few sentences.

Furthermore, television differs from newspapers in that newspapers have a collective memory in clippings (or, these days, electronic files) of past stories. Newspaper reporters are expected to consult those files, and newspapers have at least some space available to publish or review that history. Television news has neither files nor time. Tapes of past news programs are preserved for a time, but they are rarely indexed, and only raw footage is kept (in a sort of library), not reportage. TV reporters and producers rarely, if ever, review past coverage when preparing a deadline story. They would not have time to use it, and they have no time to view it. Thus, even if there is a history of coverage, it is easily lost.

Duke's use of this characteristic of television news is best understood by grouping it with a second and related characteristic:

2. *Television reporters are not likely to be expert in the stories they cover.*

Again, the problem is time. Television, especially local television, has few beat reporters—reporters who can become familiar with the stories they cover over time. Most jump from assignment to assignment, relying on quick research, a good news sense, and basic reportorial technique rather than on knowledge or research in depth.

A television reporter gets in, gets the story, and gets out. No time is set aside during the day or week for sitting in the library reading newspaper clippings, chatting with experts, or doing background analysis. TV reporters may be quick to pick up the basic shape of the story, and they may remember exactly what happened yesterday, but they are unlikely to know a lot more than that. This is not an indictment of their professionalism: they may be called on to cover a teacher's union strike in the morning, a drug-related homicide at noon, and David Duke's political race in the afternoon. How can they be deeply knowledgeable about all three subjects and another three tomorrow? The problem is structural.

These problems are compounded by viewers. The audience most dependent on television for news (those who say they rely on TV news for information, who do not often read newspapers or listen to much radio news) does not even watch TV news consistently. Though regular TV news watchers also read the newspaper and have other sources of information, they are outnumbered by the casual watchers. Moreover, even those who watch a television news story are not likely to remember much of what they saw and heard after a day or two.[4] Television's amnesia is shared by its audience.

What People Knew about Duke

David Duke was fairly well known when he got into the race for the Louisiana House of Representatives in 1989. He had been a prominent figure as a right-wing student protester who wore a Nazi uniform, as a Klan organizer and dragon, as a candidate for the state Senate in 1975, and as a contender, on a fringe-party ticket, for the presidency in 1988. And he was fairly well known as the media's favorite grand wizard, often interviewed by vignette-seeking reporters from the national print media, including the big news weeklies. Notoriety was essential for his political career, and he had cultivated it successfully.

Much of the electorate and virtually all of the news media therefore knew going in that Duke had been a Klansman, had some Nazi connections, was a racist, and was generally controversial. Probably only a handful of reporters and others who had covered or followed such stories in detail knew much more than that.

Miscalculation by Duke's Opponents: The Print Media Didn't Help

Duke's political opponents did not know much more than the news media and tended to suppose that merely repeating generalities about his past would disqualify him as a candidate. (As Douglas Rose points out in Chapter 9 of this book, Duke's opponents had a passionate desire to disqualify him, to simply take him out of the running altogether. In a way, they had trouble believing that anyone regarded him seriously—a fatal error in judgment.) When repeating general impressions about Duke's record failed to cripple him as a candidate, they were ill-equipped to launch specific attacks.

Another possible source of detailed information on Duke's political career, the daily newspaper of record in New Orleans, the *Times-Picayune*, made an early editorial decision to leave coverage of Duke's race for the Louisiana legislature in the hands of the bureau reporters assigned to the suburb where Duke was running, the East Bank of Jefferson Parish. That decision virtually precluded in-depth coverage of the candidate's past behavior, which would have required freeing up one or more experienced reporters for quite a while —a luxury a suburban bureau cannot afford.

After Duke won the House seat, media watchers in New Orleans noticed that the *Times-Picayune* had declared a kind of hands-off policy on Duke. Some people close to the newspaper's editors said that, given Duke's effective use of television publicity, it was feared that any kind of coverage would end up increasing his support. On the other hand, there were repeated rumors that a particular reporter (Tyler Bridges) was working on a massive investigative piece on Duke that would break any day. A major story by Bridges did finally appear about a month before the senatorial primary on October 6, 1990, but up to that time the daily newspaper did not function as the newspaper of record. It did not provide, for the journalistic record, the history of David Duke's career.

Thus, neither the opposing candidates nor the daily newspaper created a context in which television news could and, indeed, would be forced to pick up a researched account of Duke's past as part of its coverage. Television news was left to deal with Duke on its own terms, and television's lack of collective memory and the relative ignorance of its reporters loomed large.

TV Amnesia: A Telling Example

Duke's exploitation of the ignorance of TV reporters was evident on election night. A major network affiliate in New Orleans had assigned a weekend news anchor to Duke campaign headquarters. Throughout the evening her coverage was almost star struck, including one remarkable moment when she began touting Duke memorabilia and quoting his staff members urging people to buy their Duke T-shirts before the prices went up. But the most striking exchange occurred when Duke went on camera, one-on-one, and asserted flatly that his campaign had pulled "eight to twelve percent of the black vote in Louisiana, more than any other Republican candidate in history." If true, that would have been astonishing. It was not true. No reputable pollster or analyst has found any evidence for such numbers. Duke made it up. And the reporter did not know the difference and did not inquire further.

Perhaps the most striking successes of Duke's political campaigns were a direct result of such ignorance. In light of relatively vague charges against him, a medium with no information base, and ill-informed reporters, Duke set out to render his past ambiguous. When accusations were made, he denied them, dismissed them, or explained them away. Because the reporters had little information with which to confront him, Duke often appeared to have rebutted his accusers. When groups offended by his record protested his activities, he made their attacks on him the issue: Why are they picking on me? Why do they want to silence me? And whenever possible he would incorporate some form of his message concerning white people's rights.

Voter Response to the Duke Strategy

Duke was largely successful in muddling the issue of his record—a stunning feat of media manipulation given the things he had done and said over the years and was still doing and saying during the 1989 campaign. To his supporters he managed to present himself as a person who had put the extremist positions of his youth behind him, whereas it would be more accurate to say that his entire career up to that moment had consisted of taking extremist positions, for which, until very recently, he had attracted as much publicity as possible. Because of Duke's repeated and unrebutted denials, such information as voters had was rendered ambiguous. Voters were free to project onto Duke whatever they wanted to see, and they did. David Duke's vague and shapeless political record became a Rorschach blot that the electorate interpreted as it was predisposed to view it.

Those who were strongly attracted to his racially polarized message tended to accept Duke's own account of his past. They knew of his Klan affiliations but were unlikely to know or believe that he wore a Nazi uniform, and they thought that he was less of an extremist than his detractors claimed.

Those who opposed him, on the other hand, were quick to believe the worst though they, too, knew relatively few specifics. Most of the damning issues from Duke's record had been rendered so ambiguous that those who were against him were often confused and ill-informed about his actual history. There were a few well-informed voices crying in the wilderness, but in 1989 they still lacked the credibility needed to win over or compel media attention. One of their chief spokesmen, Lance Hill, had been for years a frequent letter writer to the newspapers, but he had neither a journalistic reputation nor a known record of scholarship. Though he later earned considerable respect precisely through his work on David Duke, that took time.

Thus, during Duke's bid for a seat in the state House in 1989, voters' opinions were formed in an atmosphere dominated by television news coverage. Such coverage was marked by the absence of any detailed consideration of Duke's record, and by repeated airings of Duke's two-part message: Why are they picking on me, and don't white people have rights, too? By the time his opponent put a research team together and began to issue information-based criticism of Duke, it was too late. Voter attitudes were already fixed.

Effective News Coverage: Too Little, Too Late

After Duke entered the legislature and embarked on his campaign for the U.S. Senate, a team of researchers emerged out of the Louisiana Republican party, Tulane University, and social groups concerned about Duke's political motivations. Over time, this team accumulated a solidly researched history of Duke's career, which slowly made its way from a kind of *samizdat* transmission of photocopied documents into the media. Some of the material had been available earlier, but from sources who did not command media attention. Little by little, that changed.

Late in the Senate race (near the end of August 1990), an enterprising reporter for the *Shreveport Journal*, Ronni Patriquin, put together articles on two of Duke's more controversial publications, *African Atto* and *Finders Keepers*. The first is a crudely prepared text, purporting to have been written by one Muhammed X, that sets forth techniques for blacks to use in attacking whites. *Finders Keepers* is a manual of sex advice for the modern woman, advocating one-night stands and adultery; one passage waxes rather eloquent about oral sex.

Patriquin's publication of these articles—considered to be a major scoop —made her one of the most aggressive reporters in the state as far as Duke was concerned. In the late days of the Senate campaign, Patriquin's stories were often reprinted and much talked about; they became the basis for coverage of the two Duke books statewide. Both articles came from material collected by the loosely allied groups that were now investigating Duke's background.

From the same research team came much of the information used by New Orleans reporter Quin Hillyer for a June 19, 1990, piece in the New Orleans newsweekly, *Gambit*, on Duke's Nazi-derived beliefs. This was also true of the questions asked of Duke by television interviewer Angela Hill and some members of her studio audience during a local New Orleans Oprah Winfrey–style afternoon talk show. Anyone who doubts that a good television interviewer can get past Duke's smooth surface need only watch this show. If the average news coverage of Duke had been of similar quality, it might have made a difference.

Television coverage in northern Louisiana followed the lead of the print media and looked intensively at Duke's controversial publications. That attracted the outraged attention of the religious right. It was in this atmosphere of increased critical attention that the New Orleans *Times-Picayune* finally broke its embargo and published a major piece on Duke by Tyler Bridges.

The latter days of the 1990 U.S. Senate race differed markedly from the 1989 state House campaign and the early stages of the Senate contest in the way the press handled information on David Duke. Careful analysis of the shifts in voter opinion in the late stages of the Senate race would be required to assess the impact of that information, but it is reasonable to speculate that it might have had a greater effect if it had appeared much sooner, partly because it is hard to change people's minds once they have formed an opinion about a political candidate.

More of Duke's Television Strategy

David Duke's ability to make a favorable impression on voters through television news was also enhanced by another structural characteristic of television news coverage:

3. *Television loves a pretty, friendly face.*

Television is a visual medium, and what the camera sees is at least as important as the words spoken. That is why more and more TV stations are using graphics or even file footage to illustrate news stories when they do not have actual footage. It is also why Duke cultivated a smiling, friendly, attractive image to enhance his message.

David Duke has long been aware of the importance of appearance in influencing others. A telling passage in his 1976 manual of sex advice concerns the usefulness of plastic surgery to increase attractiveness and self-confidence; in fact, he recommends fairly extensive cosmetic surgery, if desired. Duke himself has apparently been the beneficiary of cosmetic surgical procedures. Of these he has admitted to one, a nose job, which he says was a reconstruction after an accident of unspecified date. Careful comparison of early and recent photographs suggests that he may also have benefited from the thinning of his lower lip through liposuction, a chin implant to strengthen his profile, tucks to remove bags under his eyes, a general face-lift, a skin peel, and perhaps even smile wrinkles added beside his eyes.

Duke's theatrical awareness of his image is indicated by the fact that he has spent much of his career in costume. Early photographs—including the infamous 1970 photo of Duke picketing in a Nazi uniform—show him affecting a Hitlerian look, with hair parted on the side and a mustache.

In effect, as his political style and ambitions changed, he transformed himself into a replica of a small-city television anchor: smooth skin, straight nose, slender lips, strong chin, and a friendly, laughing face. Just as John F. Kennedy altered modern electoral politics when he wore makeup for the famous 1960 television debates (and Richard M. Nixon, to his regret, did not), Duke may have upped the ante when he made himself over as a television candidate. No doubt he was not the first politician to turn to face-lifts and hair dye, but he may have relied more heavily on such visual appeal than is usual.

This crafted visual image reinforced the crucial nice-guy appeal that was half of Duke's repeated message. David Duke's friendly, smiling, attractive, and almost familiar face (combined with a reasonable, warm tone of voice) reinforced his words: Why are they picking on me? Anyone can see I am a reasonable, good fellow.

Why Most TV Interviewers Could Not Handle Duke

The next two structural characteristics of television that Duke has exploited explain why he held his own with the best interviewers on television and made mincemeat of local reporters during his 1989, 1990, and 1991 campaigns. First:

4. *When being interviewed on television, you don't have to answer the questions asked. Even on a highly edited show, you will still get your 15 or 28 seconds of time on the tube.*

Political candidates have become increasingly aware of the preciousness of the few seconds they are allowed on the television news; they spend hours deciding exactly what message they want to deliver during those seconds. If a television reporter asks a question that points in a different direction, the skilled politician may simply ignore it to answer the question the interviewer "should" have asked: "That's not the important point, the important point is . . ." If the reporter is left to make the most of such an interview, it is easy enough to edit in the appropriate question.

On live television, the situation similarly favors the person being interviewed: the camera is rolling, the moments are passing, and all they can do is kick you out. One producer who put together a statewide televised talk show with David Duke as a guest claimed to have been reduced to sleeplessness by Duke's evasions: "I thought I had prepared my interviewer well. He had a lot of information and some very good questions. He would ask a question, Duke would listen carefully and attentively to the question, smile, make eye contact with my interviewer, make eye contact with the camera, pause for a long moment, and then deliver his pre-packaged message, which had no relation to the question asked."[5]

David Duke does not differ from other politicians in the fact that he takes advantage of this characteristic of television news, but he is more consistent in his use of it than most. Throughout his political campaigns, he has evidently regarded every moment before the TV cameras as an opportunity to deliver his primary message, and he has not allowed distracting reportorial questions to dissuade him from that important task. In this way he makes another structural characteristic of TV news coverage work for him:

5. *Television interviewers will lose the affection and respect of their viewers if they appear to be rude to the subject of an interview.*

Television, as Marshall McLuhan told us, is a "hot" medium, and when dealing with a hot medium people must remain cool. The persona of the radio talk-show host (radio is a cool medium on which performers can be hot) does not translate to television. A television interviewer who appears to be too aggressive will seem to violate an implicit code of civility and lose his audience—after all, he is sitting in everyone's living room, almost a guest in the home. Dan Rather learned this to his dismay when he coldly and efficiently pursued George Bush's evasions past the point of audience tolerance.

A corollary of this axiom is that television reporters are ill-equipped to deal with either persistent lying or evasion or with a newly minted lie, because that would require a level of persistence and aggression that might bore or alienate the audience. How many times can you ask Dan Quayle to explain how he got into the National Guard before you mark yourself as rude and obnoxious? Why are people always picking on David Duke?

The one obvious exception to the rule that you cannot be rude to the subject of a television interview helps to make this point clear. The exception is the deliberately sensational interview show, like that of Phil Donahue or Geraldo Rivera, where the interviewer cultivates a carefully crafted personality (ultra-reasonable, compassionate, or boorish and comic) that permits greater latitude. This is a form of drama, and it produces dramatic set pieces rather than news interviews.

It is, therefore, almost impossible to chase down the hare on television, except in unusually long, carefully selected, and highly edited pieces such as those that appear on "Sixty Minutes." Mike Wallace can do it (partly because he can pick his stories and edit the footage); Suzie Six O'Clock and Joe Anchorman cannot. Even Mike Wallace risks awakening our sympathies for the doomed hare, and if the hare somehow escapes, there is always the risk of seeming flat-footed and comical. Going after an agile opponent on live television is a very tricky business.

Duke masterfully used this implicit code of civility to further his nice-guy-under-attack image. If a reporter or interviewer went after him too aggressively, he would evade a couple of questions and then turn his standard message against the interviewer: Why are you picking on me? Why won't you talk about the issues? This strategy was reinforced by an atmosphere of suspicion and distrust of the media among voters generally (skillfully exploited by the national Republican presidential campaign in 1988 to counter media attacks on George Bush and Dan Quayle) and to an even greater degree among Duke supporters, who tend to distrust the media.

Even the experienced and skilled Sam Donaldson, who survived the charisma of Ronald Reagan, had trouble chasing down David Duke in a nationally televised interview. Donaldson came across to many viewers whom I talked to in Louisiana as hostile and aggressive. Viewers unsympathetic to Duke still found Donaldson's interview to be unsuccessful.

An amusing byplay took place when Donaldson went after Duke about some of the material he had published in the journal of the National White People's party. Donaldson had selected a choice piece of social planning whereby Duke's publication recommended dividing the United States into zones to which different racial and ethnic groups would be assigned. Cubans would get the southern tip of Florida, for instance, blacks would get part of Mississippi and Louisiana, and so on. As recently as 1989, in an interview with a Tulane University student, Duke had reaffirmed that he might indeed support such a proposition.

In pressing Duke for a comment on the article, Donaldson read out the proposed divisions. When he got to the suggestion that all Jews be assigned to Long Island, his sophisticated New York studio audience laughed. Duke immediately turned to Donaldson and asserted—for the first time anywhere —that the whole thing was a joke. Donaldson's look of amazement showed that he disbelieved the claim, but he was already out on a limb with his hard pursuit of Duke, and he chose not to confront the deception. The national TV anchorman was stymied, and his killer interview turned into a near-comic turn of stumbling after the hare.

Conflict: The Plot Television News Loves

Although face-to-face arguments do not play well on television, conflict has a special place in TV news:

6. *Television loves conflict, because conflict makes a good story that is easy to tell.*

One of the nagging problems for television reporters and producers is how to tell a story in the time available, which may range from fifteen seconds to three minutes, rarely more. A simple plot line is the usual answer. If one school board member starts shouting at another while discussing cafeteria rules, even the most conscientious reporter will probably throw away all the footage and notes about more complicated issues. Conflict makes a good story that is easy to tell.

David Duke took advantage of television's love of conflict by casting his campaign whenever possible as a conflict between himself and the groups or individuals whom he characterized as trying to silence him. Using this defensive technique, he neutralized the people who objected to his candidacy because of his record. His ability to do so was enhanced by the fact that some of these groups or individuals were eager to disqualify him without the burden of detailed and factual argument, a strategy that Duke easily deflected in a classic television tale of conflict. In effect, Duke made his campaign into a simple story and managed to get that story aired on television over and over. Along with his simple, repeated two-part message and his deliberate alternation of extremism and moderation, this technique was central to his success.

Balanced TV Coverage: Duke's Final Advantage

When issues are complex and feelings run high, even the most skilled and knowledgeable television reporters and producers may be uncertain just how to handle an issue fairly. What they know they can do to avoid criticism is to give both sides a chance to be heard:

7. *When TV reporters and producers are unsure how to be fair in handling an issue, they resort to being evenhanded.*

Because David Duke is highly controversial and already gets a lot of media attention, it is natural that he will attract criticism and opposition. When that happened during his political campaigns, he repeatedly asked for—and got—a chance to respond on the air. His response was almost always in the pattern of his consistent media message: Why are they picking on me? Is it to silence me when I say that white people have rights too?

Put it all together and it is a compelling strategy for turning an extremist into a mainstream candidate. To be successful, it requires a candidate with a friendly physical image, or a good plastic surgeon, and a firm grasp of the working weaknesses of television news. It also requires walking a tightrope between too much extremism and too little. And, finally, it requires a message that will attract voters once the strategy works and massive free media exposure is achieved.

Duke's Message in Pure Form

Crafted with the help of a professional media specialist, Duke's message appeared in an expanded form in two special half-hour television appeals that were aired by his 1990 and 1991 campaigns. The commercials' strongest single point is their I'm-a-nice-guy theme, which makes up a substantial part of the spoken message and is reinforced by Duke's smiling, friendly presence, the warm setting (the pieces were shot in a studio set that looks like an upper-middle-class home with library), and even a sequence with Duke playing loving father to his two attractive daughters. The message is unmistakable: David Duke can't be a Nazi or a terrible racist—look at him, he's handsome, friendly, normal looking, and has cute kids.[6]

During these political commercials, Duke casually dismisses his Nazi affiliations as incidental and long past, though they were in fact central to his career and continued up to and throughout his 1989 legislative race. He brushes off his sale of Nazi literature by suggesting that he was simply running a bookstore and did not endorse the materials he sold. (In fact, Duke's book sales operation—mostly by mail order—sold only extremist literature, including a number of classic Nazi texts and many notably scurrilous racist materials. The nature of the operation was to sell books by promoting them through glowing reviews and blurbs.)

In one passage, in the 1990 version, when he talks about Hispanics in the Southwest, Duke verges on his old KKK style. He suggests that part of the United States has become like Mexico through illegal immigration. We should therefore pull our troops out of Europe, he says, and line them up on the Mexican border *to preserve the integrity of the United States.* Done so casually, this proposal almost passes unnoticed, but it is a striking lapse. One can only believe that it was (like everything else in this half-hour political commercial) carefully crafted, perhaps to appeal to anti-Hispanic hate groups.[7]

What is most interesting about the piece is that it is a perfect representation of Duke's television strategy—almost a paradigm of the message he had already delivered through hundreds of appearances on television news. Its highly crafted character is so consistent with Duke's day-to-day offerings that one can only assume that all those seemingly casual encounters with the media were planned with equal care.

National versus Local TV News Coverage

A final and surprising note is that during Duke's 1990 and 1991 campaigns, sophisticated national TV networks did not seem much better equipped to deal with Duke's television news strategy than the understaffed, overworked local stations. David Duke has proved to be a fascinating subject for the national news, particularly for CNN, which several times sent crews to Louisiana to cover his campaign for the U.S. Senate. CNN recorded perhaps the most vulnerable moment in Duke's attempt to transfer the momentum of his successful House race to the Senate campaign by ignoring it. Duke had just decisively lost the Republican caucuses, including a shutout in his home district, to Louisiana state senator Ben Bagert, who then beat Duke decisively for the official Republican nomination. CNN declared that Duke was the incumbent J. Bennett Johnston's only real opposition in the U.S. Senate race. CNN can justify its highly editorialized coverage by noting that events proved it right, but such naive and laudatory national coverage is one reason for Duke's success.

On this issue as on others, CNN set the tone for the national media. Throughout his Senate campaign, Duke was able to take advantage of an astonishing amount of national publicity, all of it apparently motivated by surprise over his ability to mount a credible campaign, and all of it reinforcing that campaign. The national news proved no better than the local news at getting out the hard facts about Duke's career, partly because it was too busy sounding the general alarm about his shocking success and, in the process, fueling his momentum. If the engine of Duke's campaign, his alternation of bad-guy–good-guy publicity, had sputtered momentarily with the primary loss, it was once again up and running.

National news coverage of local politics compels local news coverage, and it is reasonable to say that a wave of favorable national coverage carried Duke over the lowest point in his Louisiana senatorial campaign. Just when local TV news had become supersaturated with Duke coverage and had begun to shift to strong, traditional hard news about Duke's career, the national television news teams came to town with the same structural weaknesses and provided Duke once again with the naive media forum his campaign needed.

Exceptions Prove the Rule

Even when television stations went in for deeper coverage of David Duke, it had little effect on their day-to-day news stories. Bill Elder, an investigative reporter at WWL-TV, did a strong documentary piece on Duke. In fact, I think it is the single best reporting on Duke that I have seen on television and a model for what local TV at its best can accomplish. It aired in April 1990 on Elder's irregular series, "Journal." This investigative piece, like the afternoon Angela Hill show, had little influence on other television coverage and attracted few viewers.

Even WWL—despite its documentary and the fact that it possessed the best day-to-day TV news operation in Louisiana—was no less susceptible than other stations to Duke's manipulation. The material developed in the

Elder documentary did not make it into the daily news. Daily TV news reporters just do not have time to use such material.

What made the Elder piece different from other television coverage was simple: it was well researched. Elder had the privilege—rare among television reporters—of working on a single story for a long time. Like many investigative reporters, he pursued it in addition to his usual news assignments, but he had some resources and could take his time. The result was a thorough, careful, thoughtful piece of reporting.

In the case of Angela Hill, her questioning of Duke, and that of some members of her on-the-air audience, was informed by work done by the Louisiana Coalition against Racism and Nazism. The coalition had distributed to reporters and others a document containing suggested questions for Duke, possible evasive answers based on his previous responses, and follow-up questions to press him for a more complete answer. At least half of the questions Duke was asked on the Hill show came straight from that document.

One of the most effective questions asked Duke to reconcile his ownership of an extreme right-wing bookstore with his support of a bill proposing criminal penalties for book and record sellers found guilty of violating obscenity laws. The gist of the question was this: David Duke, you sold in your bookstore and advertised in your published literature a set of so-called comedy tapes including one with the title "Die, Nigger, Die." Do you think that such a tape should be considered obscene and that selling it should be a crime? It was one of the few times in the campaign Duke was caught off guard; for once he had to think of an answer rather than recite a programmed reply.

What made the coverage of both Hill and Elder effective was research— conducted in one case by an investigative reporter and in the other by an advocate group. If it is too much to expect that television stations will allow good reporters the time to do some research when they have to cover Duke, there is still one thing news managers can do to improve the quality of coverage and that is to avoid inviting his manipulation. For example, by covering every objection to a Duke speech or appearance as if it were hot news, TV stations offer him more free air time than other candidates dream of.

Conclusion

Every defect of television news coverage described in this chapter is remediable. It is simply a matter of news managers making the decision to allocate adequate resources to do the job. There is no reason television cannot have a memory, just as there is no reason TV reporters cannot be given the time to understand the issues they cover and become subject experts. There is no reason television has to seek conflict or other easy plot lines, or rely on the 28-second sound bite, or fill itself with pretty faces. These things happen for a reason, rooted in part in the nature of the medium but determined in the end by decisions made by those who run television news operations. Such decisions matter to all of us, and the phenomenon of David Duke suggests that if a free press (including the electronic news media) is to be effective in protecting our democratic institutions, it may matter very much how the press does its job.

The reason television news, and other institutions of the free press, fall short of our expectations so much of the time is that they are not political institutions but economic institutions and perhaps cannot properly be faulted for failing to carry out public-interest functions at their own expense.[8] Nevertheless, there are professional standards that can reasonably be expected of the press, and the pressure of those standards might eventually lead creative managers to find ways to combine sound business practices with sound professional practices. In the meantime, we—as viewers of television news and as citizens—need to be aware of the structural weaknesses of TV news coverage in order to make our own judgments from a sound understanding of how the news we see has been selected and even created.

NOTES

1. For an account of Duke's early career, see Sims, *The Klan*. Video footage of Duke facing the burning cross with a Nazi salute was used in political commercials by Senator J. Bennett Johnston. Duke's sale of Nazi and racist literature during his 1989 campaign for the Louisiana legislature has been documented by Elizabeth Rickey; see her chapter (chap. 4) in this volume or Bridges, "Neo-Nazi Books Sold at Duke's Office," B4. Duke's suggestion that the United States was on the wrong side in World War II was repeated in 1989 in an interview with Tulane student Abby Kaplan; see Patriquin, "Duke: Fighting World War II Was a Mistake." On Duke's bogus military record, see Berry, "Hero of the Rice Runs." Duke's book inciting blacks to antiwhite violence was called *African Atto* and his how-to-get-a-man book was called *Finders Keepers*; see Patriquin, "Duke Poses as Black to Pen Book" and "Duke Co-Authors Sex, Exercise, Diet Book."

2. Howell, "Louisiana Senate Race Survey."

3. Early in the campaign pollster Joe Walker, working for Republican candidate Ben Bagert, estimated Duke's hard support at 12 percent. Late in the campaign Susan

Howell estimated it at 15 percent. Douglas Rose estimated it at 25 percent. All in personal communication to author.

4. See Patterson, *Mass Media Election*.

5. Valeri LeBlanc, producer of "Stateline," a statewide cable television talk show, personal communication to author.

6. Duke's half-hour television piece was produced by Rusty Cantelli, a New Orleans media consultant; a videotape is in the Amistad Research Center at Tulane University.

7. In his December 4, 1991, announcement at the National Press Club that he would enter some Republican presidential primaries, David Duke emphasized his opposition to immigration—alluding to the Hispanics in Texas—and free trade, casting a slur on the Japanese on the eve of the Pearl Harbor anniversary—"You no buy our rice, we no buy your cars." Quoted from Thomas B. Edsall, "Duke Announces Bid for the Presidency: Former Klansman Plans to Challenge Bush," *Washington Post*, December 5, 1991, A1.

8. Patterson, *Mass Media Election*, 173–74.

REFERENCES

Berry, Jason. "Hero of the Rice Runs." *Shreveport Journal*, June 22, 1990.

Bridges, Tyler. "Neo-Nazi Books Sold at Duke's Office." New Orleans *Times-Picayune*, June 8, 1989.

Howell, Susan. "Louisiana Senate Race Survey." Survey Research Center, University of New Orleans, September 1990. Mimeo.

Patriquin, Ronni. "Duke: Fighting World War II Was a Mistake." *Shreveport Journal*, December 7, 1989.

———. "Duke Poses as Black to Pen Book." *Shreveport Journal*, August 14, 1990.

———. "Duke Co-Authors Sex, Exercise, Diet Book." *Shreveport Journal*, September 21, 1990.

Patterson, Thomas E. *The Mass Media Election*. New York: Praeger, 1980.

Sims, Patsy. *The Klan*. New York: Stein and Day, 1978.

Douglas D. Rose

9 Six Explanations in Search of Support

David Duke's U.S. Senate Campaign

Why did nearly 44 percent of Louisiana voters support David Duke for U.S. senator in the fall of 1990? White supremacy, cultural racism, political alienation, social marginality, economic frustration, and maverick candidacy have all been offered as explanations. A public opinion poll on responses to David Duke, commissioned by the Louisiana Coalition against Racism and Nazism in July 1990, supports each reason. But the poll also suggests the need to explain some other highly significant aspects of Duke's Senate candidacy: that most voters already "knew" all about Duke before the campaign began (including whether they supported or opposed him), that his public support was invisible, that supporters and opponents disagreed over where he really stood, that he dominated discussion and strategy, and that he provoked intense opposition.

As interpreted by concepts recently introduced into the voting behavior literature, these results provide further insights. The new concepts suggest that voters used a running tally for evaluation, that they supported the candidate on their side of the issues, and that Duke's candidacy used symbols to rally a cultural group. These findings are particularly significant, as poll evidence suggests that most of the information voters had about Duke was in fact projected onto him from small but important bits of information about his Ku Klux Klan background and his opposition to affirmative action. The concepts also raise the question of Duke's "extremism" or "legitimacy" for voters. In fact, the crucial campaign in Duke's Senate race may have been the one for acceptability, not the one for support.

Six Explanations for Duke's Support

Why does David Duke receive support? One approach to answering that question is to find out what separates Duke's supporters from everybody else. If agreements and disagreements about Duke correspond to cleavages about some earlier, broader matters, the cleavages account for the support for Duke.

This chapter tests hypothesized reasons for Duke's support against evidence from a survey conducted during his primary election campaign for the U.S. Senate. The survey included 605 respondents, 76 percent of them white, in a sample drawn to represent all likely Louisiana voters in the October primary.[1] The sample does represent the electorate, because only 56 percent of black registrants cast votes in the Senate election, as compared to 65 percent of white registered voters. Based on my analysis of all-white and all-black precincts, Duke received under 1 percent of the black vote cast and nearly 57 percent of the white vote cast in the election.

Figure 9.1 shows, according to precinct returns, Duke's share of the vote cast along with the percentage of voters who were black. As shown at the bottom right of the figure, Duke received almost no votes in all-black precincts. His votes came from whites, but which whites? At the left of the figure, the all-white precincts show an enormous diversity in response to David Duke, as do the racially mixed precincts. What explains the variation in support among whites?

Six explanations for Duke's support can be tested. The first hypothesis is that Duke's support stems from what is most newsworthy about him, his Nazi

Duke claimed to have received 8–12 percent of the black vote in the U.S. Senate primary but actually received under 0.6 percent. This black supporter said God told her to forgive Duke for his past sins and vote for him. (Courtesy of Eliot Kamenitz)

and Klan past. In this view, Duke garners votes from people who are white racists in the old sense: they believe in white biological superiority, support racial separation, perceive excessive Jewish influence, and approve of the Ku Klux Klan. This is vintage historical racism, *white supremacy*. According to this view, Duke's background associations and current stands provide cues that racists can recognize, and the test is whether Duke's supporters agree with these views, while his opponents do not.

Racism is not always that blatant, however. For a quarter of a century, since the formal decline of segregation, politicians have been accused of using code words to elicit racist support, and Duke may fit that description. Some researchers call support for such coded racism symbolic racism, where dislike and fear of blacks are expressed through seemingly nonracial symbols and justifications. In this view, Duke's supporters would not overtly endorse flatly racist stands but would agree with his campaign stances that blame blacks for being cultural failures and seek to punish them. The key to this

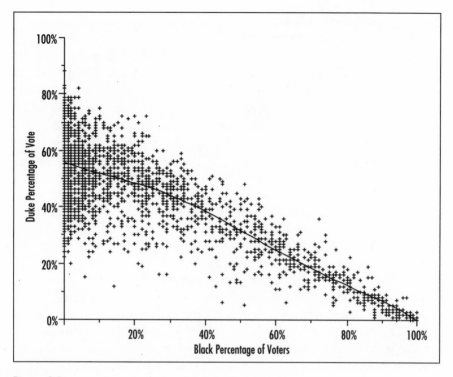

Figure 9.1

Duke's Share of the 1990 Senate Vote by Black Percentage of Voters, Based on Precinct Returns

approach is the gap between public expression and private meaning for racists. I find it difficult to use normal survey evidence to examine this hypothesis, as survey data consists of public expressions to strangers over the telephone. If respondents secretly mean something else, we do not find it out.[2]

The responses used to support the notion of symbolic racism can more persuasively be used to support *cultural racism*. This view starts from a study of American political culture, a large part of which is consensual public belief in the American Way: that every individual should have the opportunity to get ahead, and that individual efforts to get ahead should be rewarded with success. There is also agreement, though less than consensual, that people do get opportunities and that effort is rewarded. To people with these beliefs, it is personal characteristics—work habits—rather than structural ones—lack of chances—that explain the lack of success among blacks. Lack of success is inferred to mean lack of effort. Programs such as affirmative action, minority set-asides, and welfare are assumed to be ineffective because they do not improve equal opportunities.

I call this position cultural racism, as these cultural defects are attributed to blacks. Politicians who express these views—usually Republican and conservative—find voters who agree with them. If Duke's supporters and nonsupporters divide on the issues of whether blacks should get ahead on their own, whether preferential treatment exceeds discrimination, and whether government discriminates against blacks, then support fits the cultural racism rationale.

Another conjecture suggests that race actually may be incidental to Duke's appeal, which is due to *political alienation* by the electorate, a distrust of government—often related to a broader distrust of other social institutions. In Louisiana, a populistic distrust of either the honesty or the effectiveness of government has become part of the larger political culture. Opposition to programs such as welfare and affirmative action is, in this view, part of a larger hostility to government programs, suspicion of officials' motivations, and alienation from political institutions. Duke's supporters, in this view, should see government run for the benefit of the few (special interests, including blacks), distrust the media, suspect waste and theft in government, and support cuts in almost all aspects of government that do not directly benefit themselves. Nonsupporters would hold contrary views and display a more positive orientation to government.

To some supporters, neither race, nor issues, nor politics may provide the real meaning of David Duke. Instead, Duke's *social marginality* may be the key. In this view, the legitimation and acceptance of socially marginal people (such as Duke) is important to occupants of socially insecure positions, such as skilled laborers, part-time workers, union members, or people with less than a college education. Successful people in these social positions might find it reassuring to justify success by an American Ethos, hence to denigrate blacks in cultural racism, but the main motivation would be self-assurance and bolstering, not social improvement or protest. In contrast to supporters, Duke's opponents, in this view, would be the most mainstream, successful individuals.

David Duke is a protest candidate, in another view, whose specific stances are not as important as their general attack on the status quo and the promise of an improving panacea. Protest arises from *economic disappointment* and the belief that improvement is possible. Rising expectations, followed by a setback, can lead to support for a protest candidate with a chance to win. In this view, Duke's support—at least the support beyond his core voters—would be found among those with recent reverses in their economic situations and among those of low income.

Finally, David Duke may be viewed simply as another *maverick candidate*. In this view, supporters of other candidates become opponents of Duke because elections become zero-sum. In the Senate race, as in most, an incumbent ran for reelection against a challenger from the other party; Duke ran as a third candidate, an outsider.[3] According to this hypothesis, divisions among voters on the incumbent's performance in office, party identification, and ratings of the other candidates should largely determine the Duke response. People who do not support more establishment candidates are left free to support Duke on the basis of his campaign information, personal qualifications, and issue positions. In this view, Duke resembled George Wallace, another maverick, third-party, issue candidate.[4]

These explanations are not necessarily mutually exclusive. A composite answer might read: Duke is a maverick candidate challenging not only the incumbent but also both major party establishments; he focuses the distrust and disappointment of those who feel unjustly left out of the mainstream, and he uses issues to appeal for support that reflect cultural values in apparently racist fashion. Note that such a composite places Duke with George Wallace as appealing to "pseudoconservatives."[5] Pseudoconservatism lashes out resentfully at unsuccessful, dominant liberal leaders. It is the little person against the big interests. It is also one-third of America's populist political culture.[6]

EVIDENCE IN THE POLL

Survey research supports each of these explanations in part.

White Supremacy. As shown in Table 9.1, supporters of Duke differed in the aggregate from opponents and from other candidates' supporters in their attitudes toward the Klan, racial segregation, and white superiority. One-third fewer of Duke's supporters strongly condemned the Klan, strongly disagreed with racial separation, and strongly rejected the notion that whites are superior. People who take these stands are the least likely to favor Duke. However, the equation of Duke support with vintage genetic racism is incorrect. Duke supporters usually view the Klan unfavorably, reject racial separation, and disagree that whites are superior. Duke supporters lack the clear consensus of his opponents on these issues. They sometimes voice moderate rather than strong disagreement or disapproval, they sometimes proffer no opinion, and they sometimes take racist positions, but their characteristic position is as nonracist as that of Duke's opponents.

Nonobvious racism is trickier to detect. Clearly, Duke's supporters are more racist than his opponents. Yet by the standards of American public

Table 9.1

Racist Attitudes among Whites, by Support for Duke

Ku Klux Klan Evaluation

"I am going to read the names of some people and organizations. For each one, I would like you to tell me if the name is familiar and if so, whether you view that person or organization very favorably, somewhat favorably, somewhat unfavorably, or not at all favorably. . . . the Ku Klux Klan."

	Un-familiar	Favor-ably*	Somewhat Unfavor-ably	Not at All Favor-ably	Total	Percent-age of Sample
Duke Evaluation**						
Favorable	7%	13	19	62	101%	52%
Unfavorable	2%	0	5	94	101%	39
Candidate Preference***						
Johnston	4%	2	8	86	100%	37%
Bagert	2%	0	6	92	100%	13
Duke	10%	15	21	54	100%	33
Strong	14%	21	18	46	99%	19
Weak	2%	7	25	66	100%	14
Undecided	7%	6	14	73	100%	17

*This category combines "very" and "somewhat favorably" responses because of their infrequency.
**The question text (see Table 9.8) is the same as that for the Ku Klux Klan evaluation. "Very" and "somewhat" favorable responses have been combined, as have "somewhat unfavorably" and "not at all favorably" responses, and the "unfamiliar" responses have not been presented.
***Respondent's preferences were measured by two questions: "This October there will be an open primary election for United States Senator. If that election were held tomorrow and the candidates were Democrat Bennett Johnston, Republican Ben Bagert and Republican David Duke, for whom would you vote? Do you definitely plan to support that candidate, or is it still possible that you will change your mind?" Respondents indicating definite plans to vote for a candidate are labeled "strong" supporters, whereas those indicating a possible change of mind are described as "weak" supporters.

Racial Separation Is Better*

"This country would be a better place if the races were separated. Do you strongly agree, moderately agree, moderately disagree, or strongly disagree with this statement?"

Table 9.1 *(continued)*

	Don't Know	Agree**	Moderately Disagree	Strongly Disagree
Duke Evaluation				
Favorable	6%	13	26	55
Unfavorable	1%	6	15	78
Candidate Preference				
Johnston	2%	8	20	70
Bagert	0%	6	20	73
Duke	7%	16	25	52
Strong	7%	14	21	58
Weak	7%	19	31	44
Undecided	8%	6	26	60

*Rows may not add up to 100% because of rounding error.
**This category combines "strongly" and "moderately agree" responses because of their infrequency.

Whites Are Superior and More Intelligent*

"Whites as a race are biologically superior and more intelligent than blacks." [Do you strongly agree, moderately agree, moderately disagree, or strongly disagree with this statement?]

	Don't Know	Agree	Moderately Disagree	Strongly Disagree
Duke Evaluation				
Favorable	6%	25	23	47
Unfavorable	2%	8	17	74
Candidate Preference				
Johnston	2%	12	17	70
Bagert	2%	6	21	71
Duke	7%	27	25	41
Strong	8%	27	24	41
Weak	7%	26	26	41
Undecided	9%	17	25	49

*Rows may not add up to 100% because of rounding error.

opinion at the time of historical Nazism, Duke's supporters are nonracist. Standards have changed. This leads to confusion if Duke's supporters are termed Nazis or racists in the sense used a half-century ago. Perhaps, as the symbolic racism argument would have it, they would like to be forthright racists. I cannot tell from the interview summaries: their responses do not fit overt racism, and this makes them differ significantly from groups whose responses do. Given Duke's past identification with racist groups, the weakness of the clear majoritarian nonracist position among Duke's supporters implies at least the absence of impassioned condemnation of racism.

The possibility that overt positions are not quite what they seem is explored in Table 9.2. The questions are of the sort used to demonstrate weak attachments to civil liberties: support is reflected by agreement that membership in an organization does not disqualify individuals from elective office. Majorities of the sample took the civil libertarian stance. James Gibson and Richard Bingham have pointed out that support for civil liberties can be diminished by either opposition to the activities or to the groups involved, the key point here.[7] The groups most overtly concerned are blacks, who were opposed by the Klan, and whites over sixty-four years old, who engaged in active conflict with Nazis. In both cases, though voters in these groups continued to take a civil libertarian position, they were about 10 percent less libertarian than other respondents. But groups historically opposed to the Klan and Nazis are not the least libertarian groups. Strong supporters of Duke's Democratic and Republican opponents take antilibertarian positions. As the differences among candidate groups exceed differences among Duke supporters and opponents, it is possible that voicing support for a principle that would disqualify a political opponent is not wholly ingenuous. By implication, it is possible that the nonracist positions of Duke's opponents were somewhat inflated by the strategic aspects of the election contest.

Cultural Racism. Duke supporters and opponents differed even more on the issues of racial opportunity and black effort, as seen in Table 9.3. If Duke's supporters fit the cultural racism pattern, they should believe that there is little racial discrimination, especially by government, hence that special government help for blacks is unjustified. They would believe, for instance, that actual differences between blacks and whites in welfare recipiency do not reflect differences in need, and that affirmative action means preferential treatment for blacks. Here, as in the case of white supremacy issues, the general direction of differences between Duke supporters and other respondents fit the hypothesis. Also as in the case of white supremacy issues, the magnitude of differences between Duke supporters and opponents on cultural racism questions was respectable but hardly sufficient to explain attitudes

Table 9.2
Attitudes toward Klan and Nazi Membership

"Would previous membership in the Ku Klux Klan [a Nazi organization] disqualify someone from being elected to office, or would it not disqualify someone for office?"

Membership Would Disqualify Candidate from Elective Office

	Ku Klux Klan	Nazi Organization	Percentage of Sample
Blacks	31%	41%	21%
Whites	22%	35%	76
Over 64 years	32%	49%	
Duke favorable	11%	27%	
Duke unfavorable	35%	42%	
Strong Bagert	45%	61%	
Strong Johnston	44%	53%	
Weak Johnston	25%	39%	
Undecided	22%	44%	
Weak Bagert	13%	23%	
Weak Duke	5%	22%	
Strong Duke	9%	16%	
Male	15%	26%	50%
Female	29%	44%	50

toward Duke. The largest differences came on questions of government policy. On questions of preferential treatment and special government help, the supporters of the Democratic candidate were on the left, those of the Republican candidate were in the middle, and supporters of David Duke were on the right, with fairly equal sized differences. That is, Duke supporters were as much more "conservative" than Republicans as Republicans were more "conservative" than Democrats. The perception that blacks on welfare do not need it was especially distinctive to Duke supporters, rather than an extension of an existing partisan debate.

Unlike white supremacy issues, differences between Duke supporters and opponents on discrimination and effort issues sometimes reflect different characteristic positions. Whites favorable to Duke largely reject special government help for blacks, whereas whites unfavorable to Duke on balance

Table 9.3

Opinions among Whites on Racial Opportunity and Effort,
by Support for Duke

Racial Discrimination and Preferential Treatment
"How much discrimination do you feel there is against blacks—a great deal, some, not much, or none at all?"

"How much preferential treatment do you feel there is for racial minorities —a great deal, some, not much, or none at all?"

"Government officials usually pay less attention to a request or complaint from a black person than from a white person."

	There Is a Great Deal of Discrimination against Blacks	There Is a Great Deal of Preference for Racial Minorities	Strongly Disagree That Government Pays Less Atten- tion to Blacks
Duke Evaluation (Whites)			
Favorable	9%	46%	44%
Unfavorable	25%	21%	25%
Candidate Preference (Whites)			
Johnston	21%	25%	33%
Bagert	19%	36%	27%
Duke	9%	47%	41%
Strong	6%	45%	46%
Weak	14%	50%	34%
Undecided	13%	36%	41%
Black Respondents	65%	26%	15%

Preference between Federal Special Effort to Help Blacks and Self-Help
"Some people feel that the government in Washington should make every effort to improve the social and economic position of blacks. Others feel that the government should not make any special effort to help blacks because they should help themselves. Which opinion comes closest to your view?"

	Government Help	Help Selves
Duke Evaluation (Whites)		
Favorable	19%	72
Unfavorable	46%	41

Table 9.3 *(continued)*

	Government Help	Help Selves
Candidate Preference (Whites)		
Johnston	46%	45
Bagert	29%	59
Duke	17%	74
Strong	16%	77
Weak	20%	71
Undecided	25%	55
Black Respondents	67%	26

Agreement That Blacks on Welfare Don't Need It
"I am going to read you several statements. After each one, I would like you to tell me whether you strongly agree, moderately agree, moderately disagree, or strongly disagree with that statement. 'Most blacks who receive money from welfare programs could get along without it if they tried.'"

	Strongly Agree	Disagree
Duke Evaluation (Whites)		
Favorable	43%	18
Unfavorable	16%	41
Candidate Preference (Whites)		
Johnston	22%	36
Bagert	21%	38
Duke	49%	14
Strong	50%	15
Weak	47%	15
Undecided	24%	24
Black Respondents	26%	42

support it. Because the survey shows unusually little consensus on these issues, however, Duke supporters are as likely to take the popular position as they are to take the unpopular one. In this sense, the differences that show up on these issues are the more serious: they reflect current policy concerns, not consensually rejected alternatives, and they express majoritarian doubts about current policy that, directly stemming from the culture, also emerge in mainstream partisan cleavages. The magnitude of difference can still be overstated. Differences between Duke supporters and opponents on these questions comprised about 25 percent. This was half as large as the difference between blacks and whites in the racial discrimination questions.

In one respect, differences between Duke supporters and opponents do not reflect the cultural cleavage we had expected to find. If black-white differences indicated black individuals' failure to take advantage of opportunities, and if blacks—stereotypically—were held largely responsible for crime, then what should be perceived as the causes of crime? We expected that respondents would blame moral failure. Indeed, attributing causes of social events like crime to personal variables rather than situational or structural variables is so common that it is termed the "fundamental attribution error" in social psychology.[8] A folk ideology or populistic movement might be especially prone to this thinking. This error—where there is wrong there must be wrongdoing and wrongdoers—fits a pattern in American popular culture that Paul Sniderman calls "moralism."[9] Although individualism is not moralism, right-wing populism historically has been moralistic. However, Duke supporters in the poll were not moralistic; in fact, they were least likely to attribute crime to a moral breakdown. Instead, often citing the lack of jobs or opportunities, and, to a lesser extent, racial problems, they were fairly indistinguishable from other respondents on the recommended solutions (see Table 9.4).

Political Alienation. So far, it seems clear that support for David Duke corresponds both to a moderate degree of racism and to underachiever stereotyping, though little to the oft-associated moralism. The incomplete success of these racial-issue explanations opens the way for an even larger issue explanation, political alienation. As Table 9.5 illustrates, Duke supporters in the poll were suspicious of government waste, of political crookedness, and of special governmental influence by a few big interests. The differences between Duke supporters and opponents, however, were smaller than on race-related issues. Regarding the waste of taxes, for instance, Duke supporters are mainstream in Louisiana. Because there is no consensual position on the other aspects of trust in government, Duke's supporters are as mainstream as anyone else. Except as paranoia is commonplace, they do not illustrate a particularly paranoid style. Moreover, strong and weak Duke supporters do not always show the same distinction from other groups. In the poll, weak Duke supporters said that they might consider voting for another candidate. It was weak Duke supporters who, like blacks, were particularly suspicious of big business influence in government, while it was strong Duke supporters who were most distrustful about waste and crookedness. Although support

Table 9.4

Belief in the Causes of and Solutions to Crime, by Support for Duke

"Which of these would you say is the main cause of crime and drug problems—a moral breakdown, racial problems, or a lack of good jobs and opportunity?"

"What would you say is the most effective solution for crime and unemployment problems—new or expanded government jobs programs, more investment by private companies, or strengthening moral values?"

	Cause: Moral Breakdown	Solution: Strengthen Morals
Duke Evaluation (Whites)		
Favorable	47%	53%
Unfavorable	55%	52%
Candidate Preference (Whites)		
Johnston	51%	50%
Bagert	63%	54%
Duke	42%	58%
Strong	32%	53%
Weak	56%	65%
Undecided	56%	52%
Black Respondents	18%	38%

for Duke was linked to distrust of government, therefore, this distrust does not appear to explain support for Duke.

Social Marginality and Economic Disappointment. Are Duke supporters socially marginal? As shown in Table 9.6, Duke supporters in the poll were, indeed, somewhat marginal. They tended to be the master sergeants of the economy, lacking college diplomas, with a head of household in the private sector and the unionized, skilled labor force. Within the structure of American opportunities, they were enjoying the benefits to which the current generation of blacks aspire. Again, however, the explanation is inconclusive. Only a minority of Duke support was composed of marginal individuals, and the differences with Duke opponents were not large. The most significant difference was in college education, but education may have been linked to Duke

Table 9.5

Political Trust and Support for Duke among Whites

Government Waste and Crooked People in Government
"Thinking about the manner in which the government spends tax dollars, how much would you say it wastes and mismanages—quite a lot of the tax dollars, some of the tax dollars, or not very much of the tax dollars?"

"Thinking about the people in government, how many of them would you say are crooked—hardly any, quite a few, or a great deal?"

	Waste: "Quite a Lot"	Crooked People: "A Great Deal"
Duke Evaluation (Whites)		
Favorable	71%	40%
Unfavorable	67%	29%
Candidate Preference (Whites)		
Johnston	66%	29%
Bagert	57%	26%
Duke	73%	47%
Strong	80%	52%
Weak	64%	40%
Undecided	76%	39%
Black Respondents	66%	43%

Government Is Run to Benefit the Interests of . . .
"Is the U.S. Government run to benefit the interests of all people or does it just benefit a few big interests?"

[If "a few big interests"] "Which of these do you think the government is run to benefit most—the media, big business, liberals, or Jews?"

	All	Media	Big Business	Liberals	Jews
Duke Evaluation (Whites)					
Favorable	27%	8	46	8	3
Unfavorable	39%	3	36	3	1
Candidate Preference (Whites)					
Johnston	36%	2	40	4	1

Table 9.5 *(continued)*

	All	Media	Big Business	Liberals	Jews
Bagert	43%	2	31	6	2
Duke	24%	8	47	7	3
Strong	26%	8	42	6	4
Weak	21%	9	55	8	2
Undecided	27%	8	37	3	0
Black Respondents	19%	9	57	5	2

support for reasons that go far beyond marginality, such as support for mainstream candidates. Duke supporters, hence, tended to be marginal, but only to a mild degree.

The notion that Duke support is linked to disappointment is somewhat the opposite of the notion of marginality. That is, marginal individuals are doing well, given their resources, while disappointed individuals are doing poorly, compared to their past or their expectations. Table 9.7 indicates that Duke supporters in the survey did indeed tend to be disappointed. They were more likely to have low incomes, they had personal economic situations that had gotten worse in the last few years, and they were unlikely to say that their chances of getting ahead were better than the average person's. Because these differences remained modest, however, most Duke supporters looked like most Duke opponents, perhaps due to five years of an oil recession.

Implicit in the notions of marginality and—as a scapegoat—disappointment is a sense of competition between whites and blacks in which Duke presents himself as a white champion. The absence of moralism, in this approach, makes sense if Duke supporters are stimulated by perceived group competition. Social marginality and disappointment provide opportunities for perceived competition and so does physical proximity in residential areas. Historically, proximity of blacks has been a good predictor of white support of segregationist candidates. In the 1990 Senate election, Duke's support among whites peaked at 63 percent in precincts with close to a 50–50 voter registration split among blacks and whites.[10] In all-white precincts, his white support fell below 56 percent, and in nearly all-black precincts, 45 percent of white voters supported him. The pattern of ups and downs fits a competition hypothesis, but the amount of variation is small. Competition adds relatively little to marginality and disappointment as an explanation.

Table 9.6

Socioeconomic Marginality and Support for Duke among Whites

	Skilled Labor	Union (Private)	College Graduate
Duke Evaluation (Whites)			
Favorable	27%	9%	24%
Unfavorable	16%	4%	46%
Candidate Preference (Whites)			
Johnston	22%	5%	31%
Bagert	7%	0%	62%
Duke	28%	12%	24%
Strong	31%	12%	18%
Weak	24%	11%	33%
Undecided	21%	6%	28%
Black Respondents	25%	7%	16%

A Maverick Candidate. The evidence for viewing Duke as a maverick candidate, the sixth explanation, is presented in Table 9.8. The table shows that, aside from a few "Strong Democrats," party identification was not linked to evaluation of David Duke by whites. This means Duke's support was not that of a maverick in the basic sense of appealing to those with no place in the political spectrum. Instead, it was closely linked to voter orientations to the candidates. On election day, of course, this is often something of a truism: supporters of one candidate are opponents of another. Outside the immediate heat of a contest, however, voters are rarely polarized except by long-standing, broad orientations such as party, racial identification, and ideology.[11] Duke causes special electoral polarization above and beyond the more common Democratic-Republican split. He is more likely than the other candidates to be evaluated not at all favorably, to be ignored as a second choice, and to be found unacceptable as a voting alternative. Put another way, the cleavage on Duke was largely a cleavage among supporters of Johnston and Bagert and supporters of Duke: the stronger the support, the more the cleavage. The maverick candidate explanation fits some of the facts, but it is insufficient by itself to explain Duke's support.

Determining the Best Explanation. As we have seen, all of these explanations account for some of Duke's support. The least powerful are those picturing

Table 9.7
Disappointment and Support for Duke among Whites

"Will you tell me please which of the following categories best represents your total family income [for 1989]?"

"In the last few years, do you think your own personal economic situation has gotten better, gotten worse, or stayed about the same?"

"Compared to the average person in America, do you think that your chance of getting ahead is better than the average person, worse than the average person, or about the same as the average person?"

	Income <$20,000	Worsened $	Chances >Average
Duke Evaluation (Whites)			
Favorable	21%	33%	28%
Unfavorable	15%	26%	37%
Candidate Preference (Whites)			
Johnston	20%	25%	28%
Bagert	11%	29%	43%
Duke	23%	35%	30%
Strong	27%	37%	26%
Weak	16%	31%	35%
Undecided	25%	30%	23%
Black Respondents	31%	34%	17%

Duke primarily as a populist candidate who draws on distrust of government among marginal and disappointed citizens. More powerful are the explanations focusing on racism and stereotypes. A minority that is "soft" in opposition to the Ku Klux Klan is disproportionately made up of Duke admirers, as is the group that denies that blacks are discriminated against. These aspects of racism and stereotypes are those most closely linked to Duke's past and his platform. The most powerful account, however, treats Duke as a maverick candidate, whose votes, in the absence of a partisan base of support, depend on his appeal and his opponents' lack of appeal. Voters can be attracted to Duke as a candidate without firm agreement with his views, and racism alone, unmatched with approval of Duke, does not produce votes for Duke. To some degree the explanations are overlapping, so that the results do not cumulate.

Table 9.8

Partisanship and Support for Duke among Whites

Favorable Evaluation of Duke*
"I am going to read the names of some people and organizations. For each one, I would like you to tell me if the name is familiar and if so, whether you view that person or organization very favorably, somewhat favorably, somewhat unfavorably, or not at all favorably. . . . David Duke."

	Very Favorably	Somewhat Favorably	Somewhat Unfavorably	Not at All Favorably
Johnston Evaluation (Whites)				
Favorable	15%	27	16	35
Unfavorable	44%	32	8	9
Party Identification (Whites)				
Strong Democrats	24%	23	11	30
Weak Democrats	23%	32	15	23
Independents	26%	33	11	25
Weak Republicans	25%	31	11	24
Strong Republicans	29%	22	15	26
Black Respondents	2%	4	9	65

Voting Plans Regarding Duke*
"Thinking just about David Duke, do you definitely plan to vote for him in the election for Senate, will you consider another candidate, or do you definitely plan to vote against him?"

	Definitely For	Will Consider Him	Definitely Against	Don't Know
Duke Evaluation (Whites)				
Favorable	49%	32	3	16
Unfavorable	1%	13	78	7
Johnston Evaluation (Whites)				
Favorable	16%	23	46	15
Unfavorable	51%	27	10	12
Candidate Preference (Whites)				
Johnston	2%	21	65	12
Bagert	2%	34	54	10

Table 9.8 *(continued)*

	Definitely For	Will Consider Him	Definitely Against	Don't Know
Duke	76%	22	0	3
Strong	97%	3	0	0
Weak	45%	48	0	7
Undecided	4%	32	15	49
Black Respondents	4%	10	70	15

*Rows may not add up to 100% because of rounding error.

Which is the best explanation? The observed power of the explanations roughly corresponds to their logical proximity to a vote for Duke. A drop in personal income, for example, needs to be seen as the government's fault, with a solution matching Duke's, before it can produce a vote for Duke. By contrast, intense dislike of the Klan needs only an awareness of the Duke-Klan link to produce opposition to Duke, a single additional logical step. Any questions explicitly mentioning Duke and any explanation that starts from an orientation to Duke are likely to be more powerful explanations. Which is the best explanation that does not directly mention Duke or voting?

A combination of racism and stereotype best predicts, using the technique of discriminant analysis, voting support for and opposition to David Duke among whites. Duke's opponents, those who say they would not consider voting for him, can be predicted from their statements that membership in the Klan disqualifies a candidate from being elected to office and that the federal government should help improve blacks' position. Duke supporters can be predicted by agreement that whites are superior to blacks and by the denial that there is racial discrimination against blacks. Using these four questions and a threefold categorization of voting support, neutrality, and opposition to Duke, respondents can be correctly placed 60 percent of the time, a 38 percent reduction in the error that would occur with random predictions.

Although this accuracy is adequate for most purposes, it is disappointing here, where so much information is available to predict a single response for each voter. For instance, some of those stating that Klan membership disqualifies Duke from election were simply expressing general antagonism to Duke, so that the "prediction" of opposition to Duke was actually a "postdiction." The six explanations, while correct, then, are unsatisfactory.

Intensity, Extremism, and Opposition

What the explanations leave out are some of the most obvious and charac-teristic features of the outcome of the Senate race, notably its unlikeliness. Without the support of a political party, Duke launched himself as a credible candidate. Without spending much money to communicate his messages to voters, he became the best-known candidate, the one to whom voters freely attributed issue positions. Duke, not the incumbent or the Republican chal-lenger, dominated the election and was the focus of intensity. The literature on congressional elections stresses the difficulty of doing what Duke did—challenging an incumbent and becoming known.[12]

One way to gauge the extent of Duke's achievement is to compare him with the other challenger in the Senate race, state senator Ben Bagert. Bagert was a typical quality challenger. A professional politician first elected when the incumbent, J. Bennett Johnston, first ran for statewide office, Bagert was known mainly for his environmental legislation. Though as recent a convert to Republicanism as Duke, he easily defeated Duke for the party's nomina-tion by out-organizing both him and the party regulars in statewide caucuses. But Bagert found it difficult to raise his name recognition from a bare major-ity of the electorate even to the 70 percent range, which is low for a serious Senate challenger. Money remained hard to raise; professional advisers de-serted the campaign. Why? Because Bagert seemed likely to lose.

Johnston clearly would be hard to beat because he had a head start: as an incumbent, he was known, funded, experienced, and organized. Attempting to catch up during a short campaign, Bagert, like any challenger, was prone to err and falter. Yet the psychology of challenge requires that the challenger, when known beforehand to be behind, appear always to be gaining momen-tum, catching up. Because the challenger's potential to close the gap is—to realists—the reason to support him, such campaigns tend to go boom or bust. The better the campaign does, the more promise it shows and the more resources it can garner. Conversely, once Bagert's collapse began, there was little to stop it: there were few committed Republican partisans, few voters who knew him well, few citizens whose intense dislike of Johnston would lead them to support any opponent, and few reporters who reported on the candidate rather than the failing candidacy.[13]

By September, Bagert had no funds. Duke, in contrast, had plenty. Cap-ping his own experience with the techniques of mail solicitation among targeted potential supporters that had been developed so fully during the 1980s by right-wing groups, he raised over $1.5 million.[14] Bagert started out known to half of the electorate; Duke became known to all of it. Bagert's support was sparse, unconcentrated, and wavering; Duke's support was widespread, firm, and predominant even among Bagert's target groups. Unsurprisingly, the negative advertising that signals the incumbent's fear of the challenger was aired, not against Bagert, but against Duke. Two days before the election, Bagert withdrew from the race.

The big question is why. Why did many voters connect with Duke? One way to understand that is to probe one of the most striking characteristics of the campaign, Duke's opposition. Using opponents' perceptions to check supporters', it becomes clear that vast amounts of voter projection, the issue of extremism, and conflicts of deep-rooted cultural symbols underlay this election.

DUKE'S OPPOSITION

Many novice politicians have enthusiastic supporters. What makes Duke different is the scope and intensity of the voters who oppose him. In the Senate race, the level of Duke's support four months before the primary—33 percent of whites—was not unusual. However, 31 percent of whites and 66 percent of blacks already found him unacceptable. In contrast, whites rated Bagert and Johnston unacceptable by only 11 percent and 6 percent, respectively, blacks by 1 percent. Of those who said that they viewed Johnston unfavorably, 35 percent found him unacceptable; 79 percent (76 percent among whites) of those viewing Duke unfavorably, however, also find him unacceptable.

The 1990 survey data, in fact, suggest that intense opposition to Duke signaled the basic strategic fact about the election: it was Duke's contest. Supporters added to intense opponents were 64 percent of whites and 66 percent of the electorate, about the amount garnered by Bagert and Johnston put together. Duke's opponents, hence, were crucial in making the election a referendum, transforming an ordinary Senate race into the David Duke election.

The character of the opposition is also unusual. U.S. Republican presidents do not normally oppose Republicans, as George Bush and Ronald Reagan did in Duke's House race. Nor do candidates commonly have whole organizations created to oppose them, as Duke did. Even stranger, the opposition arose—without much help from preexisting organizations—despite superficial news coverage and limited voter information.

Who are the opponents of David Duke? The poll suggests that their characteristics are the reverse of those of Duke's supporters. As noted, social liberals and critics of economic individualism oppose Duke to some extent. Jewish and black individuals respond negatively to what they see as Duke's attack on people like themselves. Mainstream identifiers oppose Duke as someone who will upset the applecart. Supporters of other candidates oppose him. In the poll, intense opposition was about 60 percent white and 40 percent black.

What requires clarification is the intensity, uniformity, and behavior of this opposition. As shown in Table 9.9, reporting responses to three separate questions, two-thirds of Duke's opposition fall into the most extreme available categories. The numbers suggest that the election served to elicit and organize the opposition to Duke. Three-quarters of those not at all favorable to Duke cared a great deal who won.

Duke opponents had no doubts, because, like his supporters, they had little information that could raise doubts. As indicated in Table 9.10, from two-thirds to three-quarters of the public had no beliefs about various controversial charges against Duke's actions or stands. Those who had beliefs were divided both for and against him. Belief on the matter of Duke's Nazi membership was firmer but only loosely corresponded (negatively) to Duke approval. The vast majority of respondents did believe that Duke had been a member of the Klan, but both supporters and opponents believed that.

It should also be noted that a majority of likely voters volunteered Klan-racism connections as a reason not to support Duke. Duke opponents are similarly overwhelmingly likely to believe that Duke was a Klan member: of those "not at all favorable" toward Duke, 99 percent were "not at all favorable" toward the Klan. Klan membership, hence, appears to be a central, consensual bit of information about Duke, especially for opponents. For opponents, Duke represents old-fashioned racism—white supremacy and segregation—symbolized by the KKK and its leadership.

DUKE AS A PROJECTION

Projection caused the responses of Duke's supporters and opponents to be more uniformly polarized than they would have been with information-based responses. Table 9.11 shows polarization on pro-Duke arguments. By supporters, Duke was praised for outspoken honesty. Opponents, while favoring candor, were unlikely to praise him for it. They were highly skeptical that his programs would stop waste in government, while supporters tended to believe that Duke would be effective. Groups most suspicious of waste in government were those most likely to believe that Duke would help with the problem. Supporters in part saw Duke as a voice for whites, in the same sense that minorities have spokespersons. (By implication, this leaves out any special majoritarian role for whites.) Opponents of Duke neither saw a need for a special white voice nor believed that Duke speaks with "the" white voice. Supporters believed that false fears were raised about Duke in the state

Table 9.9
Intense Negative Orientations toward Duke among Whites

	Not at All Favorable to Duke	Duke Unacceptable*	Definitely against Duke
Johnston Evaluation (Whites)			
Favorable	35%	43%	46%
Unfavorable	9%	10%	10%
Duke Evaluation (Whites)			
Favorable	0%	2%	3%
Unfavorable	67%	76%	78%
Candidate Preference (Whites)			
Strong Johnston	61%	70%	82%
Strong Bagert	58%	67%	59%
Weak Johnston	33%	46%	42%
Weak Bagert	33%	39%	50%
Duke	0%	0%	0%
Undecided	16%	19%	15%
Black Respondents	65%	66%	70%

*"Are any of these candidates unacceptable—is there one for whom you would never vote?"

representative election, while opponents believed that the fears were realistic. Cleavages on these issues among supporters and opponents dominated the responses. The less the question was contaminated by implications pushing all responses to one side—disbelief that any single senator can stop waste, for example—the purer the division along pro- and anti-Duke lines, reflecting pure projection.

Table 9.12 reflects similar projection on whether Duke is a divisive hater, a kook pretending to be normal, an embarrassment to Louisiana, and a discouragement to new industry. His supporters overwhelmingly disagreed with these portraits of Duke. The continuum of election support—from the strongest supporters of other candidates, through undecided, to the strongest Duke supporters—largely overlapped the agree-disagree continuum with anti-Duke statements. This is consistent with the support causing the agreement—through projection—rather than vice versa, for most voters. Black respondents were, as a group, similar to the strongest supporters of Johnston and Bagert, except on the question of Duke's abnormality. While Duke's positions are generally beyond the acceptable limits in discussions among black

Table 9.10

Beliefs about Duke

"From what you know, did David Duke say the Holocaust didn't happen and that Jews have too much influence in America, or did he not say that?"

"From what you know, does David Duke advocate breeding programs to improve the race involving voluntary sterilization of people with below-average I.Q.'s, or does he not advocate such programs?"

"From what you know, did David Duke advocate a program to relocate ethnic groups into separate nations, or did he not advocate this?"

"From what you know, has David Duke hired neo-Nazis and Klansmen to work on his campaigns, or has he not done this?"

"From what you know, has David Duke lied about his military service, or has he not lied about his military service?"

"From what you know, did David Duke publish a book which encouraged whites to attack blacks, or did he not do this?"

"From what you know, was David Duke ever a member of any Nazi organization?"

"From what you know, was David Duke ever a member of the Ku Klux Klan?"

	No	Yes	Don't Know
Does Duke Advocate . . .			
There was no Holocaust?	17%	12	71
Lo-IQ sterilization?	14%	19	66
Separate ethnic nations?	15%	13	72
Did Duke . . .			
Hire Nazis for campaign?	13%	13	74
Lie about military service?	10%	12	78
Urge whites to attack blacks?	10%	12	77
Was Duke a member of . . .			
a Nazi organization?	34%	32	34
Duke supporters	49%	23	28
Duke opponents	23%	46	31
the Ku Klux Klan?	9%	74	17
Duke supporters	14%	71	15
Duke opponents	2%	89	9

Table 9.11
Strong Agreement with Pro-Duke Beliefs among Whites

"[I will read] some statements people have made about politics. After I read each one, please tell me whether you strongly agree, moderately agree, moderately disagree, or strongly disagree.

'David Duke has the courage to say things others are afraid to say. We need that kind of honesty in government.'

'As Senator, David Duke would help put a stop to the wasteful spending and mismanagement that have wrecked our economy.'

'Blacks and other minorities have a voice in America; David Duke represents a voice for white people, and it's about time that someone spoke up for them.'

'A lot of people were afraid of David Duke when he was running for State Representative, but now that they have had a chance to see him in action, they feel a lot better about him.'"

Duke is (will) (was):	Candid	Stop Waste	White Voice	Falsely Feared
Johnston Evaluation (Whites)				
Favorable	37%	14%	19%	23%
Unfavorable	73%	34%	42%	41%
Duke Evaluation (Whites)				
Favorable	73%	34%	38%	48%
Unfavorable	17%	3%	9%	3%
Candidate Preference (Whites)				
Strong Johnston	16%	4%	11%	10%
Strong Bagert	21%	13%	14%	17%
Weak Johnston	30%	7%	18%	20%
Weak Bagert	32%	5%	22%	8%
Undecided	49%	14%	23%	21%
Weak Duke	76%	33%	31%	44%
Strong Duke	92%	54%	47%	64%
Black Respondents	24%	9%	13%	15%

persons—as, for example, Louis Farrakhan's are in discussions among white persons—they were close to the limits of the normal among Louisiana whites, leading whites to be more reluctant than blacks to label Duke a simple kook.

Further evidence of extensive projection comes from a factor analysis of responses to the entire Duke questionnaire, which reveals one unusually large factor. *Factor analysis* is a statistical technique that represents responses as if they were the consequence of a relatively few, independent factors, each of which influences responses to one or more questions. Although a factor analysis attempts first to find a single, overarching factor, it is unusual to find one in survey data. The one large factor in the questionnaire can only be called the "Duke factor"; any question that mentions Duke reflects this dominant division among the respondents.[15] The only other pattern is for social stratification as a base for Duke's populist support, including income, education, occupation, union membership, economic disappointment, distrust in government, simple racism, and beliefs that achievements reflect hard work and equal opportunity. This factor lacks much explanatory power.

The Duke factor corresponds to the polarization noted around support and opposition to David Duke, with extensive projection providing the actual survey responses. The relative size of the factor suggests that reactions to Duke dominated almost all responses, drowning out other aspects of the Senate election contest and even the latent social base for a populist insurgency. In turn, the electoral question—the vote—was the largest and strongest aspect of responses to Duke.

A discriminant analysis conducted to uncover the best reflectors of voting stance toward Duke among whites revealed instead the influence of projection. The most accurate predictor of voting is reaction to the statement that Duke would stop "wasteful spending and mismanagement that have wrecked our economy." Additional predictive power comes from reactions to the statement that Duke is a "kook" and the statement that people now feel better about Duke, having put aside false fear. All these statements explicitly mention Duke in an election context. All have strong elements of projection, since there was little factual evidence available to citizens that could "prove" any of them one way or the other. Together, they allow a 68 percent accuracy in predicted support-neutrality-opposition to Duke, a 52 percent improvement over chance. Strikingly, these statements make no explicit reference to race, welfare, the Klan, or Nazism, the more overtly dominant aspects of reaction to Duke. Although "waste" reflects Duke's policy stances as well as implicit populist suspicion, the actual statement focuses on Duke's projected effectiveness, rather than his stance. The "kook" and "false fear" questions refer to Duke's candidacy, rather than to issues or groups, and the main

Table 9.12

Disagreement with Anti-Duke Beliefs among Whites

"David Duke is a hater and will only divide people if he is elected Senator."

"David Duke is a kook who is trying to pretend that he is a normal politician."

"David Duke has already become an embarrassment to Louisiana around the country. His election would affect the economy of the state."

"The state can't afford to have David Duke as Senator. Economic development, new industry and jobs that want to move to Louisiana won't if we elect someone like Duke to the U.S. Senate."

Duke is (will mean)	Hater	Kook	Embarrass	No Jobs
Johnston Evaluation (Whites)				
Favorable	53%	61%	46%	49%
Unfavorable	79%	82%	76%	80%
Duke Evaluation (Whites)				
Favorable	86%	86%	81%	85%
Unfavorable	30%	42%	22%	27%
Candidate Preference (Whites)				
Strong Johnston	34%	38%	23%	24%
Strong Bagert	25%	33%	30%	25%
Weak Johnston	44%	62%	40%	39%
Weak Bagert	56%	70%	52%	58%
Undecided	56%	64%	51%	57%
Weak Duke	88%	93%	83%	92%
Strong Duke	95%	95%	91%	93%
Black Respondents	31%	23%	19%	25%

contention is over whether or not Duke is too far out to be an acceptable candidate.

DUKE AS EXTREMIST

In the usual analysis of public opinion and voting, relatively extreme ideological stands are important only because they distance the candidate from potential supporters. Voters choose the candidate closest to their position, and extremists take positions that are far from those of most voters. Yet a directional theory of issue voting by George Rabinowitz and Stuart Elaine Macdonald suggests that such stands are important, conferring either special benefits or harsh penalties. Their approach is here adapted to the analysis of candidates, in this case, David Duke.[16]

The which-side-are-you-on approach suggested by Rabinowitz and Macdonald is categorical rather than spatial. Voters support candidates on their side of the issue, not, as per traditional theory, the candidate "closest" to their position in hypothetical issue-space. Rabinowitz and Macdonald imply that a process of opinion-definition into "sides" occurs, involving a push toward clear-cut categorization into dichotomies, especially by voters and reporters. Voters see a "weak" proponent of their side—one reflecting all the ambiguities and reservations of their own opinion—as worse than a "strong" proponent of their side, though both are seen more favorably than any spokesperson for the other side. Hence, Democrats and Republicans can successfully nominate candidates who hold more extreme stands on divisive partisan issues than do the relatively centrist party voters.

David Duke certainly appears more extreme on race-related issues than his supporters. In the whose-side approach, such a spokesman is not necessarily hurt by being more extreme than his potential voters. In fact, he is helped— who wants a wishy-washy advocate?—except for the issue of extremism. Though Rabinowitz and Macdonald are not clear about the process, they suggest that some positions are too extreme to be the most-favored positions for voters on the same side of the issue. These extreme positions become rejected. If seen as an extremist by potential supporters, Duke would lose the considerable support that, in directional theory, falls to any strong spokesperson for the majority side.

For an individual such as Duke, who is near the margin of acceptability, the question of extremism thus becomes crucial. If he is legitimate, then he becomes the preferred, strong spokesperson for a side, garnering massive support. If he is not legitimate, then he loses. Consider the effect on election day, when New Orleans's RDO (Regular Democratic Organization) —formerly an organization of the segregationist wing of the Democratic party—endorsed Senator Johnston: "This is a difficult choice for many people. One candidate [Duke] seems to say everything they want to hear. But the messenger himself is an extremist with dangerous ties to sinister elements. He would be isolated and ineffective in Washington."[17] The accusation of extremism is presumed damning, because, as in the case of which-side models, if extremism is an issue, it is *the* issue: voters need to decide upon it before they can vote their preferences.

The two theories—who's closest to my position versus which side are you on—lead to two entirely different election strategies. In the more conventional who's-closest model of voting, of course, opponents of one candidate could also try to pin an extremist label on that candidate. Because Duke, as an ideologue, would be viewed as a weak candidate, opponents would find his challenge negligible and would assume it would be easy to paint him as an extremist. In a whose-side approach, however, Duke appears to be a strong candidate—outspoken, issue-oriented—and very dangerous to his opponents. In taking stands unpleasant to opponents, Duke maximizes those stands' chances of victory. From this perspective, it is rational for opponents to resist Duke intensely, to see him as an unusually potent rallying point, and to worry about whether voters' indifferently racist views will be converted into support for a solidly racist candidate. It is crucial for opponents, in this approach, to both raise the extremism issue and make it stick.

Raising the issue, however, is risky, because it helps Duke dominate the election, especially since debate on Duke's extremism logically precedes debate on whether he ought to be the preferred candidate. The issue of Duke's acceptability thus took center stage in the Senate race, washing out, for instance, the relative qualifications of Bagert and Duke. Duke dominates debate, albeit by being the focus of it.

Duke's opponents needed to voice their opposition in order to label him an unacceptable extremist, and, to some extent, they did. Two major efforts linking Duke to consensually unacceptable groups or ideas developed by the end of the Senate campaign. The first came in Duke's campaign for the Louisiana state House, when George Bush, Ronald Reagan, and Lee Atwater declared him to be an unacceptable Republican. During the second attempt, in September 1990, newspaper articles and advertisements seemed more successful; the approach was also amply documented and factually up-to-date, largely due to research and publicity by the Louisiana Coalition, made available to reporters in a bound "media kit." It was reportedly buttressed by door-to-door campaigning: "About 5,000 people who are members of the coalition or sympathetic to its aims have been out in their neighborhoods, telling their neighbors they are opposed to Duke and giving them information about him. Coalition leaders believe that, next to the media kit, this has been their most effective weapon against Duke."[18] Along with newspaper stories, this unusual voicing of opposition affected the climate of opinion, perhaps anticipating the gubernatorial election's more dramatic bandwagon effects among the most socially isolated voters and a spiral of silence that quieted Duke supporters as belief in their ultimate representativeness dimmed.[19]

How do people decide whether Duke is an extremist? Among respondents, opponents are well suited to discuss Duke's unacceptability, since what they know about him is what makes him unacceptable to them. The focus of the question of Duke's acceptability is on racism and his KKK background. In a poll commissioned by Bennett Johnston and conducted by Garin-Hart during July 9–12, 1990, with 601 respondents, 64 percent of likely voters volunteered reasons to have reservations about Duke, with 51 percent of likely voters identifying the Klan and racism as the sources of the reservations.[20] In response to a direct question, 47 percent indicated "major doubts" about supporting Duke because of his Klan leadership and racism appeals, while 30 percent had no real doubts. As indicated above, these are the factors underlying Duke evaluations and projections by opponents. They are also the focus of the acceptability questions.

By contrast, Duke's supporters are quiet. They are usually undercounted in polls and underrepresented in public discussions, particularly on the issues of Klan-Nazi connections, which form the core of the extremism case. While some are "soft on racism," even the hard-core supporters disclaim white supremacy and genetic racism and are not in the main motivated directly by racial issues. Though they are moved by symbolic and cultural racism, the Klan and Nazism are largely irrelevant to their voting concerns. Why, then, should supporters change their vote based on protests about Duke's background, especially when voiced by his opponents?

Duke's support is unusually firm. Generally only candidates whom an electorate knows well—presidents who have served a term, for example—have support that cannot be swayed by new information. Duke, however, fits this pattern. In the July Louisiana Coalition poll, voters first were queried about their voting choices in the Senate campaign and then were asked to answer nearly fifteen minutes' worth of further questions about Duke and his issues. These included hypothetical judgments that introduced potent anti-Duke information. After receiving this new information, the voters were again asked about their Senate voting preferences. Among whites, support for Duke dropped from 33 percent to 30 percent and "don't know" increased from 17 percent to 21 percent. The changes came almost entirely from Duke supporters who had initially agreed that it was "still possible that you will change your mind." That is not an impressive amount of change, especially considering that political campaigns rarely receive a voter's full attention for a block of fifteen minutes. Commercial advertisers, of course, pay a great deal for a lesser opportunity.

How could extremism as an issue penetrate that? An extremism issue makes change easier than does the usual information about issue stands, group ties, and personal characteristics. This requires a brief explanation of why changing votes is particularly difficult. As has been recently discussed by Milton Lodge, Kathleen McGraw, and Patrick Stroh, people's responses tend toward consistency and continuity in many ways, including response set, which mirrors how people generally do act and think. Instead of creating new responses to each new situation, people adjust their ongoing responses. One reason why new arguments about Duke have so little apparent impact is that people do not recalculate their stance at every opportunity: instead, they use a running tally, an on-line, ongoing evaluation, in which new information mixes in with an existing evaluation.[21] What counts is the total evaluation, not its components. Further, because people forget or ignore the original source of an evaluation, the "refutation" of a reason for support does not erase the reason, then erase the support. In this model, any accepted positive information is equal to any other such information—it adds to the total— making distinctions difficult.

Voters' on-line evaluation for questions touching their intended actions— such as "Which candidate do you prefer for Senator?"—renders them fairly immune to targeted, "key" bits of information. Basically, the whole net information mass must be changed for the voter's preference to be changed.

Extremism, however, creates an issue, rather than adding information to an old one. The decision on extremism is a new decision; information already used by voters in forming opinions about Duke may not be available to refute extremism claims. For opponents, of course, extremism is not a new topic. It is new, however, for many supporters. Duke's Klan-Nazi connections are not what they are really interested in and so come through in a rather vague blur. The Coalition's survey used hypothetical questions on Duke's Klan-Nazi connections in an attempt to get inside this blur.[22] How would voters be affected by information on the issue? Table 9.13 indicates that, among those who already knew about Duke's Klan and/or Nazi membership, strong supporters were unswayed. There were too few disbelievers in Duke's Klan membership for analysis; among those who disbelieved in his Nazi affiliations, the responses were similar to those among believers, though less extreme. Supporters were more likely to indicate possible impact, while opponents were less likely. Most, except for diehard Duke supporters, conceded the membership to be potentially important. Few (2 percent) indicated that Nazi or Klan affiliation made them more likely to vote for Duke.

DUKE AS A SYMBOL

Duke's supporters seemed relatively persuadable by an "extremism" campaign that opponents were well placed to conduct. Additionally, Duke's socially marginal supporters were those most vulnerable to an extremism appeal. Yet the extremism campaign did not prevent him from capturing 57 percent of the votes cast by whites. What made the opposition so intense? What else was going on?

Intensity of this degree with so small an apparent stake is neither common

Table 9.13

Impact of Hypothetical Membership on Voting among Whites

[If Duke believed to be a member] "Does that make you more likely to vote for Duke for U.S. Senate, less likely, or have no effect on your vote?"

[If Duke not believed to be a member] "If you knew that David Duke had been a member of a Nazi organization [the Ku Klux Klan], would that make you more likely to vote for Duke, less likely, or have no effect on how you vote?"

Percentage responding that membership in the organization would make a vote for Duke "less likely" among those believing/disbelieving in Nazi and Klan membership:

Was Duke a . . .	Nazi?		Klansman?	
	No	Yes	No	Yes
Johnston Evaluation (Whites)				
Favorable	63%	80%	(Too	64%
Unfavorable	26%	36%	few	32%
Duke Evaluation (Whites)			responses	
Favorable	32%	36%	for	26%
Unfavorable	79%	91%	analysis)	85%
Candidate Preference (Whites)				
Strong Johnston	82%	93%		85%
Strong Bagert	74%	100%		100%
Weak Johnston	87%	86%		73%
Weak Bagert	52%	81%		64%
Undecided	48%	58%		42%
Weak Duke	34%	36%		26%
Strong Duke	21%	0%		4%
Black Respondents	53%	85%		86%

nor unprecedented. Moral issues, issues of life-style, and issues of culture are all often emotional, intense political issues. Because political conflict involving them is not overtly over material goods and services, such politics is often termed *symbolic politics*. In its opposition's intensity, Duke's candidacy, therefore, strongly suggests symbolic politics.

Symbolic politics can be a slippery term. One meaning I do not intend is deceitful politics.[23] As with symbolic racism, "symbolic" may connote deception, perhaps collusion to mislead. Symbols in this meaning are delusory, as when the symbol of a judge's robe cloaks coercion, hiding it from sight. Opponents of any issue, candidate, or movement are often convinced that support for the other side must be based on delusion, if not deception. Thus a charge that support is based on empty symbols is commonplace. I do not mean that Duke's support or opposition is delusory or that symbols are used to deceive. A second nonmeaning stems from the truism that any politics is symbolic politics—only politics without language or any form of representation would be nonsymbolic.[24] The concepts of politics often refer to realities, such as political parties, whose importance is grounded not in some physical existence but in their existence as symbols in the minds of people.

Symbolic politics involves the use of symbols in a nondenotative, though not misleading, way. The symbols do not symbolize what they usually stand for. On the other hand, no deception is involved, as what the symbols represent in this instance is also widely understood.

In symbolic politics, the referents of symbols are real and understood, and the real consequences of symbolic acts (such as prohibiting the production and consumption of alcohol) are intended by supporters.[25] Denotative, "factual" consequences, however, are not the motivating force on at least one side of the controversy. It is precisely the social status of symbols in the minds of people that is the motivating issue on at least one side. Symbolic politics thus can be a politics of principle and of morality or a politics of hate and of contempt. In politics such as flag-burning controversies or abortion controversies, the social status of symbols is treated as an ultimate reality by participants. The more important a symbol is as a source of meaning and identification to an individual, the more potential that symbol has for involving the person in symbolic politics. The controversy would involve the treatment of the symbol—and, by implication, the individual affirming or identifying with the symbol—by other people. National holidays, as in the case of Martin Luther King, Jr., Day, involve the affirmation of a symbol, hence of the people and of the way of life of the people identified with the symbol.[26]

To opponents, the symbols of David Duke are overtly racial. Nazi, Holocaust, Klan, and cross burning are what Duke means to them. They reject and wish to discredit these things or wish to reaffirm the rejection of them. Because these are the symbols most important to opponents, they assume that they are also the symbols most important to supporters, that Duke supporters wish to elevate and affirm and identify with Nazis and Klansmen. As they are fairly certain that what they oppose most Americans also oppose, Duke's opponents are puzzled, shocked, and offended by the support Duke receives. To them Duke usually symbolizes a way of life—segregation and racial discrimination—that has clearly been both put aside and denigrated. To them he is a kook, an extremist, a voice of the past. The active response by his opponents is to attempt to educate his supporters by giving them the "facts" about Duke's past associations with Nazis and the Klan. The syllogism runs:

People vote on the most important issue, which is the Klan.

David Duke represents the Klan, hated by almost everyone.

Duke should get almost no support.

As Duke does get support, opponents assume the weak link is that supporters do not know that Duke represents the Klan. The next step is to assume that his supporters actually like the Klan. In fact, however, supporters usually do know about Duke's Klan links and they do not like the Klan. The last assumption to be changed is the most basic one, the definition of the most important issue as Duke's past racist associations.

To supporters, Duke symbolizes support for the American Creed and economic individualism. To supporters, these represent threatened values and an endangered American Way that they identify with their own way of life. To supporters, the retrospective issues of Duke's background are much less important than the issues he raises about how to defend their values. Duke's symbolic politics reflect cultural politics, and his issue campaign is a cultural crusade.[27]

But Duke's is an odd cultural candidacy. Unlike some other defenses of a way of life, particularly in the South, Duke has few compatriots with equivalent support. No broad movement is behind him like Prohibition or segregation. Nor are his defenders notably forthright. Whereas Roman Catholic or fundamentalist pro-life demonstrators flaunt their intensity, Duke's supporters at the same times and places often obscure where they stand and how much they care. Aside from anonymous polls, support becomes evident in intense, surprising bursts of conviction during a conversation. The implicit awareness of widespread disapproval and opposition to Duke makes the support silent, despite its intensity.

The disapproval expected by Duke's older supporters is not entirely new. Despite Ronald Reagan and a revived social conservatism, the actual people and values being upheld have had a rough twenty-five years. White southerners in general have been the objects of disapprobation, particularly on the questions of their values and their treatment of blacks. They are sensitive to issues of "special treatment," for good or ill. Perhaps the high point of Duke's popularity occurred when he defended the homestead exemption—the exclusion from taxation of $75,000 of an owner-occupied house. Defenders of the homestead exemption include white suburban homeowners identifying their life-style with the postwar American Way, while opponents include businesses whose property is not eligible for exemption and big-city renters, who believe that their rent is high because of property taxes. The homestead exemption is attacked as a special privilege. To Duke supporters, however, the real special privileges are being received by the opponents of the homestead exemption.

Reagan Republicans, after running on behalf of neutral procedures and against special treatment, were by 1990 perceived as a party of unequal opportunity, with success based on favoritism rather than hard work. While Duke did not explicitly tap into the anticorporation vehemence of his supporters, ties to the "special interests" of political action committees were a widespread criticism by his supporters of the incumbent Senator Johnston. Duke instead explicitly attacked "special treatment" for blacks in minority set-asides, another sensitive side of his supporters' sense of being unfairly put upon.

If Duke's intense opposition involves the symbols of racism, his intense support involves the symbols of populism, the American cultural political movement of last resort. Duke taps into only the right-wing potential of this potent combination of distrust and righteousness.

David Duke is thus a cultural candidate, symbolizing in the 1990 Senate race an alternative culture to that offered by the other two candidates. According to a regression analysis of parish data, Duke ran best in areas reflecting the old, white, populist Louisiana. He received more than twice as many votes as Bennett Johnston in areas with concentrations of white registered Democrats, while he received few votes in areas with numerous black voters and garnered about one-half of the white votes among Republicans who did not represent the old Louisiana populistic values. Yet he could not garner the broad support that George Wallace, for instance, received in outstate Louisiana. Only 1.7 percent of Louisiana's 3,261 precincts gave Duke 75 percent or more of the vote. Crucially, because he was unable to convince women to support him as much as men, he did not yet have the appearance of a community candidate—the representative of all the people like "us," who is on "our" side.[28]

DUKE AS THE FUTURE

Duke's successes and failures reflect dynamics that can happen elsewhere. The particulars are Duke's. These include his relative inability to tap two potential veins of support: hostility against illegitimate economic gains by businesses and sponsorship by a unified cultural group. They also include the special liability of his associations with neo-Nazis and the Ku Klux Klan. The latent appeal of a David Duke is not limited to Louisiana, however. Neither is the intense opposition. Indeed, non-Louisiana reactions seem most to stress that Duke would be labeled "unacceptable" rather quickly in other locales. Perhaps.

It might be useful to remember that Duke's Senate campaign indicates what can happen when a candidate taps into aspects of public opinion that the usual institutions of media, opposition candidates, and political parties are not used to handling. The fact is, normal practices did not control opinion and voting in Duke's Senate election, because they did not fit the actual dynamics of public opinion. Special practices, such as the last-minute withdrawal of the official Republican candidate and the organization of a "No Dukes" campaign on Duke's acceptability, did. When campaigns draw as fully on projection, directional voting, and cultural politics as Duke's did, then this 1990s election in Louisiana may prove to be a model for unconventional support and opposition.

NOTES

1. The survey was conducted on July 7–8, 1990, by Penn and Schoen, a Washington, D.C., political consulting firm. The data were made available by the Louisiana Coalition against Racism and Fascism, which bears no responsibility for this analysis or interpretation. According to random sampling theory, with a sample size of 605, there is a 5 percent chance of a difference at least as large as 4 percent between the sample and the population on any particular estimate. In practice, errors are likely to be larger than sampling theory alone would expect, so small numeric differences should usually be ignored unless they form a pattern or conform to a theoretical expectation.

2. Although experienced interviewers can recall times when respondents indicated a private racism far beyond normal responses, there is no way of knowing whether this accounts for 1 percent or 99 percent of Duke's support. The underestimate of racist voting by about 6 percent in other surveys suggests that hidden support for racism is notable but not major. In the analysis below, likely hidden Duke supporters are examined for their correspondence to hypothesized reasons for Duke support. Thus, if an answer fits acknowledged Duke supporters, we check to see whether it also fits possible hidden Duke supporters.

3. Formally, the October 6 "primary" election was not partisan. Any candidate receiving 50 percent of the vote won office, making it in fact a general election for office rather than a primary election for nomination. In a Louisiana single-seat contest, such as the Senate election, if no candidate receives 50 percent, there is a runoff election between the top two candidates, regardless of party. J. Bennett Johnston ran as a Democrat, while both Duke and Ben Bagert ran as Republicans in an "open" election where all candidates competed among all voters for a single stake,

a seat, so it was not a partisan election. However, Democrats endorsed Johnston and Republicans endorsed the winner in special party caucuses held long before the fall election. Bagert overwhelmingly defeated Duke in the caucuses, partly because his supporters were Republicans and activists and partly because of superior organization. In all but formality, Duke ran as an Independent candidate, opposing the Republican, just as he did in his state representative election, as well as the incumbent Democrat. Bagert's withdrawal two days before the election left Republicans without a candidate, and only 51 percent of registered Republicans voted in the Senate election, as opposed to 69 percent of white registered Democrats. I arrived at the turnout estimates by ecological regression of voting results on registration data, by parish.

4. Converse et al., "Continuity and Change."

5. Sniderman, *Race and Inequality*, 75. The use of the term *pseudoconservatives* follows Hofstadter, *Paranoid Style*.

6. Populism may take the form of support for broader participatory democracy, as during the 1960s; it may take its usual form of support for existing majoritarian institutions; or it may take the form of a right-leaning insurgency, as appears to be the case for David Duke and as it was for the "taxpayer revolt" in referenda a decade earlier. Populism is always assertive of voter sovereignty and majority rights and values and hostile to nonmajoritarian institutions and movements. A particular instance of populism is left, center, or right depending on its specific stances: does it involve change toward greater equality? resistance against change toward increased benefits for the minority have-mosts or have-nots? or change toward inequality that hurts the minority have-nots?

7. Gibson and Bingham, "Conceptualization and Measurement."

8. Ross and Fletcher, "Attribution and Social Perception."

9. Sniderman, *Race and Inequality*.

10. These results derive from a fourth-order polynomial regression of Duke's vote on the percentage of white election-day sign-in for precincts in the 1990 Senate election. Duke's black vote is estimated at the 0.5 percent he received in all black precincts. This permits use of the regression coefficients to derive estimates of his share of the white vote presented.

11. See, for example, McClosky and Zaller, *American Ethos*.

12. Jacobson, *Politics of Congressional Elections*.

13. The problem of challengers is particularly acute in Louisiana due to the election structure. What is called the primary—actually a general election in which most incumbents win reelection—occurs a month after Labor Day, when voters are settling back into their yearly routines after the summer. In most states it is not necessary to get voters' attention during the summer, as only the primary elections are held early in the fall. In Louisiana, by contrast, a challenger has to have built enough support by early October to keep the incumbent from receiving 50 percent of the vote by default. To be in position by September, the challenger must have prepared the way in the summer, raising funds and organizing workers, and must have kept rising in the polls. Yet challengers find it almost impossible to do these things in the summer without the

veteran's strong base. Hence, challengers often enter the final month ill-equipped to garner the publicity and support needed.

14. Sorauf, *Money in American Elections*.

15. Responses to one-half of the questions asked are notably related (loading .4) to the factor. Under reexamination (oblique rotation), the Duke factor reveals a voting component, including questions relating Duke to neo-Nazism, and a related ($r = .34$) component of reaction to Duke alone, including evaluations of Duke and support for racial stereotypes.

16. See Rabinowitz and Macdonald, "A Directional Theory."

17. Campaign endorsement mailer in the author's possession.

18. Kelso, "Unmasking of David Duke."

19. Noelle-Neumann, *Spiral of Silence*. The process of forming a public opinion about a candidate's extremism, however, has few of the organizing devices of the equivalent process of forming a public opinion about which candidate should win. There are no clear rules for when the process stops or how the votes are counted. As in the case of Oliver North, information elites may prove poor guides as to public judgment. Indeed, publics in one locale are often a poor guide to the views of publics in another area. The class, region, and life-style overtones of the extremism issue suggest that the crucial publics for extremist individuals are people like themselves. The rural cosmetologist may be more influential than the metropolitan newscaster, though we do not know this.

20. Coded responses to question 9b, p. 6, of the interview schedule with summary percentages. Garin-Hart Strategic Research, Study no. 3168.

21. Lodge, McGraw, and Stroh, "Impression-Driven Model."

22. There are reasons to suspect the efficacy of hypothetical questions. Individuals are not skilled at keeping separate truth and fiction on the same topic when they have the same evaluative implication. Belief is most successfully suspended on imaginary or new topics rather than established realities. For respondents who already believe the hypothesized information, no new thinking—or action—is implied, so their responses are not equivalent to respondents who already resist the message. Individuals are not good at predicting their own mental responses, their thinking yet to come, under the best of circumstances. When extremism is involved, they are also required to predict changes in how they would go about deciding how to evaluate Duke, as well as the outcome.

23. Edelman, *Symbolic Uses of Politics*.

24. Mitchell and Mitchell, *Politics*, chap. 4.

25. Gusfield, *Symbolic Crusade*.

26. Devine, *Political Culture*; Lipset, *First New Nation*; Chidester, "Civil Religion."

27. See Bennett, *Public Opinion in American Politics*, chap. 13, for a discussion of the myth-election-culture linkage.

28. All evidence indicates that women give Duke less support than do men. Women appear to be less supportive of extremist candidates and more supportive of more socially acceptable candidates. However, it is not clear whether the gender

differences found in surveys are matched by equal differences in voting. Duke's voting support is underreported in surveys. Some of this is due to misreporting of preference, and a large part of the misreporting may trace to a desire of individuals to appear socially acceptable. Hence there is this problem: does the hypothesized extra social sensitivity of women mean a lot less support for Duke or merely a lot less *reported* support for him? In the 1991 gubernatorial runoff, voting among women was 5 percent less pro-Duke than was voting among men, a much smaller difference than the 12 percent gap found in the Louisiana Coalition's telephone survey in 1990.

REFERENCES

Bennett, W. Lance. *Public Opinion in American Politics*. New York: Harcourt, Brace, Jovanovich, 1980.

Chidester, David. *Patterns of Power*. Englewood Cliffs, N.J.: Prentice-Hall, 1988.

Converse, Philip E., Warren E. Miller, Jerrold G. Rusk, and Arthur C. Wolfe. "Continuity and Change in American Politics: Parties and Issues in the 1968 Election." *American Political Science Review* 43 (December 1969): 1103–5.

Devine, Donald. *The Political Culture of the United States*. Boston: Little, Brown, 1972.

Edelman, Murray. *Symbolic Uses of Politics*. Urbana, Ill.: University of Illinois, 1967.

Garin-Hart Strategic Research. Interview schedule with summary percentages. Study no. 3168, July 16, 1990. In author's possession.

Gibson, James L., and Richard D. Bingham. "On the Conceptualization and Measurement of Political Tolerance." *American Political Science Review* 76 (1982): 603–20.

Gusfield, Joseph. *Symbolic Crusade: Status Politics and the American Temperance Movement*. Urbana, Ill.: University of Illinois, 1963.

Hofstadter, Richard. *The Paranoid Style in American Politics*. New York: Vintage Books, 1967.

Jacobson, Gary C. *The Politics of Congressional Elections*. 2d ed. Boston: Little, Brown, 1987.

Kelso, Iris. "The Unmasking of David Duke." New Orleans *Times-Picayune*, September 29, 1990.

Lipset, Seymour Martin. *The First New Nation*. New York: Basic Books, 1963.

Lodge, Milton, Kathleen M. McGraw, and Patrick Stroh. "An Impression-Driven Model of Candidate Evaluation." *American Political Science Review* 83 (1989): 399–420.

McClosky, Herbert, and John Zaller. *The American Ethos*. Cambridge: Harvard University Press, 1986.

Mitchell, Joyce M., and William C. Mitchell. *Politics: Problems and Outcomes*. Chicago: Rand McNally, 1971.

Noelle-Neumann, Elisabeth. *The Spiral of Silence*. Chicago: University of Chicago, 1986.

Rabinowitz, George, and Stuart Elaine Macdonald. "A Directional Theory of Issue Voting." *American Political Science Review* 83 (1989): 93–121.

Ross, Michael, and Garth Fletcher. "Attribution and Social Perception." In *Handbook of Social Psychology*, 3d ed., vol. 2, edited by Gardner Lindzey and Elliot Aronson, 73–122. New York: Random House, 1985.

Sniderman, Paul, with Michael Gray Hagen. *Race and Inequality: A Study in American Values*. Chatham, N.J.: Chatham House, 1985.

Sorauf, Frank J. *Money in American Elections*. Glenview, Ill.: Scott, Foresman, 1988.

Douglas D. Rose with Gary Esolen

10 | DuKKKe for Governor

"Vote for the Crook. It's Important"

On Sunday morning, October 20, 1991, Louisianians found con-
firmed as fact what had begun long ago as a hope or fear and had been
delivered as truth the night before in exhausting election returns coverage.
The choice for governor was David Duke or Edwin Edwards. In his last
reelection attempt in 1987, three-term governor Edwards had managed to get
28 percent of the vote. In 1991 he climbed to 34 percent, edging Duke (32
percent) for first place in the runoff. For the two-thirds of the voters
who supported them, the runoff was unexpected good news, as neither had
seemed likely to have such an easy runoff opponent. For the one-third of the
voters who supported Republicans Buddy Roemer (27 percent) or Clyde
Holloway (5 percent), they faced their worst fears, the choice between two
evils. Many spoke of not voting.[1] The 29 percent of registered voters who
had not voted in the primary already included many unenthusiastic about the
choices, even before they were narrowed down.[2] On unregistered voters, the
primary outcome had the opposite effect. During the two days allowed for
voter registration between the primary and the runoff, 64,485 new voters

registered, upping the rolls by 3 percent.[3] The increase was greatest in Orleans Parish (4.6 percent), where Duke had run most poorly and Edwards had run best, but pro-Duke parishes had also swamped their registrars.

The Major Candidates

The basic structure of the election was that there were three well-known, often first-choice candidates: Governor Roemer, former governor Edwards, and Representative Duke. The multitude of other candidates (nine on the ballot, about as many who were announced candidates or sent up trial balloons at some time during the campaign) were unlikely to be able to overcome the initial support for these three. Because none of the three could win a majority in the first election—the "primary"—a runoff would occur between the top two finishers if the second candidate wished one.

Early polls indicated that Roemer would be the runoff preference of many more voters than would choose him in a primary (see Table 10.1). If Roemer could get past the primary into the runoff, he would win. Edwards and Duke, by contrast, polled close to their maximum strength (except against each other) in the primary. They hoped to avoid facing Roemer in a runoff. Duke and Edwards had, until both made the runoff, an informal coalition, because neither could win unless they jointly kept Roemer's primary vote down.

Buddy Roemer, like earlier reform governors, delivered too well on his explicit promises of change (reform) and too little on his implicit promises of improvement. Roemer had been elected on a surge for his promised "Roemer Revolution," which had started well but lost steam within a year.[4] Roemer, elected as a Democrat, pushed a Midwestern Progressive Republican brand of clean government and economic conservatism: lower business taxes, stop favoritism in contracts, enforce environmental regulations, "scrub the budget," improve bond ratings, restrict campaign contributions, and present a realistically balanced budget. Roemer's take-it-or-leave-it approach to policy-making alienated potential allies. He appeared unable to convert broad public support into policy accomplishments. By 1991, most of his original "Roemerista" team had left for other positions.

Though voters gave Roemer decent job ratings, they were not enthusiastic and often made him their second or third choice. Voters have only one vote, and they cast it for their first choice. Consequently, in trial heats, Roemer could defeat any other single candidate but still was in danger of losing the election. Roemer could have won a runoff that he could not qualify to get into. If many candidates ran, each the first choice of some voters, Roemer's vote in the first election would be held down, perhaps enough to keep him out

Table 10.1
Early Primary and Runoff Preferences for Governor, 1991

	Primary (December)*	Runoff (December)	Primary (March)**	Runoff (March)
Roemer	26%	45%	31%	47%
Edwards	27	33	24	39
Duke	11	15	13	NA

*Poll conducted by Ed Renwick for the Baton Rouge *Morning Advocate*. Reported in Iris Kelso, "Is Edwin Edwards Back in Favor?," New Orleans *Times-Picayune*, January 29, 1991, B11.
**Poll conducted by Southern Media and Opinion Research of Baton Rouge for the Louisiana Association of Business and Industry (LABI). Reported in Jack Wardlaw, "What the Latest Statewide Poll Shows," New Orleans *Times-Picayune*, April 10, 1991, B7.

of a runoff. Roemer needed a solid base of support, and this appeared to be Republican voters. During the winter and spring of 1991, he discussed becoming a Republican with the White House and with his allies. Roemer's consultants told him that if he switched parties and there were no candidate to the right of him, he would win. He switched. In April, Roemer was the choice of 45 percent of Republicans, Duke was preferred by 14 percent, and Republican nominee Holloway was the pick of 8 percent, with the remainder undecided.[5] Throughout the primary election, Roemer was the overwhelming preference of Republican voters, while Holloway and Duke drew primarily Democratic support.

Republicans were too small a base; they constituted 18 percent of registered voters. In contrast, Duke and Edwards were the first choice of large, polarized groups of voters—Edwards of blacks and yellow-dog Democrats, Duke of resentful whites—as well as the last choice of equally large groups of voters. But, in elections, who is a voter's last choice is less important than who is a voter's first choice. Duke and Edwards might each have enough first choices to make a runoff, where their negatives might begin to hurt them. Duke was the only likely runoff opponent whom Edwards might defeat and Edwards was the only likely runoff opponent whom Duke might defeat. They wanted each other. The way to get each other was to encourage a host of minor candidates to run and to attack Buddy Roemer. Duke and Edwards followed this strategy.

For Edwards and Roemer, the 1991 election was in part a reprise on the 1987 election. During his first term in the mid-seventies, Edwards had been an outstanding governor, bringing in a consensual state constitution, garnering revenue with a severance tax adjustment, bringing into power blacks for the first time, and putting labor's agenda into law. By the end of sixteen years, Edwards's world had shrunk to himself and his enemies. In 1987 Edwards was the incumbent, at the end of an unsuccessful third term, plagued with a recession, a huge deficit, indictments, unpopular proposals, and a record of gambling with suitcases full of cash. He had a strong core of black and labor support but was widely viewed as a last choice. A Republican, Congressman Bob Livingston, was the other well-known candidate with a core of support. Three Democrats vied for the support of the ABE (Anybody but Edwards) Democrats, the large, middle group of voters. Whichever could break out and become known and favored would win, getting into a runoff against Edwards or Livingston, either of whom would be chopped up by a fresh face. If none of the three could break out, Edwards would face Livingston in the only runoff either could win.[6] With a late media blitz and newspaper endorsements, Roemer benefited from a bandwagon within the ABE Democratic constituency. Edwards saved his money, not contesting the runoff, thereby reducing somewhat the legitimacy of Roemer's election. So again in 1991, Edwards needed to maneuver a weak Republican opponent and himself into the runoff in order to win. This time the opponent was David Duke. Unlike in 1987, in 1991 Roemer started as a well-known candidate who could not create a last-minute surge. He had to hold support.

Edwards attacked Roemer at every opportunity from 1987 onward. Using allies in the legislature, Edwards sponsored investigations and protests about most reforms. He was successful in opposing Roemer's plan for a teacher evaluation, an issue of voting intensity only to teacher unions, who opposed it. While Duke opposed Roemer's pro-business tax reforms and environmental reforms as anti–middle class and anti–oil industry, Edwards charged that the tax and environmental reforms that affected his campaign contributors were ineffective. The aim was to picture Roemer as just another politician, nothing special, not really representing a major change. Duke endorsed Roemer's intent but faulted his performance, while Edwards attacked on all fronts. Conversely, Edwards and Duke handled each other gently, finding opportunities to praise each other, such as for sincerity and graciousness. Edwards did not discuss Duke's past and Duke did not discuss Edwards's past.

Duke's strategy was similar to Edwards's. Both were well known, with an established appeal to a significant minority of the electorate. Unlike in 1990, Duke did not feel that he needed to become known, so his campaign was low-key until the fall. Much of the public controversy and media attention was gone. Instead, Duke cultivated his Senate contest constituency through direct mail and occasional appearances at rallies. Because Roemer had stressed low-tax, scrub-the-budget, anticorruption themes in the 1987 campaign and in his administration, Duke did not criticize Roemer on intent, only on performance, saying that Roemer had not gone far enough. Duke addressed little-people concerns with environmental issues, opposing regulation to preserve wetlands, to reduce runoff from farms, and to disinfect human waste dumped into Lake Pontchartrain.

Roemer's strategy was to defend his record as solid accomplishment, to remind voters of how much worse off they had been under Edwards. The difficulty with this strategy was that it ill-fit what voters liked in Roemer and what they had come to believe about him. His original support was linked to his rhetoric, his ability to picture in glowing terms a rosy alternative and to mobilize dreams on behalf of action. Roemer's rhetoric was not used in his reelection attempt, which focused on the past rather than the future. In defending that past, Roemer's campaign stressed his accomplishments. However, voters believed that Roemer was largely a case of missed opportunities, unfulfilled potential, and might-have-beens. Voters did not believe that Roemer was a good politician. His job ratings in polls were strongest in the areas of intention and weakest in results. In the face of unanimous criticism from Duke, Edwards, and Republican nominee Holloway, Roemer could not convince voters that his results alone deserved reelection.

The Coulda, Woulda, Shoulda Candidates

Roemer, Edwards, and Duke were known to be candidates for governor by a year before the election. Edwards had been running from the day he left the governor's mansion. Duke rolled straight from his Senate primary loss in 1990 to a consideration of bigger elections. Though he might have easily won an office such as lieutenant governor, he aimed for the more symbolic gubernatorial spot. If he lost, he would begin campaigning for the Republican nomination for president.

A number of potential and minor candidates had some impact on the election. The Louisiana Republican party officials were looking for a candidate. While Roemer's economic conservatism appealed to the rank and file, he vetoed a stringent antiabortion bill backed by social conservatives in the party hierarchy.[7] State Central Committee chairman Billy Nungesser and seven others sponsored a poll showing a high negative rating for Roemer, which they used to try to talk prominent Republicans into running against the incumbent.[8] Former governor David C. Treen—a Republican defeated by Edwards and the brother of John Treen, whom Duke had beaten for a House seat in District 81—floated his name. As governor, Treen had signed a bill requiring the teaching of creationism, which was later overturned in court as unconstitutional. Though he had long been the father figure of the Republican party in Louisiana, Treen's 13 percent showing in an early poll was a mirage, reflecting familiarity more than support, so he withdrew. Richard Baker, a Republican congressman, was more of a formula candidate: attractive, credentialed, respectable, and fortyish. He had run television spots during the 1990 fall campaign despite facing no opposition for his seat. But Baker never got above a few points in the polls. With Roemer, Duke, maybe Treen, and finally Clyde Holloway in the race, there was not much room for an additional Republican. By the time Roemer converted to Republicanism, Baker was no longer a factor.

A number of Democrats ran but dropped out before the primary election. Public service commissioner Louis Lambert, a populist who had lost a gubernatorial runoff to David Treen, garnered up to 16 percent in trial heats, but potential financial backers did not believe that he could actually win. In addition to the high-name-recognition candidates, several attractive candidates tried to move up from less visible spots. Aaron Broussard, mayor of suburban Kenner (which includes the New Orleans airport), shared Edwards's politics and style but not his support. Public service commissioner Kathleen Blanco reached double digits in the polls in early summer. However, Blanco did not fit her potential mainstream female Democratic candidacy. Elected to the public service commission as a consumer advocate, she had become a business advocate, but she was running against the pro-business Roemer. When Roemer's veto of the pro-life bill was overridden in the summer, Blanco clearly stood with the extreme antiabortion forces. Her candidacy died in September. Had a female candidate more oriented to women's issues run, the Clarence Thomas–Anita Hill Senate hearings the weekend before the election might have provided a propulsion for an insurgency.

Of the low-odds candidates, only Clyde Holloway survived to make a dent. Holloway initially had become involved in politics due to a school integration/busing controversy, when he organized opposition and alternative education. He opposed a liberal black female opponent in his third try for Congress and won. But Louisiana lost a House seat due to the 1990 census, and Holloway occupied a centrally located district, which was carved up and split around in the spring 1991 redistricting. At this time, he decided to run for governor, punishing those who had left him out in the cold. The Republicans endorsed their candidates by caucuses, and attendance at these required either intensity or organization, neither of which Roemer supporters had. Holloway, a populist, pro-life conservative Republican similar to Duke on the issues, was endorsed by the fundamentalist and pro-life groups that dominated the caucuses.[9] But Holloway had no chance to win. He started in single digits with low name recognition and ended in single digits with high name recognition. Compared to the other candidates, he was inexperienced in state government, was unattractive on television, had no distinctive issue stances, and lacked a demographic base. As the nature of the three-candidate race became clearer, voters moved away from Holloway to the major candidates.

In the end, eight other candidates were also on the ballot, each receiving under 1 percent of the vote but clamoring for equal time in debates and forums. Because each challenger had to oppose the incumbent, the nonviable candidates operated as a Greek chorus of despair about the state of the state. As Holloway drew his vote primarily from Democrats and disproportionately from pro-lifers hostile to Roemer, his main effect was that his status as Republican nominee gave credence to his attacks on Roemer. The televised debates, which featured the three challengers criticizing the incumbent, served to discourage the governor's supporters, who turned out at low rates in the primary. The minor candidates tended to obscure the actual election, which involved the incumbent against two opponents, Edwards and Duke. The primary vote was Edwards, 34 percent; Duke, 32 percent; Roemer, 27 percent; Holloway, 5 percent; and the remaining candidates, 2 percent.

Campaign Financing

In the 1991 race, campaign spending was vastly reduced from earlier gubernatorial elections. In 1983 the top two contenders, Edwards and David Treen, had spent over $18 million between them in the primary. In 1991, spending was one-third of that. The decline of oil prices had shrunk the available money, especially risk money. One of Roemer's reforms limited campaign contributions to $5,000 (except for political parties). This restricted the role of "smart" money, which places large bets on the likely winner in expectation of a payback. Without a tradition or structure in place for raising small- to medium-sized contributions, financing lagged in the primary.

Roemer led in fund-raising, having both the support of the national Republican party and the support of college-educated, middle-income voters. He was the only candidate who could afford serious television spot advertising. Yet six weeks before the election, when decisions had to be made about production, media time buying, endorsements, GOTV (get out the vote) phone banks, printing, and the rest, Roemer had raised only $2.1 million.[10] With ten days to go, he had raised $2.9 million, not a large amount for an incumbent governor.[11] It was also not enough for saturation advertising, needed for his ads to change people's minds about him.

Edwards raised less than 40 percent as much as Roemer. Neither in 1987 nor in 1991 was Edwards able to raise the funds to afford a strong GOTV effort among New Orleans blacks, who turned out on primary day at slightly less than a 60 percent rate. Duke raised least among the major candidates, with the fewest large contributors but a strong base of small-amount givers, most stimulated by his direct mail campaign. By October 10, Duke had $826,000 in contributions, listing (in the late period) four contributions over $5,000 and thousands of small ones.[12]

The standings of the three major candidates were not changed by campaign financing. All were already well known, received plenty of news coverage, and engaged in widely televised debates. In 1991 no one came from nowhere as Roemer and Edwards each had on their first tries for gubernatorial office. In theory, limits on campaign financing may have a greater impact on minor candidates, who need to vastly expand their recognition and ratings before the last month of the campaign. The problem was hardly just financing, however, as having to overcome three disparate, well-known, intensity-provoking candidates posed a major barrier to winning even for a well-financed unknown.[13]

The Campaign Strategy of David Duke

David Duke's main fund-raising was by direct mail, which also served to recruit supporters and spread his message. His direct mail campaign for governor relied on proven techniques of right-wing fund-raising.[14] These techniques depend on a sense of immediacy and urgency, heightened by conversational language and a call for action. The psychology of direct mail is involvement, built by asking the recipient to participate, to send something off or agree to take some action. Even more than for his Senate campaign, Duke's mailings were targeted, personalized, immediate, emotional, and participatory.

EARLY DIRECT MAIL

In December 1989 Duke sent out a Christmas card cosigned with his daughters.[15] The card featured a drawing of the daughters, behind them Duke, and behind him the state capitol building. The card personalized Duke by picturing him with his daughters. The most political part was a poem, underneath the Louisiana seal, praising risk-taking thought and speech—"be his cause strong or weak." As an insert in this mailing, a two-page letter on a mimicry of school notebook paper announced that Duke would "probably run for the U.S. Senate against Bennett Johnston. And I need your advice." The letter used techniques such as identifying enemies—"Johnston and his left-wing cronies like Jesse Jackson and Ted Kennedy" who "are selling-out America to the welfare-cheats, radical leftists, and liberal special interests." The intended effect was to create a sense of similarity and kinship with a person and to involve the reader psychologically in the campaign. This and other early mailings had many of the direct mail hallmarks: indented paragraphs (often containing only one sentence), single-spaced text, use of blue-pen signature, overblown language, the request for participation beyond contributions, specified uses of solicited money, laser-printed "handwritten" return envelopes, and personalization.

By mid-campaign, Duke had employed more of the characteristics of right-wing direct mail. His mailings included more than a half-dozen items encouraging the recipient to get involved, at least to the extent of sorting through all the packets. The cover envelope of one of these mailings denotes authority—"Representative David Duke," the Louisiana seal, "Postmaster: Official correspondence. Please hand deliver." But it also implies personalization and urgency through the word *CONFIDENTIAL* printed in red, a window envelope revealing the individual's personal code number and address, and an actual stamp (albeit bulk rate). Clearly, Duke was using his office to lend credence to himself and gain access, but the conspiratorial tone spoke more to pseudoconservatism than to respect for authority. The contents include a "copy" of an aide's memo to Duke with the candidate's blue-pen, laser-printed, hand-scripted instructions, "Send a few copies to our best supporters. . . . David." The mailing requests that the supporter review a secret "Campaign Victory Plan" and return a "VERIFICATION RECEIPT REPLY" to reassure the campaign that the plan has been delivered unopened. The plan, "FOR YOUR EYES ONLY," has a "security code registration" that is the recipient's identification number in the mailing file. The reader—"one of my most loyal and energetic supporters"—is enjoined, *"DO NOT LAY THESE DOCUMENTS ASIDE* even for a moment."

The personalization increased from early mailings to later ones. Who did Duke thank? "YOU." "I have not been able to personally and formally thank you for your generous help. . . . If I sent you a thank-you letter every day for the rest of my life, it wouldn't be enough." The personalization technique of direct mail helped to overcome one of Duke's vices, a tendency to ignore people and get too involved in issues, not realizing when he is beginning to turn people off. The mailings, by remaining personal and sticking to well-worn conservative issue appeals, avoided Duke's weakness and bolstered his strengths.

As Duke's campaigns progressed, both the form and the substance of the mailings increasingly overlapped nationwide right-wing appeals. The basic letter continued to be single-spaced but by 1990 extended to the recommended format of at least four pages, front and back. Additionally, a full-fledged "plan" specified uses for the solicited funds during the campaign. The issues mentioned were school prayer, affirmative action (Ted Kennedy's bill), workfare, tax increases, and gun control. The authority theme continued with a "Representative David Duke" letter format complete with picture, committee assignments, and seal. The urgency of the appeals was pitched to the closeness of the contest and the nearness of election day.

THEMATIC APPEALS

David Riesman suggested that American political participants are either moralizers or inside dopesters.[16] Moralizers are not usually involved in politics—are normally contemptuous of it—but when they participate, they do so with the aim of correcting abuse. Involvement is purposive. By contrast, the inside dopester follows politics to be in the know or to get ahead and has few strong opinions. Duke's mailings appeal to both strands.

The overt issue appeals of David Duke are moralistic, for example, welfare cheats and unfair hiring rules. The implicit purpose of involvement is to reform the system. However, the constant stress on winning and power speak to twentieth-century sensibilities of the other-directed and the inside dopester. Is he acceptable? The stress on Duke as "official" emphasizes his acceptability. Can he win? Duke directly spoke to this in the Senate campaign:

> The polls say I can win. Even Bennett Johnston says he fears my candidacy the most. (December 22, 1989)

> The polls show we have an excellent chance of winning. (August 6, 1990)

The stress on winning makes most sense to other-directed inside dopesters, who do not wish to be caught on the "wrong" side, the losing side:

> . . . according to the Baton Rouge *Morning Advocate* Johnston is only nine points ahead. . . . What's more, Susan Howell . . . said "You can't accurately poll David Duke's support because he flies below radar." In other words, Johnston and I are running neck-and-neck!

Though supporters of extremist movements are not known for their social sensitivity, Duke, as indicated by William Moore in Chapter 3 of this book, has attempted to mainstream extreme themes to a mass clientele, whose concern for social approval and correctness is greater than that of members of extremist groups. While the basic appeal is moralistic, the emphasis on authority appears reassuring, and the emphasis on winning and confidentiality speaks to the wish to be an insider.

MAILINGS IN THE ELECTION FOR GOVERNOR

In the gubernatorial election, Duke developed his direct mail campaign into an entirely right-wing mailing. In building his mailing lists, he started a "House list" with his core of early supporters, including 18,000 subscribers to the *NAAWP News*, adding those who contacted him during his tenure as representative and contributors to his Senate campaign.[17] In addition to milking this House list, Duke purchased additional "prospect lists" using the statewide registered-voter files. Prospects received targeted mail: whereas recipients from the House list were addressed as "valued friend and supporter," registered Republicans received a "[b]ecause you are a conservative Republican" introduction, with a "Thank You" for this 44 percent Senate vote "because of Republicans like you."[18] As is usually the case with targeted direct mail, most of the appeal was repeated across lists, with targeting limited to a few items. As the campaign progressed, respondents to the prospect mailings were added to the House list. As the list grew, the cost per mailer decreased.

The major characteristics of Duke's direct mail continued: the window envelope, the legislative seal-picture-address, return address, and letterhead; the use of the term *official* on the envelope; the multi-item mailings; the stress on participation (a spurious "poll") and personalization ("for your family"); printed instructions to the "Postmaster"; the laser-printed handwritten note; the contribution form listing suggested amounts from large ($500) to expected ($25); and newspaper reprints of "success" stories, especially voter support. The single-spaced, multi-page letters simulated a typed letter (with underlining, double exclamation marks, and asterisks for emphasis). Prose tended to become hyperventilated—"Left-wing money from Hollywood to New York City is pouring in for my opponents." The emotional appeals took shortcuts with the facts, as when Duke claimed that a 3 percent swing would have won the U.S. Senate election for him without explaining how 3 percent can make 45 percent into a majority.[19]

Additionally, Duke added new elements: the "teaser copy" on the enve-

To: **Representative David Duke**
500 N. Arnoult Road
Metairie, LA 70001

**Please return your Survey
to me within 5 days of receipt!
Thank You.**

12A

CAR-RT SORT**CR36

NEW ORLEANS

8-4059

DAVID DUKE OPINION POLL

INSTRUCTIONS: Look at the boxes below and select the one which best reflects your opinion. Then remove the flag sticker above that matches the box you have selected and affix it to the appropriate box.

| I Support David Duke | **I SUPPORT:** | David Duke's stand against higher taxes, to reform the liberal welfare system, and for the true equal rights for all. |
| I Surrender | **I SURRENDER:** | It's OK with me if state government taxes me more and and is ultimately controlled by the Black Caucus/Liberal Coalition. |

Please answer the following questions:

1. I support David Duke's efforts to end racial quotas, and reverse discrimination . . . . □ YES □ NO

2. I support David Duke's efforts to require welfare recipients to work, to have drug testing for welfare recipients, and reduce the illegitimate welfare birthrate . . . . □ YES □ NO

3. I support David Duke's efforts to cut the budget and oppose additional tax increases . . . . □ YES □ NO

4. Who would you most like to become Governor of Louisiana. _____

My phone number is: Home: (_____) _____ Work: (_____) _____

CONTRIBUTION FORM

YES, David, I support you all the way! I want to help you raise the money you need to get your message on TV. That's why I'm enclosing a contribution made payable to the Duke Campaign.

| _____ $5,000 | _____ $1,000 | _____ $ 500 | _____ $ 250 |
| _____ $ 100 | _____ $ 50 | _____ $ 25 | _____ Other |

For a contribution of $25 or more I will send a souvenir Duke Campaign doubloon. If you contribute $250 or more you will receive a beautifully minted solid silver campaign coin.

I want to help the Duke Campaign:

_____ Put up a yard sign at the following location(s) _____

_____ Display a bumper sticker

_____ Volunteer or offer other services: _____

Paid for by Duke Campaign Committee. Contributions are not tax-deductible for income tax purposes. $5,000 maximum contribution allowed by law.

A direct mail piece used in Duke's gubernatorial campaign features a white flag sticker for surrender and an American flag sticker for Duke support. (Courtesy of Douglas D. Rose)

lope describing the mailing—"David Duke wants to know *your* opinion" or "DAVID DUKE NEEDS TO KNOW: WILL YOU FIGHT OR SUR-RENDER??," the statement that the individual's response would be brought to Duke's "personal attention," reprints of newspaper headlines or articles validating Duke's claims, the choice of using either an American flag sticker to choose "I Support David Duke" or an "I Surrender" white flag sticker to choose big government/higher taxes/rule by the Black Caucus, and the request for home and work telephone numbers "so I can let you know of campaign developments." In the spring, mailings worried that "Louisiana taxpayers are not organized to protect themselves" against the legislature. An insert attempted to get respondents to register as Republicans and to support Duke in the spring caucuses (which ultimately endorsed Congressman Clyde Holloway). By the fall, Duke was opposing "forced integration and busing," gun control, and "special interest control."

From late July through mid-October, Duke averaged three mailings a month.[20] He identified himself with Roemer's supporters ("the hard-working, tax-paying, law-abiding, middle-class citizen") who believed Roemer's promises to " 'scrub and balance the budget,' reduce the bureaucracy, fight the special interests, and, if a tax 'raised its ugly head,' to 'chop it off!' " The mailings portrayed Roemer as betraying his constituency, siding with Edwards on behalf of "the parasites that feed on political corruption, brutal crime, and welfare fraud and abuse." Roemer as well as Edwards was a "taxer and spender," and "both made the Welfare bureaucracy even bigger [and] are members of the NAACP, and both openly support the racial discrimination of quotas and set-asides." Duke promised to fight "personal or small business tax increases," "require able-bodied welfare recipients to work, get the drugs out" of welfare and public housing, and "reduce the illegitimate welfare birthrate."

Duke attempted to broaden his appeal by positioning himself on national, state, and local issues. "Positioning an issue" involves explicitly sharing the voters' views of problems, stating concern and promising to try hard to deal with them, and, if there is a clear majority, indicating a general orientation to solutions. The message targeted to residents of Jefferson Parish emphasized local concerns: "1) DRAINAGE . . . to alleviate the flooding problem . . . 2) TOLLS [on] the Mississippi River Bridge . . . 3) NO NEW TAXES . . . 4) SAVE THE LAKE [Pontchartrain] . . . 5) CRIMINALS OFF THE STREETS . . . more jail space." Duke avoided promises, except for bridge tolls, which he vowed to "work to remove . . . by the end of my first term."

A final bulk mailing was prepared by the Duke Campaign Committee for delivery two weeks before the primary election. Following earlier patterns for eve-of-election direct mail, the "URGENT ELECTION GRAM" stressed immediacy of need and the chance to win. The opposition was "spending millions to stay in control. They're frantic"; Duke needed to go "on TV the last crucial days." The need was $165,000, the bank account was $20,000. For minimal givers, the Dukegram suggested $25. Personalization involved more "I" than "you": "I'm working 20 hour days and am extremely tired," "I'm coming on strong in the Governor's race," and "They're attacking me and my family," on the "I" side, and "I had to get this to you right away," "Without your help, I can't buy TV," and "You've been so good to me already," on the "you" side.

The direct mail campaign was the core of Duke's primary election effort, providing funds, strengthening voting commitments, presenting issue appeals, and allowing unfiltered contact with a broad base of registered voters. To gain votes, candidates need some kind of contact with voters—through word of mouth, mail, or the mass media. With over two million registrants, personal contact was not going to get Duke enough votes. And though he excels in use of the media, his "neat tricks" still leave his issue appeals narrow and do not permit him to control the target audience or the message. Direct mail, backed by media-stimulated interest in what Duke would say, provided a controlled yet effective method of contact. The weakest method of contact, used at the start of the campaign, was word of mouth.

"STAY AWAY FROM THE 'N' WORD"

The Duke supporters most likely to talk up his campaign were also those who most closely fit opponents' image of beer-belly racist rowdies in pickup trucks. Though Duke claimed to have changed from his extremist "youth," his campaign was supported by his old organizations. In the summer the *NAAWP News* (published by the National Association for the Advancement of White People, which Duke founded) went out in a two-color, tabloid format to an expanded mailing list overlapping the Duke campaign list. The only name on the masthead was David Duke's, and two stories featured him. In the story on Duke's appearance before the NAACP candidate-endorsement forum, the text quoted Duke's stock remarks on welfare and affirmative action, plus the reporter's tag: "David Duke's viable solution for making race relations better is stated quite simply 'Equal Rights for All.' "[21] Another story covered Duke's address at Boston's Old South Meeting House, featuring the friendliness of "good, working people" of "the People's Republic of Tax-achusetts" and the unfriendliness of the "far-left," "Marxist hooligans," and media.[22]

When individuals were reluctant to overtly support Duke, even though they agreed with him, his organization had difficulty in targeting potential supporters, maximizing contributions, and keeping the faithful up-to-date on issues and events. His campaign urged supporters to speak out, connect, and convert, but the potential social embarrassment held back adherents. One *NAAWP News* article discussed the proper way of "coming out" of the closet as a racialist:[23]

> Just be *reasonable*. Start off slowly . . . they can be persuaded, but they need help. What they've been conditioned to look for in people who talk openly about racial issues are clues to "hatred," which is a definite "no-no" for most well-intentioned folks. So, if for no other reason than this (and also because it's rude and insensitive), *STAY AWAY FROM THE "N" WORD* and anything like it, even if others in your conversation use it. Hearing it is the easiest way for someone, who might otherwise be open to suggestion, to suspect that your arguments are based upon hate and not principle and reason.

This advice followed Duke's successful campaign tactic of stressing his coolness and his opponents' emotionalism. Because potential supporters "wanted some reassurance that there wouldn't be some stigma attached to their voting for him," they should find out that "you haven't lost your job . . . because you are a NAAWP member"—but do not push too hard as "one sure fire way to turn them off is to make them think you're trying to hit them up for money." The author recommends letters and telephone calls to public officials and letters to the editor in addition to personal conversations.

The Duke campaign found vocal supporters for public occasions. Duke rallies were raucous. At the September televised debate in Baton Rouge, the audience was dominated by Duke backers calling "Duke, Duke, Duke" after his statements. Radio call-in shows relied on protesters to build an audience. One radio show advertised for call-ins on the gubernatorial election with the pitch: "Don't get mad, GET EVEN with those who are paid to serve you. TALK WITH RON. You can beat rip-offs and powerful politicians. Every voice counts."[24]

DIRECT MAIL LINKAGES

The direct mail campaign worked in combination with advertising and public appearances. Duke's appeals were largely repeated from one forum to the next. In the Senate campaign, his speech had run one hour, but for the gubernatorial campaign, he honed it to a more effective one-half hour. The speech matched a thirty-minute television advertisement, opening with his daughters followed by an appeal for a "fair hearing." On the days before the ad aired, newspaper advertisements promoted it, inviting viewers to hear "The Candidate for Governor *ALL* of Louisiana is Talking About!" On the air and in speeches, Duke repeated material from the direct mailings—for example, the Howell quote about Duke being "below radar" was used to promote the idea that he would win despite poor standings in the polls.

Fund-raising was another link between direct mail and televised advertisements. During the 1990 Senate campaign, Duke had briefly used a 900-telephone-call device to raise funds from his televised advertisements. This innovative technique was banned by the Federal Election Commission. In 1991, Duke varied the technique. Over the air, he raised funds using a traditional 800 number, encouraging the use of credit cards to provide the campaign with instant access to the contributions. Additionally, Duke advertised the 900 number to get information about his "free" *DAVID DUKE REPORT*. The direct mail campaign in late September 1991 used this approach, urging telephone calls (1-900-PRO-DUKE) at $5 a minute that guaranteed "a free 6-month subscription" to the report. Curiously, the subscriptions normally cost $20 for six months and $50 for a year. Duke claimed that "subscriptions to the DAVID DUKE REPORT do not constitute a contribution to the David Duke Campaign, a separate entity." Respondents went on the campaign's mailing list.

Direct mail was the largest expense and also the largest fund-raiser for Duke's primary campaigns. For example, in the first quarter of 1990 his Senate campaign received over $450,000, mostly in small, nonitemized contributions of less than $100. These were primarily responses to the direct mail campaign. Of the 15 percent of contributions that were itemized, over one-half (107 of 209) were from Louisiana, followed by Florida (14) and other large states (New Jersey, Michigan, Illinois, New York, Pennsylvania, Ohio, and Washington). If these are representative of the smaller contributions, then Duke's mailings concentrated on Louisiana but went out nationwide to his old mailing list of pre-Republican contacts. Direct mail similarly accounted for most of the listed disbursements, with nearly $200,000 paid to DMS (Direct Mail Services) of nearby Ocean Springs, Mississippi. Parallel to the direct mail campaign was a telephone campaign.

Duke's conversion to conservative tactics went beyond direct mail and fund-raising. Imitating George Bush's Willie Horton ads, he attacked Roemer for paroling a prisoner who later committed a violent crime. Duke would dress down for a press-the-flesh opportunity, removing his expensive suit to don blue jeans and T-shirt and hold a beer. Despite his lack of military service, he used the flag and military victory as touchstones. While Congressman Clyde Holloway disgustedly termed Duke a phony, voters supported Duke's message.

Duke added a fundamentalist appeal. He invoked Jesus, Christ, and the "Christian nation" at the beginning and end of his talks and letters—"With your help and God's grace we will win. Sincerely, David Duke."[25] His initial message in the gubernatorial race was that he had repented his past, that Christianity involved forgiveness of David Duke and no one should cast a stone at him. As the campaign progressed, he elaborated on this apparently successful theme, speaking of a personal conversion and reform. He used to blame minorities for their problems, Duke said, but now he regretted it because he knew the liberal Democratic welfare system was at fault.

His techniques during the gubernatorial campaign fit the descriptions used elsewhere in this volume. For example, Gary Esolen's and Ronald King's discussions of "neat tricks" (see Chapters 8 and 11 of this book) can be extended to include Duke's televised request for a "fair hearing"—do not judge him on his past, he is changed—combined with a repetition of the same appeals that he has used since the 1970s: he lambasted Roemer and Edwards for being members of the NAACP (Duke accused the rakish Edwards of being "in bed with" the NAACP) and railed against the "forced busing" of little children, illegitimate births to welfare mothers, and welfare spending and affirmative action. In the fall of 1991, Duke declared: "I've become more moderate, but I'm not afraid to say I believe in white rights. I do say that because I believe in protecting our nation's western, Christian culture, but now I can also say I believe in black rights, in equal rights for all."[26] Duke could take implicitly contradictory issue stances because his basic appeal was as a group representative, and the group itself held partly inconsistent beliefs about majority rights and minority rights.

More than in previous campaigns, Duke's message was delivered in pure form to voters. Because he was well known and the campaign was relatively well financed, he did not have to rely on news coverage to the extent that he had during the Senate campaign. Direct mail, televised advertisements, and televised debates provided Duke the opportunity to deliver a technically impressive package to his readers and listeners.

On the Airwaves

Duke's primary use of television included a thirty-minute advertisement, televised debates, and two thirty-second commercials on taxes, welfare, and affirmative action.[27] The most widely viewed debate was broadcast statewide on the largest network affiliates in New Orleans, Baton Rouge, Shreveport, and Lafayette. The debate had a lighter side. Discussing allegations about his past, Edwin Edwards gave repeated assurances that (1) he did not really do it, (2) it was not so bad, (3) someone else was worse, and (4) he would never do it again, though . . . (go to 1). Having Edwards and Duke on the same bill for the televised debate in Baton Rouge provided a large dose of repentance and revival and charm.

As in the past, Duke's opponents underestimated him. Roemer attempted to dismiss Duke with generalizations applying to all the challengers. Duke rebutted with specifics and with the charge that no one would discuss his issues—indeed, neither the panel of reporters nor the other candidates addressed welfare or affirmative action.

Duke was the candidate of white anger and angry whites, and one of his problems was the need of his supporters to justify their backing of Duke to themselves and to others. What justifies anger is moral outrage. In the debate, Duke argued that affirmative action and the welfare system were morally outrageous, and he used the unwillingness to address these issues as a reason to express anger at the press and the political process. They were treating him unfairly, he said, picking on him. To his supporters, Duke symbolized how they themselves, individually and as a group, were treated unfairly and picked on. His emotions mirrored their own; his anger repeated and awakened their anger.

One of the dangers of such an appeal to anger is that it can make even its supporters uneasy. To quell that uneasiness, Duke continued his strategy of making himself look friendly and virtuous. He relied on references to Jesus and to Christian culture, images of himself with his attractive daughters, and his polite manner. In his half-hour television advertisement, he devoted a substantial amount of time to an endorsement by James Meredith, the black former civil-rights-activist-turned-conservative. Because Meredith has no political influence in Louisiana, that might seem curious, but the ploy served its purpose. It delivered an implicit message: if Duke is acceptable to a black with a civil rights background, then his racial anger (and, by extension, that of his supporters) cannot be all that bad.

For a campaign involving more than two major contenders, the gubernatorial primary contained a surprising amount of negative airtime. In a multi-candidate contest, it is usually less worthwhile to attack an opponent than to promote yourself, as a vote lost by one opponent helps you less than a vote won for yourself. With many challengers to an incumbent, the challengers sometimes informally agree to attack the incumbent in order to avoid a primary victory, allowing one of the challengers—a player to be named later—to oppose the incumbent in a runoff. This happened in the 1991 primary, when all the challengers attacked incumbent Buddy Roemer, the front-runner. Roemer, on the other hand, perceived Edwards as his main opponent and so denounced him. Finally, independent expenditures were, as usual, negative—in this election, mainly involving an assault on Roemer, in a half-million dollars worth of television commercials, and his replies.[28] Of this negativity, little went Duke's way. On radio, three Vietnam veterans censured him for draft dodging, and on CNN his opponents got some time, but in the most visible forums his opponents left him alone. Their belief was that Duke could not be attacked successfully.

The positive advertisements of Duke's opponents were not persuasive. Roemer's ads included a seven-minute video on women's issues.[29] Again, this is curious. Though Roemer polled well among women, this was partly due to their opposition to the other candidates rather than to his position on issues and primarily traceable to style and intent. Roemer came across as honest and "clean" and sincere, but his campaign "put little emphasis on integrity" and style.[30]

Media coverage of the election focused on the "horse race"—who was ahead and why, who would win and how. Because David Duke was obviously one of the three leading candidates, and because his vote was difficult for standard polling techniques to estimate, most of the media coverage was concerned with him. As the election approached, growing estimates of Duke's hidden vote seemed to create a bandwagon effect, a self-fulfilling prophecy.

Trial Heats

The percentage share of the support—measured in poll "trial heats" pitting the candidates against each other—gained by the top three candidates slowly increased from the low sixties to the mid-sixties in the late spring, to the low seventies in September, to the high seventies in October, and finally to the low nineties on election day. This was largely due to the removal of minor candidates. Of more interest is the split of the vote among the top three candidates. As shown in Figure 10.1, Roemer held a clear lead from December 1990 through the spring, then lost ground during the summer and fall, most dramatically during the final weeks of the campaign. Edwards remained fairly stable. Duke, who trailed the other two early, enjoyed an October surge that carried through primary day. The dynamics of Roemer's slide and Duke's surge are intertwined with the concept of a "hidden vote" for Duke.

From the beginning of the gubernatorial campaign, most commentators expected a hidden vote for Duke that would not show up in opinion polls. The unexpectedly strong vote he received in the Louisiana House primary and runoff and in the U.S. Senate primary matched an overcount in telephone surveys and exit polls for black candidates such as Douglas Wilder of Virginia and David Dinkins in New York. Voters seemed to be presenting themselves as more politically correct, more racially tolerant than they actually

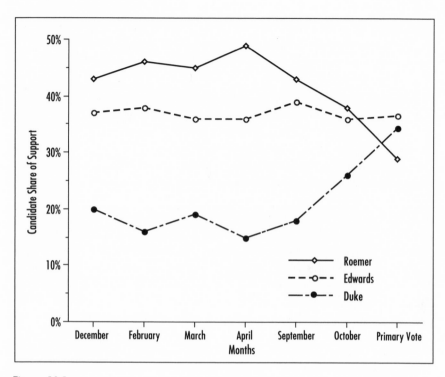

Figure 10.1

Support for the Top Three Candidates in the 1991 Gubernatorial Primary, by Month

were. In Duke's case, the undercount of his support could be attributed in part to high turnout among his supporters. An additional consideration of unknown impact is the refusal to be interviewed, which tends to be concentrated among alienated individuals, lower-middle-income elderly voters, and those who distrust the media. These groups are fertile ground for Duke appeals. Whatever the share of closet support, high turnout, and refused interviews, the polls—especially inexpensive random digit dial surveys—were expected to undercount Duke's support. His mailings and ads regularly capitalized on this expectation, claiming that he was winning or about to win.

In the late stages of the primary campaign, most pollsters made some attempt to estimate the hidden Duke vote.[31] Results are indicated in Table 10.2. The polling techniques varied from allocating to him undecided white voters who were not anti-Duke to categorizing respondents who had anything good to say about him as Duke supporters (partly at Roemer's expense).[32] The impact was to increase the estimated support for Duke, moving him to a

Table 10.2

Guessing Up the Hidden Duke Vote, September–October 1991

Pollster

	Ed Renwick	Susan Howell	Mason-Dixon	Mason-Dixon	Ed Renwick	Susan Howell	Silas Lee	Bernie Pinsonet	Gus Weill
	6–12 Sept.	17–24 Sept.	27–29 Sept.	Final Projection					
Roemer	34%	30%	30%	31%	31%	35%	32%	34%	35%
Edwards	27	28	29	30	32	30	29	32	31
Duke	27	24	28	29	27	30	25	27	25

Sources: New Orleans *Times-Picayune*: Jack Wardlaw, "Polls Show Dissatisfaction of Voters Is Widespread," September 22, 1991, B7, and "La. Governor's Race Stumps the Pollsters," October 17, 1991, B1; "Edwards' New Ads Attack Roemer," October 1, 1991, B4; Tyler Bridges, "Duke Can Get in Runoff, Poll Shows," October 3, 1991, B3.

closer third place in the polls, which was much more realistic. None of the guesstimates had him overtaking Roemer.

The Primary Outcome

Duke's showing of 32 percent in the gubernatorial primary in 1991 was better than the 44 percent he obtained in the senatorial election of 1990. Despite the lowered percentage, his votes were more impressive in the governor's contest. His opposition—an incumbent governor and a former governor —was stronger in the gubernatorial race. On the record, Edwards had previously defeated J. Bennett Johnston for governor, and Roemer had defeated Edwards; Duke, on the other hand, had lost to Johnston, so to defeat Roemer and run close to Edwards in the primary was to improve on his performance. Duke's earlier opponents had been no match for him before a crowd or the camera, but Edwards and Roemer could please both. When Duke "won" the mostly widely watched televised debate, he beat two of the three best vote getters in the state.

Why had Duke become stronger? First, and most important, the main reason to oppose him—his extremist past—had become less relevant. In 1991 Duke's immediate past was his 44 percent of the vote for U.S. Senate, preceded by his term in the legislature, then by his victory in the House contest, and only then by his neo-Nazi and KKK involvements. There was greater distance from his extremist past in 1991 than in 1990, crowded down the list by the statewide campaigns. Second, votes legitimate candidates. Widespread voter backing earns any candidate some respect. To denigrate a candidate is to denigrate his or her supporters. In a democratic culture, voters are all legitimate and what they prefer deserves a hearing. Duke was more acceptable by virtue of his widespread support. He had also broadened his appeals to include more mainstream issues.

REPUBLICAN DISARRAY

In addition to Duke and his supporters, Republicans contributed to Duke's entry in the runoff against a candidate he might defeat. Nationally, the White House cheered when Roemer switched from the Democratic to the Republican party in March 1991. It was the first party switch by a sitting incumbent governor. In Louisiana, however, incumbents had been moving to the Republicans for some time—it was a main element of the party-building strategy of state chairman Billy Nungesser's predecessor, George Despot.[33] But the party officials selected in 1988 had stressed issue purism and activist support, rather than appealing candidates. With Roemer's defection to the Republicans under national sponsorship and his veto of an antiabortion bill, which served as a lightning rod for antiabortion forces, state GOP officials were in a quandary by April. They had isolated themselves from the presidential party by their inept handling of Duke as a state representative and as a candidate in the Senate race, their central committee was packed with pro-life born-agains, and their chairman had led the opposition to Roemer. Though Republican voters preferred Roemer, party officials decided in December 1990 to use caucuses to decide which candidates to endorse. While Chairman Nungesser publicly welcomed Roemer to the party, there was no change in his private distrust of the governor, and the meeting between Nungesser and Roemer to discuss Republican endorsement ended in "mutual cussing."[34]

Consequently, Roemer benefited little from his conversion. The pro-life groups dominated the caucuses and endorsed Clyde Holloway. Roemer already was strong among Republican voters but could not shut the door on additional Republican candidates. Instead, he lost some moderate Democratic support that otherwise would have been available to him. Edwards was left as the only Democrat in the race, in the end picking up more white support than he had shown in the polls.

After years of growth, the Republican party of Louisiana fell on hard times, starting with the loss of Senate candidate Henson Moore to John Breaux in 1986. The next year, the Republican gubernatorial candidate Bob

Livingston finished third in the primary to Edwards and Roemer. In 1988, the Pat Robertson born-agains took over the party organization. In 1989 Duke won as a Republican, defeating John Treen. In 1990 Republican candidate Ben Bagert—backed by the pro-life forces for the nomination—withdrew from the Senate contest due to low support. In 1991 the Republican candidate for governor, Holloway, tallied 5 percent of the vote, helping to defeat the Republican incumbent and putting Duke and Edwards in the runoff. " 'We are the best state party the national GOP has,' said Mr. Nungesser. . . . 'Our party is on a roll.' "[35]

In the 1991 primary, Republicans and pro-life candidates were in trouble up and down the ticket. Twenty-year state representative Woody Jenkins, leader of the pro-life movement, faced a runoff against first-time candidate Sandy Ashby, leader of the pro-choice lobby. Strong Republican candidates ran second for lieutenant governor, attorney general, and insurance commissioner. Democratic voters seemed reluctant to vote for Republicans, especially including Duke-backed candidates, who usually trailed badly. An anti-incumbent mode seemed to pervade the election—term limits passed two to one in New Orleans—so the poor performance of challenging Republicans and antiestablishment Dukists is even more striking. The disarray of the Republican party helped Duke and hurt Roemer.

THE DUKE CONSTITUENCY

The basic nature of Duke's constituency was unchanged from the Senate contest to the gubernatorial primary. Figure 10.2 indicates that the parishes supporting him were the same in both elections. The Orleans Parish precincts each gave him about two-thirds of the votes they had delivered in 1990. An exit poll at the runoff indicated that 92 percent of his Senate supporters voted for him in the runoff.[36] As his opposition changed from a conservative, northern Louisiana Democratic incumbent to a moderate, northern Louisiana Republican incumbent and a liberal, southern Louisiana Democrat challenger, the stability of Duke's support was not due to the similarity of his opponents across elections. His core support depended little on opponents or offices: one-third of his runoff voters said they would definitely vote for Duke for president and one-half said they would consider it.

The interpretation of Duke's support continued to vary. Because of the diversity of reasons to vote for Duke, many explanations can be backed up with evidence, especially if not tested against all the evidence and if competing explanations are ignored. In the best press story on Duke support, each of the six major explanations were illustrated by specific voters.[37] The reasons for his support in the Senate contest (discussed in Chapter 9 of this book)

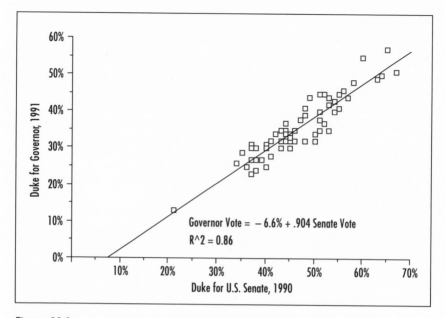

Figure 10.2

Comparison of Duke Votes in the 1990 Senate Election and the 1991 Gubernatorial Primary, by Parish

hold for the gubernatorial election as well. With Duke's narrowed backing in the 1991 primary, his supporters more closely resembled his core backers in 1990—less hostile to the Ku Klux Klan, less drawn from the New Orleans metropolitan area, and less well educated—but the differences were incremental rather than dramatic. As earlier, supporters and opponents created consistency in their individual views by projecting interpretations onto ambiguous evidence. Duke's supporters indicated belief that he had changed his views; Edwards's supporters indicated belief that Edwards would change his ways. As before, the support preceded the belief.

Edwards's primary election support was heavily concentrated among blacks, who gave him 90 percent of their votes. Among whites, by contrast, Edwards ran poorly (14–18 percent), especially in Republican areas. According to precinct and parish voting data, Roemer in the end received an impossibly high percentage (100+) of the Republican vote. What this indicates is that in locations with many Republicans, all types of whites voted for Roemer in large numbers; thus, Edwards did not win his usual 25–31 percent of the white Independent and Democratic vote. For example, in suburban Jefferson Parish, the Edwards vote fell to under 4 percent in all white precincts with sizable numbers of Republicans. Roemer received an estimated 7 percent of the votes of blacks, 7–13 percent of the votes of white Democrats, and almost no votes from white Independents. Duke took 43 percent of the white vote but an estimated 54–57 percent from white Democrats; he received few or no votes from blacks and Republicans. His strongest support (over 69 percent in Jefferson Parish) came from whites who were not registered as Democrats or Republicans. This pattern of Duke support is similar to his contest for the House of Representatives against John Treen (see Chapter 2 of this volume) and to the Senate primary.

Runoff Strategy

In the runoff, the available votes were those of Roemer, Holloway, and nonvoters, and both Edwards and Duke strove to gain them. However, Roemer's voters did not like their choices. Before the primary, only 10 percent of Roemer supporters gave positive ratings to Edwards and only 9 percent rated Duke positively; the views were overwhelmingly negative.[38] When asked for their second choice, only 15 percent identified Duke and 14 percent chose Edwards. The question among Roemer supporters in the week following the election was, "Who are you going to vote against?"

Edwards moved to firm up his support by promising to continue the Roemer policies he had earlier denounced. He would continue to fund the environmental agency and would not fire the corruption investigator, William Lynch. To men, he pitched that Duke was bad for business; to women, he played up the unacceptability of Duke's extremism. Business groups endorsed Edwards and guaranteed funding. Due to Roemer's campaign finance reform, limiting contributions to $5,000, large businesses could not actually make the necessary contributions, but they could promise their support and begin arrangements for the funds to be provided.

These moves were greeted with some skepticism by the press:

This column regrets any observation over the years that could have been construed as implying that Edwards is a corrupt, cold-hearted, skirt-chasing, gambling-addicted demagogue, a champion of polluters and crooks and a reckless administrator who left the state in shambles four years ago.[39]

But if you believe Edwards would continue Gov. Roemer's brand of environmental enforcement or that he would allow a Bill Lynch to nose around wrongdoing in his administration, forget it. If you believe that, you can believe Duke is a born-again Christian and no longer has racist views.[40]

Duke had in Edwards the sponsor of most of the policies he complained about—welfare and affirmative action. It was widely believed that Edwards depended strongly on black voters and rewarded their support with favorable stands on policies and with contracts or positions for organizations. In the face of this inviting target, Duke was initially silent. Roemer's voters were against payoffs but not specifically payoffs to blacks, and the Duke campaign took some time to ponder the problem. In the meantime, Duke went after lesser issues, complaining that public money was being spent to help register black students to vote.[41] His strategy became twofold: on the positive side, attract Roemer voters by emphasizing his issues such as economic conservatism, reform, and environmentalism; on the negative side, emphasize Edwards's past association with corruption and fiscal irresponsibility.

A Mason-Dixon poll conducted within a week of the primary had put Edwards ahead of Duke 46 percent to 42 percent, with 12 percent undecided.[42] The pollsters attempted to minimize a hidden vote for Duke by asking if respondents were registered and likely to vote and by counting undecided whites favorable to Duke as likely to vote for him. The remaining undecideds, who did not include any whites favorable to Duke, were somewhat more anti-Edwards than anti-Duke: 70 percent felt that Edwards's past was worse than Duke's, and 58 percent felt that Duke was more trustworthy and honest. If votes followed these ratings, then the election was too close to call. The outcome would depend on turnout, not a hidden vote.

As in all his elections, Duke's voters would turn out at high rates. If opponents stayed home, it could be a landslide, whereas Edwards could win a high turnout election. The main question of the runoff became, Would Roemer supporters who disliked Duke more than Edwards vote or would they stay home? Because dislike is usually not a good motivation for turning out to vote, Republicans began to try to convince themselves of the virtues of Edwin Edwards.

The Runoff Campaign: Early Days

For a week after the primary, the state was alive with perceptions, quotations, insights, calls from relatives elsewhere, reporters, and new theories about David Duke, Edwin Edwards, and Louisiana. One teacher saw it as "a choice between a crook and a scoundrel. I'll choose the crook."[43] Buddy Roemer repeated the observation that the voters trusted Roemer but did not like him, while they liked Edwards but did not trust him. Then the choice became an accepted reality. Roemer and Holloway voters formed their preferences between Edwards and Duke. Neither candidate was an unknown, so once the need arose to support one of them, most voters could decide fairly quickly.

The initial response of Republicans to both candidates was cool. Nationally, the White House declared noninterest in the choice. Statewide, party heads David Treen and Billy Nungesser indicated no interest in backing Edwards—Nungesser claimed that the rules prohibited it.[44] National committeeman Hayward Hillyer chose "Edwin Edwards, who is against everything our party stands for" because Duke was the more serious danger.[45] Holloway and Roemer stayed neutral between "unacceptable" alternatives.[46] David Treen and most of Roemer's associates came out for Edwards before the end of October.[47] Everyone fell in line eventually. Edwards's "experience" became an asset instead of his "record" being a liability.

Duke's supporters increased their fervor and visibility during the runoff campaign. The New Orleans media devoted space and time to the election in proportion to the immense voter interest. The *Times-Picayune* ran daily front-page stories featuring both candidates and a daily editorial opposing Duke. The increased coverage of Duke brought his supporters into the limelight for the first time. The context of a close contest heightened their positive perceptions of him. Rather than a protest, support for Duke became an affirmation. Supporters believed that their "David" was going to produce a meaningful change:

I think David Duke will go as far as it takes to get things done.[48]

Forget the past and give the man a chance to clean up this mess![49]

Duke has a format for change in these areas. Let's give it a try.[50]

He has a platform and others do not.[51]

While opposing welfare fraud and abuse, Duke also championed "those who have worked hard and have paid taxes all their lives [yet] are often denied the decent retirement and proper health care they have truly earned."[52] After hearing Duke and Edwards debate, the state convention of the American Association of Retired Persons booed Edwards and endorsed Duke.[53]

The Runoff Campaign: In Full Stride

In the first televised debate of the runoff, Duke pitched his appeals to undecided Roemer voters, focusing on Edwards's negatives. Duke held up copies of pardons granted by Edwards—had the violent criminals been put on the streets in exchange for money, or (worse) was it done for free? He expressed concern for the environment and pointed out Edwards's past record of encouraging the dumping of environmental waste. Duke raised anew charges of corruption and favoritism under Edwards, and he attacked Edwards as a free spender. Roemer was particularly proud of his record in cleaning up environmental politics, targeting education funds to the classroom, reducing fraud, "scrubbing the budget," being fair but tough on crime, and running a clean administration, and Duke appropriated Roemer's issues.

To the national news media, the story started out to be Duke's past associations. Unprecedented numbers of reporters arrived or telephoned to cover an aspect of the story, and local papers also increased their coverage. After early duplications, the press began to turn up new information, especially about Duke's current orientations and affiliations. Print reporters—notably Tyler Bridges of the *Times-Picayune* and Roberto Suro of the *New York Times*—uncovered a rich lode of new material. By contrast, the television coverage demonstrated all the weaknesses discussed in Chapter 8 of this book. Phil Donahue, Larry King, and the "Today" show all gave Duke easy access to free media to reach his voters. Indeed, Duke's strategy of attracting Roemer voters relied on free TV: the televised debates on in-state stations and national programs carried by local affiliates. Duke faltered when pressed by well-briefed print reporters on *Meet the Press* and in the second televised debate, when several "you're not answering the question" comments from reporters unsettled him. Even so, of the 7 percent of exit poll respondents citing the debates as a factor in their voting, more than two-thirds chose Duke.

The national coverage, however, interfered with Duke's runoff strategy. The issue appeals to Roemer voters were not the issues the national audience wanted to hear about. So Duke reverted back to his earlier messages: Why are they picking on me? I've changed. I'm against welfare abuse. Affirmative action is unfair. My opponent is responsible for the mess we are in. The white middle class gets no respect. Those who oppose me are the real racists. This focus lost Duke his best opportunity to draw Roemer voters, but it gained him a national audience. The night before the runoff election, Duke was on "Nightline," defending himself before late-night viewers instead of mobilizing 6:00 A.M. voters in Louisiana.

For opponents, Duke's association with genetic racism continued to be the main issue. Blacks, Jews, and liberal Democrats interpreted support for Duke as support for old-fashioned racism, as espoused by Hitler and the KKK. Hence, Duke became "DuKKKe" to opponents. Because Duke supporters were—aside from the first week after the primary—invisible in most areas, opponents examined every face for clues of Dukism. In the voting line, there were new faces, grim faces—were they Duke supporters? Jews looked at blond types and thought, "Are you the ones?" Blacks imagined every strange white to be a Duke supporter. Both groups saw Duke supporters as people who condemned Jews and blacks from the moment of birth, as genetic racists. The most poignant moment of the runoff came during the second televised debate, when Norman Robinson, a black television reporter, stepped out of role and directly asked Duke to apologize for his past. Duke did but in the same sentence presented himself as identical to anyone who had ever had a racist thought.

Duke supporters, by contrast, dismissed his past and announced their support for his policies—against welfare and affirmative action. Was he still a racist? They accepted Duke's claims of a break from the past, a conversion from hatred to fairness, because they agreed with him on the issues most important to them, such as welfare abuse. They identified with his message and accepted the messenger at face value. Immediately after the primary, supporters felt legitimated and became open about their preference. But as the weeks progressed and the negative pressure from press and friends increased, isolated Duke supporters retreated back into silence. When local or national attention concentrated on Duke's past, his supporters saw it as unfair coverage, which ignored the "real" David Duke in order to focus on irrelevant issues. To supporters, the overwhelming national media condemnation of their candidate appeared ill-informed, arrogant, and biased.

The top state and local reporters, followed by the more astute regional and national reporters, focused on issues of potential importance to Duke's supporters. In the second televised debate, Duke was asked to identify his church and minister. Duke calmly named a nonexistent "Evangelical Bible Church" and a nonminister "Reverend" Rongstad.[54] He met with fundamentalist ministers and dated his conversion to age thirteen—before the past associations that the conversion purportedly convinced him to repent.[55] His state coordinator quit with a widely publicized accusation that Duke lacked Christian faith.[56] These revelations provided an acceptable new reason to stop supporting Duke for boosters who wished to bail out. (Among white fundamentalist and born-again voters, Duke received 69 percent of the runoff vote; among other white Protestants, he received 58 percent.)

Finally, Duke as a maverick candidate hit his peak in the runoff. Support for Duke because of his opposition peaked. Conservative Republicans were the largest group of available voters. They agree with his complaints against welfare and affirmative action but disliked his past associations. To those who supported Duke, Edwards was the key. A variety of excuses were offered. One was "send them a message," though the message-as-sent (cultural racism: work harder) differed from the message-as-received (genetic racism: blacks are inferior). Another was that Duke could be controlled and disposed of more easily than Edwards. Still another was resentment of outside "interference." The support of conservative Republicans was crucial to Duke but hard for him to get. They were not casting protest votes or experiencing hard times or threatened by affirmative action or fond of Hitler or the KKK. Republican support for culturally racist themes lacks the intensity that Duke supporters bring.

Edwards's approach to Roemer voters was more traditional, starting with meetings with leaders of groups concerned with the governor's issues; this led to policy concessions and eventually to endorsements. Edwards stressed the contrast between his own experience and expertise and Duke's. In southern Louisiana, however, his main theme became the economic impact of Duke's election on business development generally and on the tourist industry in particular.

The Runoff Campaign: Final Days

Local preoccupation with the upcoming election was unprecedented—at the level of Watergate, the death of a president, or Pearl Harbor—and sustained for weeks. Almost every conversation of a minute or more included references to the candidates. Moods, jobs, and friendships depended on preferences and poll standings. The front page of the newspaper was dominated by election news every day for four weeks. As the runoff approached, the cumulative pressure became oppressive. New Orleans, "The City That Care Forgot," was a place of foreboding and grim determination. The town's favorite bumper sticker became "Vote for the Crook. It's Important." Plans to leave the state if Duke were elected were a common private preoccupation and topic of public discussion.

Statewide absentee voting set a new record, exceeding the old one by 26 percent. As the election approached, Duke's support appeared to become increasingly racist and angry. Signs of racial antagonism and disdain increased. Duke's most visible support is also his most racist support, and reporters sought out visible racists. In retrospect, his support also seems to have shrunk back to a more racist core. Duke's supporters who did publicly justify their preference took more extreme positions, thereby either revealing a standing bias or increasing their bias under the pressure of a contest. Though campaigns respond to voters' concerns, they also amplify them for those intensely involved. The intensity of the election and the starkness of the options may have created consistency in the two armies.

The Outcome

The runoff outcome was an enormous victory for Edwin Edwards, a display of the magnitude of anti-Duke feeling, a public relations disaster for David Duke, and a solid base for Duke's next electoral efforts. While the national media story was a simple "Louisiana Rejects Racism" morality play, the lead story to professional politicians was the surprising power of fear to bring voters to the polls.

THE MOBILIZATION AGAINST DUKKKE

Edwards's runoff victory was stunning in its unexpected magnitude. In a record turnout election (77 percent of registered voters), Edwards buried Duke 61 percent to 39 percent.[57] Edwards more than doubled his primary vote, taking 50 percent of the votes of Republican nominee Holloway's primary election supporters, 61 percent of the votes of those who had not voted in the primary, and 75 percent of the votes of Roemer backers. Though Edwards had been predicting a landslide win, uncertainty remained high until the exit poll results and turnout information became available by the middle of election day.[58]

Edwards won it his way—the traditional Democratic party way—by mobilizing turnout, by putting together a biracial coalition, and by stressing economic issues. In an election in which almost all observers had been uncertain about their predicted result and were surprised by the outcome, Edwards had believed in organizational methods and stuck with them. In the primary, Edwards and the Democratic party had spent nearly half a million dollars on election turnout expenses such as transportation, and in the runoff they went first class—even the mail to voters was first class—spending over three-quarters of a million dollars to transport voters to the polls.[59]

The record turnout produced the landslide, and Edwards had organized the get-out-the-vote effort from the beginning of the runoff. Black turnout rates exceeded white turnout rates for the first time in a statewide election for office. All organizations in the black community helped get out the vote. Though blacks constituted only 28 percent of registered voters, they represented 31 percent of runoff voters and 49 percent of the voters for the winner. Edwards captured the majority of votes among whites with a family income over $50,000 or with some college education. The economic issues he stressed were the top ones cited by voters in explaining their preferences.

What was not traditional was the importance of fear in mobilizing turnout. Black turnout for Edwards jumped twenty points between primary and runoff in Orleans Parish, and fear of Duke was the primary motivation. Normally apolitical groups—car dealers, the tourism industry, and law firms, for example—stung by the anticipation of the damage that Duke's election could do to business, contributed money, distributed endorsement letters for Edwards to employees, and even placed signed political advertisements in newspapers. A locally unknown group produced the widely discussed "Hot Damn!" television advertisement, which had a self-identified Texan chortling "all those jobs in Louisiana, come on down."[60] In elections, negative economic votes are traditionally retrospective—punishing the incumbent for unemployment or inflation. Future economic fears are not significant, except as they correspond to recent economic downturns. In the 1991 Louisiana contest for governor, however, fear of loss of business due to Duke's election was the second most often cited reason for voting. In Orleans Parish, the focus of economic fears, Duke support had dropped from the high of 21 percent (43 percent of whites) in the Senate contest to 13 percent (28 percent among whites) in the October primary, as white voters opted for Roemer. In the runoff, Duke remained flat at 13 percent (29 percent among whites) rather than returning to the level of his 1990 Senate election support.

Fear and negatives usually reduce turnout, not increase it. Specifically, it is hard to use an opponent's negatives to increase the turnout for an otherwise unattractive candidate. Yet this was exactly what happened in Louisiana, and Edwards was not in control of it. Similarly, fear inspired a deluge of over $3 million in contributions in the last three weeks—money that could not even be spent in time. "If we had known we were going to make that kind of money, we would have spent it," Edwards's campaign treasurer Lamar Poole said.[61] His campaign benefited from economic fears, but the persuasion came from voices outside the campaign. The more widespread fear, fear of Duke's racial views, owed little to the Edwards camp but underlay the turnout surge, especially among black voters. While Duke had increased turnout among his opponents before (see Chapter 2 of this volume), the runoff was unprecedented. The intense fear of David Duke, when focused on a single alternative to a viable Duke candidacy, produced a landslide.

THE REASONS BEHIND THE VOTES

Both Edwards and Duke held their primary voters (see Table 10.3). To his base, Edwards added 541,000 votes and Duke over one-third as many. The additional votes each gained closely matched the votes described in the exit polls as a vote cast mainly against the opponent. The runoff vote decisions were negative ones. Duke voters stressed the anti-Edwards theme of government corruption. Edwards voters focused on the economy and Duke's racial

Table 10.3

Exit Poll Results for the 1991 Gubernatorial Runoff

	Percentage of All Respondents*	Edwards Voters	Duke Voters
Vote Was Mainly			
For candidate	56%	55%	45
Against opponent	41	70%	30
Primary Vote			
Duke	26%	6%	94
Edwards	32	94%	6
Roemer	26	75%	25
Holloway	5	50%	50
Didn't vote	10	61%	39
Most Important Issue			
Candidates' racial views	24%	81%	19
Louisiana economy	34	69%	31
Government corruption	19	18%	82
Something else	16	67%	33
Which Two Factors Mattered Most?**			
Experienced	35%	95%	5
Strong leader	32	66%	34
Lesser of two evils	31	72%	28
Cares about people like me	20	42%	58
Will shake things up	19	11%	89
Racial Preference in Hiring			
Opposed	71%	49%	51
Favor	27	90%	10
Duke Racial Views			
Same as KKK days	60%	91%	9
Changed	37	13%	87
Edwards Corruption			
Guilty	62%	41%	59
Not guilty	33	95%	5

Source: Based on surveys conducted with 1,675 voters at 30 precincts on November 16, 1991, by Voter Research and Surveys. See "A Portrait of Louisiana's Voters," *New York Times*, November 18, 1991, A8, and "How They Voted," New Orleans *Times-Picayune*, November 17, 1991, A6.

*This column may not add up to 100% for each question because minor categories have been omitted.

**Many respondents chose only one factor.

views. Particularly among Roemer voters, Duke's negatives were larger than Edwards's. When the most important issue was the candidates' racial views, Duke was clobbered 81 percent to 18 percent (69–31 percent among whites). Sixty percent of the voters believed that Duke's views remained unchanged since his KKK days, and, among this group, 91 percent voted against him.

Some presumed reasons for voting for Duke were not borne out by the exit polls. Voters on all sides were outraged, including moderates, who decried the absence of a centrist candidate—only 3 percent cited "not too extreme" as an important factor in their vote. Duke's vote was no more a protest vote than Edwards's was—that is, Duke was the focus of protest as much as the beneficiary of it. Forty-three percent of Duke's voters cited "Will shake things up" as one of the two most important factors in their vote. Duke's vote was not a hard-times or recession vote. As a maverick candidate, Duke benefited from opposition to Edwards, especially among Republicans, but not as much as his opponent benefited from opposition to Duke, especially among Republicans. Twenty-two percent of Duke's voters and 37 percent of Edwards's voters cited "Lesser of two evils" as a voting factor. On issues of genetic racism, Duke was heavily outvoted. Duke did receive the votes of the whites who were socially proximate to blacks: those living in the same rural region and having the same education, income, and religion. However, it is not clear that these were responding to a perceived economic threat from black programs such as affirmative action. Among the one-sixth of voters who cited quotas in hiring blacks or minorities as one of the two issues that mattered most to them in deciding how to vote, Edwards received 57 percent of the votes. The "threat" issue did not mobilize white support. In contrast, Duke's other persistent issue, the call for reform to halt welfare abuse, was cited by 23 percent of voters as one of the top two issues and by 47 percent of Duke supporters. The welfare issue resonated with Duke's voters.

The reasons behind the votes are other than they appear at first glance. Duke's supporters projected their own preferences onto Duke, believing that he had changed his views, despite abundant evidence to the contrary. These professed "reasons" for supporting Duke are spurious. A basic source of Duke's support is the notion that he is on the voter's side. In preelection polls, the critical question used to predict Duke support was whether he was the candidate who cared most about people like the respondents—was he for them? Duke's past plays a double role in this support, threatening it because of extremism yet affirming the basic cleavage. Though supporters usually wish to disassociate themselves from his past, it serves to clearly label which side he is on. As long as a projected belief that Duke has moderated his views allows supporters to perceive him as acceptable, the past signals that he is a strong supporter of their side. To his core supporters, he symbolizes the maintenance of their "American" values—God and Country, hard work, self-reliance—against the perceived values of the advancing social group below them. Affirmation of Duke is affirmation of the identity of their values with America's.

DUKE FALLS SHORT OF EXPECTATIONS

Duke ran about average in groups he had hoped to do well among. His 55 percent among whites was down from 58 percent in the Senate primary. Republicans (56 percent for Duke), white weekly churchgoers (57 percent), those believing Edwards guilty of corruption (59 percent), Catholics (52 percent), whites with unemployment in the family (54 percent), those opposed to racial preferences in hiring (51 percent), whites who were worse off than four years before (58 percent), and Cajuns (56 percent) did not show the gains Duke anticipated. Duke lost his House district in suburban Jefferson Parish and almost the entire metropolitan New Orleans area. The core of Duke's support—in the northeastern (Monroe) area of Louisiana most like the rural Deep South—stayed with him. These included whites with a high school education or less (68 percent for Duke), white born-agains or fundamentalists (69 percent), and, to a lesser extent, whites with a family income between $15,000 and $50,000 (61 percent). This core had provided the traditional support for the Ku Klux Klan, which Duke abandoned because of the narrowness of its base. With only this support for Duke, his opponents could continue to label him "DuKKKe."

The three biggest failures for Duke were the failure to match expectations of a close election, the failure to hold Edwards under 60 percent, and the failure of a hidden vote for Duke. Duke had taken 57 percent of the white vote and 43.5 percent of the total vote in the 1990 Senate race and was expected to at least match those results. In the primary, he had come within 2 percent of Edwards, a candidate who appeared to have exhausted his base. Preelection polls implied that Duke should get 46 percent of the vote, but uncertainty was pervasive. Duke failed to meet these benchmarks. At 8:00 P.M. on election night, Duke supporters were stunned at the announcement that their candidate had lost by a large margin.[62] The failure to meet expectations is widely assumed to pose a problem for any candidate who depends on a perceived chance to win for his success. In fact, Duke lost in an apparent landslide. Sixty percent has now become the standard for a landslide, and Edwards received 61 percent. Moreover, the defeat of Duke was decisive, unlikely to be easily reversed: turnout was high, most voters had clear preferences, individual voters' attitudes toward Duke were firmly unfavorable, and the issues contributing to the outcome were enduring rather than transient.[63] By normal standards, Duke had failed badly.

Further, his secret weapon—the hidden vote or stealth vote—had in prior elections confused and discouraged his opponents, but in the runoff it seemed impotent. In raw data, Duke's share of the expressed preferences ranged from 33 percent (Howell) to 37 percent (Renwick) in final preelection polls. With preferences plus one-half of the undecided voters, Duke's expected share of the vote in the raw data was close to the actual vote: between 37 percent (Howell) and 40 percent (Renwick). By contrast, those attempting to count the hidden Duke vote gave estimates of 46 percent for Duke, which were less accurate than the raw results. In fact, because these final polls were taken a week before the election, at the peak of Edwards's support (which was followed by a slide), according to Edwards's tracking polls, the overestimate of Duke support was higher than it appears to be. There had been three explanations of the hidden vote—closet Duke supporters, uninterviewed Duke supporters, and high turnout by Duke supporters—and only the third matched the runoff results. When turnout was high among Duke opponents, there was little hidden vote. The failure of the hidden vote to materialize disheartened Duke supporters and made Duke seem a less fearsome opponent.[64]

Building a Base for the Future

Despite the election outcome, the gubernatorial campaign succeeded in increasing Duke's support. In Louisiana, Duke's support rose from 485,000 primary votes to 671,000 runoff votes. The number of his runoff votes was 10 percent higher than the number of his 1990 Senate votes. The number of Duke's supporters grew. In part, the setback in the runoff was merely temporary. His hidden vote should reappear whenever opponents' turnout drops to normal. The anti-Duke turnout will disappear whenever Duke faces multiple opponents. Despite the high turnout and the failure to capture the largely white Roemer vote, Duke received 55 percent of the white vote. And despite intense negative media coverage and investigative reporting, Duke escaped relatively unscathed, with few new damaging revelations about his past. The particularly forceful economic arguments about the loss of New Orleans convention business would be less important in almost any other election setting.

Having made the runoff, David Duke acquired national media coverage, which he exploited exactly as well as he had exploited local coverage in the past.[65] Duke appeared on numerous television shows, including "Larry King Live," "Donahue," "Crossfire," "Today," "Nightwatch," "Nightline," and "Meet the Press." By the middle of the runoff campaign, his national name recognition was 58 percent, and 15.5 percent of the national voting-age population approved of him.[66] His approval base exceeded that of any declared presidential candidate except George Bush. Repeatedly, he solicited contributions on air, and his mailing list grew apace—to a reported 400,000.[67] According to his October 27, 1991, campaign finance report, 47 percent of his contributors were from outside Louisiana, and over 26,000 contributors were indicated.[68] Within minutes of his concession speech, Duke was on camera telling television reporters that, although he had no "plans" to run for president, the decision was yet to be made. His record has been one of pushing his message to broader and broader audiences. The 1991 runoff campaign positioned Duke to reach a national audience.

If David Duke has built a base for the future, so have his opponents. The breadth and intensity of public opposition was demonstrated in the gubernatorial runoff. Fully half of the $3 million the Louisiana Democratic party raised in 1991 came in opposition to the candidacy of David Duke, much of it from outside the state.[69] Spontaneous anti-Duke groups formed and already-organized groups took new anti-Duke action. The research that had been conducted earlier cumulated and was disseminated to a broader public. As communications were established among independent anti-Duke groups and as correspondents learned about Duke, the anti-Duke techniques and the media research and interviewing practices that proved to be failures were dropped and the search went on for effective methods.

During the gubernatorial campaign, most of the obstacles to coping effectively with David Duke continued. As in the past, politicians and the media resisted changing their normal behavior to deal realistically with David Duke, preferring instead to try to use him to their advantage within the confines of business as usual. Edwin Edwards used David Duke to win office, Phil Donahue used him to win viewers. Highly partisan political participants treated Duke as a tool with which to belabor their Republican/Democratic or liberal/conservative or white/black or print/video competitors. The interpretations of Duke's significance tended to be self-serving: Republicans claimed that he had subverted a valid agenda, while Democrats claimed Bush's agenda was as racist as Duke's; liberals blamed Willie Horton ads, while conservatives blamed liberal programs. Blacks saw white racism in Duke's support, while whites saw black bloc primary votes for Edwards as the source of Duke's chance to win. Print journalists noted Duke's exploitation of television, while electronic partisans saw his dominance of print news. The difficulty is not the attention Duke receives nor an unwillingness to act; rather, it

is an unwillingness to learn, change, and think anew, to give up the comfort
of old enemies and yesterday's truths.

NOTES

1. Nicholas, "Roemer Fans Bitter," A1.

2. The statewide and parish voting totals are from Zisk, "The Governor's Race,"
October 21, 1991, A8, and Walsh and Bridges, "Votes," A8. Voter registration data,
summarizing registration as of September 27, 1991, the close of the registration
books for the primary election, are from the office of Jerry Fowler, Commissioner of
Elections, Department of Elections and Registration, State of Louisiana. Precinct
registration data for Jefferson Parish as of October 19, 1991, were made available
through Sam Altobello, Registrar of Voters of Jefferson Parish. Precinct voting returns for Jefferson Parish were made available through Jon Gegenheimer, Clerk of
Court, Jefferson Parish. Precinct returns for Orleans Parish were originally made
available through the Louisiana Secretary of State. All calculations have been made
by the author. To arrive at estimates of voting by registration groups—race and
party—the votes have been regressed on registration data by parish, weighted to
population, then converted to a percentage share of the vote cast (double regression).
This is the methodology mandated by the U.S. Supreme Court in *Thornburg v.
Gingles* for analysis of racially polarized voting. For precinct data, weighting has
been omitted.

3. Anderson, "2-day Voter Sign-ups Set Record," A1. Calculations by the author.

4. Grant, "Roemer's One Hundred Days."

5. April 1991 poll conducted by Southern Media and Opinion Research of Baton
Rouge. Reported in Wardlaw, "Holloway's Entry into Race," B4.

6. Liebkemann, "Issues in the 1987 Louisiana Gubernatorial Election."

7. For the economic conservatism of Republican party identifiers in Louisiana,
combined with less pro-life conservatism than that of Louisiana Democrats, see
Theodoulou, *Louisiana Republican Party*.

8. Nungesser, telephone conversation with the author.

9. Abortion views ended up being unrelated to candidate preference for governor
in the runoff. Of the 26 percent of exit poll voters preferring legal abortions in all
cases, 65 percent voted for Edwards. At the other extreme, 23 percent of voters
thought abortions should never be legal, and 60 percent of these voted for Edwards.
The splits between candidates within pro-life and pro-choice groups simply mirrored
the statewide splits.

10. Wardlaw, "Duke Ranks 3rd in Raising Money," B5.

11. Anderson, "Roemer Still Leads Big in Campaign Money," B1.

12. "Reject Lottery Computer Bid," B2.

13. Money alone changes few votes. Jack Kent, owner of Marine Shale, a com-

pany continually in hot water with Roemer's state Department of Environmental Quality and the federal Environmental Protection Agency, ran an expensive ($508,000) negative advertising campaign against Roemer. When Roemer counterattacked, linking Kent to Edwards through campaign contributions, Kent pleaded for "politics" to be taken out of the pollution business. Wardlaw, "Edwards: Confident of Endorsement," A1. No analyst attributed Roemer's loss to this campaign, despite the closeness of the primary outcome.

14. For an excellent summary of its characteristics, see Sabato, "How Direct Mail Works."

15. The direct mail pieces described are in the author's possession.

16. These categories were derived from the "inner-directed" and "other-directed" character types. "Indifferents," according to Riesman, comprise two additional types, new-style and old-style, both largely nonparticipatory. Riesman, Glazer, and Denney, "The Indifferents."

17. Marcus, "White-Supremacist Group Fills a Corner," A12.

18. Duke persists in his claim that he received a sizable proportion of black and Republican votes, although there is no evidence to support it. According to polls and analyses of voting returns from the primary election, Duke obtained little black support, and he has been the least favorite candidate of Republicans, even when his only opponent was a Democrat. Duke's support is disproportionately white, Democratic, and male. National media personnel who are new to the story take his claims at face value.

19. The statement is misleading but not false; had 72,000 of Johnston's supporters voted instead for Duke, he would have won; this would have been a shift of 5.2 percent of the vote cast—but only 3.3 percent of the registered voters. Why nonvoters should be included for a hypothesized change involving only voters is not clear. Contorted recounts to reverse outcomes are common in losers' accounts of elections.

20. Perlstein and Bridges, "New Reports of Racism Dog Duke," A1.

21. Boutte, "Duke Speaks at NAACP Governor's Forum," 5.

22. Montecino, "Ford Hall Forum Hosts Duke Speech," 6.

23. Kranz, "A White 'Coming Out,'" 10.

24. Advertisement for Ron Hunter show, C15.

25. "The Time Has Come: DUKE Governor."

26. Suro, "David Duke Has Become a Legitimate Candidate."

27. "Roemer Fights Back at Marine Shale Owner's Ads," B8.

28. Ibid.

29. "Reject Lottery Computer Bid," B2.

30. Kelso, "The Campaign Commercial Awards," B11.

31. "Edwards' New Ads Attack Roemer," B4; Bridges, "Duke Can Get in Runoff," B3; Wardlaw, "La. Governor's Race Stumps the Pollsters," B1.

32. The currently preferred technique for measuring opinion on socially sensitive topics is termed *randomized response*. With this method, it is unclear whether a particular subject is responding to a sensitive question or an innocuous one. In the

aggregate, however, the innocuous and sensitive questions can be sorted out, so that randomized responses provide an improved measure of public opinion on a specific question. None of the polls or pollsters used randomized response to measure support for David Duke before the primary election.

33. Theodoulou, *Louisiana Republican Party*, chaps. 5–6.

34. William Nungesser, telephone conversation with the author.

35. Hallow, "Louisiana Debacle Leaves GOP Second-guessing," A1.

36. Voter Research and Surveys, "Louisiana Runoff 1991."

37. Walsh and O'Byrne, "The Duke Voters," A1.

38. Poll conducted by Elliot Stonecipher, October 8–14, 1991, for the Roemer campaign. See "The Roemer Voter," A1.

39. Gill, "Promises, Promises in the Runoff," B11.

40. Kelso, "Mr. Edwards in the Driver's Seat," B11.

41. Varney, "Runoff Turns to Racial Issues," A1.

42. Wardlaw, "Polls Show It's Still Anybody's Race," B11.

43. Hodge, "Thousands Rush to Claim Right to Vote," A1.

44. Anderson, "Treen to Give Runoff Statement," B5.

45. Kelso, "Two Legislators on Duke Problem," B9.

46. Anderson, "Roemer: No Good Choice," A1.

47. Kelso, "Treen's Decision of Conscience," B11.

48. Rhoden and Hill, "Duke's Supporters Saw Success Coming," A1.

49. Gresse, "Duke Result 'Sensational,'" B7.

50. Link, "Time to Change with Duke," B7.

51. Stephens, "Six Reasons to Vote for Duke," B7.

52. "The Time Has Come: DUKE Governor."

53. Anderson, "Retirees Back Duke at Forum," A1.

54. An Evangelical Free Bible Church mainly serves impoverished children in the Desire housing project. See "Some Claims by Edwards," B1.

55. Schleifstein and Grisset, "Religious Leaders Doubt Duke's Christianity," A1; Kelso, "Shaky Stand on Religion," B7.

56. Suro, "Aide in Duke's Campaign Quits," A12; Perlstein and Bridges, "New Reports of Racism Dog Duke," A1.

57. Sources for election statistics are various and sometimes redundant. Corrected totals are from Anderson, "McKeithen Declared the Winner," B1. Parish returns are from Zisk, "Governor's Race," November 18, 1991, A8. Results for an exit poll (1,675 voters, 30 precincts) conducted by Voter Research and Surveys are from "Portrait of Louisiana's Voters," A8. Additional exit poll results are found in "How They Voted," A6. Vote totals are from Suro, "Defeat Need Not End Duke's Message," A8. *The Hotline*, an electronic network election news summary service, provided summary statistics under "Louisiana Governor: The Exit Poll." Voter registration data by parish, party, and race as of the close of the books, November 1, 1991, were furnished by the office of Jerry Fowler, Commissioner of Elections, Department of Elections and Registration, State of Louisiana. The registration data provided the basis for my regression analysis of turnout.

58. For uncertainty, see Applebome, "Louisiana Race Turns on Whose Backers Vote," A1. For Edwards's black turnout effort, see Kelso, "Black Solidarity Wins," B5. For Edwards's forecast, see Frazier and Cooper, "Edwards's Forecast," A11.

59. For Edwards's expenditures, see Jantze, "Getting the Vote Out," A1. For Democratic party expenses, see Anderson, "La. Demos Top $1 Million," B4. For the use of first-class mail, see Suro, "Louisiana Campaign Rivals Intensify Pace and Vitriol," A1. For the runoff transportation expenses, see Bridges, "Edwards More Than Doubles Duke's Campaign Spending," B1.

60. Suro, "In Louisiana Race, a Message of Hate," A11.

61. Bridges, "Edwards More Than Doubles Duke's Campaign Spending," B1.

62. Cooper, "Disappointment Hits Duke Voters," A1.

63. Kelley, *Interpreting Elections*, 29.

64. Bridges, "Edwards Leads Duke in 3 Polls," A1. Respondents did tend to give more socially acceptable responses, but in terms of their behavior on clear norms (turnout), not in terms of their views on contested matters (candidate preference). Among exit poll voters, turnout in both the gubernatorial and senatorial primaries was overreported. As the turnout surge was primarily an anti-Duke one and as admitted nonvoters were usually Edwards supporters (60 percent and 63 percent), it appears that overreporting inflated exit poll reports of Edwards's and Roemer's share of the primary vote by about 1 percent apiece and deflated Duke's reported share correspondingly. If all the reported voters had actually voted, Edwards would have received 35 percent, Duke 30 percent, and Roemer 29 percent in the primary. Duke's Senate vote was even more affected by the overreporting of turnout.

65. Applebome, "Was Duke Made for TV," A8.

66. "Most Know Duke, Few Like Him," A11. The 15.5 percent is calculated from 58 percent recognition times 27 percent approval among those who recognized him.

67. Disaffected aide Robert Hawks said that Duke claimed a 400,000-name list. See Perlstein and Bridges, "New Reports of Racism Dog Duke," A1.

68. For the October report, see Hevesi, "Duke Forgiven His Past by Out-of-State Donors," A11. For the final number of contributors, see Bridges, "Edwards More Than Doubles Duke's Campaign Spending," B1.

69. Anderson, "Demos Cashed In on Duke Campaign," B3.

REFERENCES

Advertisement for Ron Hunter show on WSLA. New Orleans *Times-Picayune*, November 10, 1991.

American Political Network, Inc. "Louisiana Governor: The Exit Poll." *The Hotline*, November 18, 1991 (vol. 5, no. 44), 15.

Anderson, Ed. "Roemer Still Leads Big in Campaign Money." New Orleans *Times-Picayune*, October 10, 1991.

———. "Roemer: No Good Choice." New Orleans *Times-Picayune*, October 23, 1991.

————. "Treen to Give Runoff Statement." New Orleans *Times-Picayune*, October 24, 1991.

————. "2-day Voter Sign-ups Set Record." New Orleans *Times-Picayune*, October 24, 1991.

————. "Retirees Back Duke at Forum." New Orleans *Times-Picayune*, October 31, 1991.

————. "La. Demos Top $1 Million in Past Month." New Orleans *Times-Picayune*, November 15, 1991.

————. "McKeithen Declared the Winner." New Orleans *Times-Picayune*, November 21, 1991.

————. "Demos Cashed In on Duke Campaign." New Orleans *Times-Picayune*, January 7, 1992.

Applebome, Peter. "Louisiana Race Turns on Whose Backers Vote." *New York Times*, January 15, 1991.

————. "Was Duke Made for TV, or Made by It?" *New York Times*, November 20, 1991.

Boutte, Paul. "Duke Speaks at NAACP Governor's Forum." *NAAWP News*, no. 63, [Summer 1991].

Bridges, Tyler. "Duke Can Get in Runoff, Poll Shows." New Orleans *Times-Picayune*, October 3, 1991.

————. "Edwards Leads Duke in 3 Polls." New Orleans *Times-Picayune*, November 14, 1991.

————. "Edwards More Than Doubles Duke's Campaign Spending." New Orleans *Times-Picayune*, December 31, 1991.

Cooper, Christopher. "Disappointment Hits Duke Voters." New Orleans *Times-Picayune*, November 18, 1991.

Correction, New Orleans *Times-Picayune*, October 25, 1991.

Duke campaign direct mail samples. In author's possession.

"Edwards' New Ads Attack Roemer." New Orleans *Times-Picayune*, October 1, 1991.

Frazier, Liza, and Christopher Cooper. "Edwards' Forecast: 58% Runoff Victory." New Orleans *Times-Picayune*, November 15, 1991.

Gill, James. "Promises, Promises in the Runoff." New Orleans *Times-Picayune*, October 27, 1991.

Grant, Robert A. "Roemer's One Hundred Days." Honors' thesis, Tulane University, 1989.

Gresse, Charles F. "Duke Result 'Sensational.'" New Orleans *Times-Picayune*, October 30, 1991.

Hallow, Ralph Z. "Louisiana Debacle Leaves GOP Second-guessing: Blamers in State Party Cite National Tilt to Left." *Washington Times*, November 19, 1991.

Hevesi, Dennis. "Duke Forgiven His Past by Out-of-State Donors." New Orleans *Times-Picayune*, November 15, 1991.

Hodge, James. "Thousands Rush to Claim Right to Vote." New Orleans *Times-Picayune*, October 23, 1991.

"How They Voted." New Orleans *Times-Picayune*, November 17, 1991.

Jantze, Michael. "Getting the Vote Out." New Orleans *Times-Picayune*, November 15, 1991.

Kelley, Stanley, Jr. *Interpreting Elections*. Princeton, N.J.: Princeton University Press, 1983.

Kelso, Iris. "The Campaign Commercial Awards." New Orleans *Times-Picayune*, October 20, 1991.

———. "Two Legislators on Duke Problem." New Orleans *Times-Picayune*, October 24, 1991.

———. "Mr. Edwards in the Driver's Seat." New Orleans *Times-Picayune*, October 27, 1991.

———. "Treen's Decision of Conscience." New Orleans *Times-Picayune*, October 31, 1991.

———. "Black Solidarity Wins It for Edwards and Louisiana." New Orleans *Times-Picayune*, November 18, 1991.

———. "Shaky Stand on Religion May Have Cost Duke Votes." New Orleans *Times-Picayune*, November 24, 1991.

Kranz, Stephen. "A White 'Coming Out.'" *NAAWP News*, no. 63, [Summer 1991].

Liebkemann, Kevin. "Issues in the 1987 Louisiana Gubernatorial Election." Honors' thesis, Tulane University, 1988.

Link, Sally. "Time to Change with Duke." New Orleans *Times-Picayune*, October 30, 1991.

Marcus, Frances Frank. "White-Supremacist Group Fills a Corner in Duke Campaign." *New York Times*, November 14, 1991.

Montecino, Glenn. "Ford Hall Forum Hosts Duke Speech." *NAAWP News*, no. 63, [Summer 1991].

"Most Know Duke, Few Like Him." New Orleans *Times-Picayune*, November 13, 1991.

Nicholas, Peter. "Roemer Fans Bitter about the Leftovers." New Orleans *Times-Picayune*, October 24, 1991.

Nungesser, William. Telephone conversation with the author, November 19, 1991. Summarized in "Editing Notes Oct. 91," in author's possession.

Perlstein, Michael, and Tyler Bridges. "New Reports of Racism Dog Duke: Ex-aide Saw Little Faith." New Orleans *Times-Picayune*, November 13, 1991.

"A Portrait of Louisiana's Voters." *New York Times*, November 18, 1991.

"Reject Lottery Computer Bid, Dent Urges Roemer." New Orleans *Times-Picayune*, October 12, 1991.

Rhoden, Robert, and John C. Hill. "Duke's Supporters Saw Success Coming." New Orleans *Times-Picayune*, October 31, 1991.

Riesman, David, Nathan Glazer, and Reuel Denney. "The Indifferents." Part II, Chapter VIII, Section 1, of *The Lonely Crowd*. Garden City, N.Y.: Doubleday, 1955.

"Roemer Fights Back at Marine Shale Owner's Ads." New Orleans *Times-Picayune*, October 16, 1991.

"The Roemer Voter." Staff graphic. New Orleans *Times-Picayune*, October 24, 1991, with a correction in *Times-Picayune*, October 25, 1991.

Sabato, Larry J. "How Direct Mail Works." In *Campaigns and Elections: A Reader in Modern American Politics*, edited by Larry J. Sabato, 88–99. Glenview, Ill.: Scott, Foresman, 1989.

Schleifstein, Mark, and Sheila Grisset. "Religious Leaders Doubt Duke's Christianity." New Orleans *Times-Picayune*, November 13, 1991.

"Some Claims by Edwards, Duke Don't Jibe with Facts." New Orleans *Times-Picayune*, November 10, 1991.

Stephens, E. L. "Six Reasons to Vote for Duke." New Orleans *Times-Picayune*, October 30, 1991.

Suro, Roberto. "David Duke Has Become a Legitimate Candidate." *San Francisco Chronicle*, October 4, 1991.

———. "Aide in Duke's Campaign Quits, Questioning Religious Conversion." *New York Times*, November 13, 1991.

———. "Louisiana Campaign Rivals Intensify Pace and Vitriol." *New York Times*, November 14, 1991.

———. "In Louisiana Race, a Message of Hate." *New York Times*, November 15, 1991.

———. "Defeat Need Not End Duke's Message or His Career." *New York Times*, November 18, 1991.

Theodoulou, Stella Z. *The Louisiana Republican Party, 1948–1984: The Building of a State Political Party*. Tulane Studies in Political Science. New Orleans: Tulane University, 1985.

"The Time Has Come: DUKE Governor." Campaign pamphlet. In author's possession.

Varney, James. "Runoff Turns to Racial Issues." New Orleans *Times-Picayune*, October 24, 1991.

Voter Research and Surveys. "Louisiana Runoff 1991." In author's possession.

Walsh, Bill, and Tyler Bridges. "Votes." New Orleans *Times-Picayune*, October 21, 1991.

Walsh, Bill, and James O'Byrne. "The Duke Voters." New Orleans *Times-Picayune*, November 10, 1991.

Wardlaw, Jack. "Holloway's Entry into Race Hurts Duke, Poll Indicates." New Orleans *Times-Picayune*, May 2, 1991.

———. "Duke Ranks 3rd in Raising Money for Campaign." New Orleans *Times-Picayune*, September 21, 1991.

———. "Polls Show Dissatisfaction of Voters Is Widespread." New Orleans *Times-Picayune*, September 22, 1991.

———. "La. Governor's Race Stumps the Pollsters." New Orleans *Times-Picayune*, October 17, 1991.

———. "Edwards: Confident of Endorsement." New Orleans *Times-Picayune*, October 29, 1991.

————. "Polls Show It's Still Anybody's Race to Win or Lose." New Orleans *Times-Picayune*, October 31, 1991.

Zisk, James. "The Governor's Race: Parish Returns." New Orleans *Times-Picayune*, October 21, 1991.

————. "The Governor's Race: Parish Returns." New Orleans *Times-Picayune*, November 18, 1991.

Ronald King

11 | On Particulars, Universals, and Neat Tricks

Newspaper and other journalistic accounts are constructed under enormous time pressure. They tell their stories briefly and focus primarily on the sequence of events as they unfold. Their reports are akin to scorecards at a ball game, recording the winners and losers, who got the big hits, and who was knocked out of the box. Scholarly accounts come somewhat later and seek to go beyond the immediate, looking for patterns, regularities, trends, and explanations. The chapters of this volume do much to help extend our understanding. David Duke's election to the Louisiana state legislature from District 81 outside of New Orleans, his serious campaign for the U.S. Senate, which netted 44 percent of the overall vote (60 percent of the white vote), and his success in the Louisiana gubernatorial primary, which won him a place in the runoff against Edwin Edwards, cannot be dismissed as mere sideshows in the spectacle of electoral politics. The contributors to this volume have launched a discussion about the emergence of racist candidates and racially based campaigns that represent an ominous aspect of American democracy.

Rather than discuss the chapters individually, I will attempt to look at the enterprise as a whole, seeking common threads and inherent disagreements, within two general points of discussion. The first concerns the context, distinguishing those features of the David Duke phenomenon that are particularistic from those more universal in society. Only on that basis can we assess the underlying reasons for his appeal and the extent to which they are generalizable, the degree to which circumstances in Louisiana are unique, and the degree to which they portend danger for America as a whole. The second point of discussion concerns the players, examining the political strategies of David Duke and of those who chose to deal with him. Only on that basis can we understand how a former member of the Ku Klux Klan and avowed racist could exploit existing conditions and become so popular.

I

As shown by the contributions of William Moore, Lance Hill, and Elizabeth Rickey, David Duke not only held, but continues to hold, beliefs far outside the mainstream of American thought. He claims that the Holocaust was a myth concocted by Hollywood, that Josef Mengele and Adolf Eichmann were mistreated by history, that Rudolf Hess should have been awarded the Nobel Peace Prize. He contends that races have genetically different behavioral propensities, that nationality is the product of biology, that high culture can be sacrificed through intermarriage. Duke fears that revelations about his past would "stir up the Jews." All of this should sound alien to the American people, whose founding constitutional principle is that individuals are created equal and whose chief lesson from World War II is that Nazi racial doctrines have no place in a democratic world order. Yet a surprisingly large number of Louisiana voters found David Duke an acceptable and legitimate candidate. To them, the symbols he generated were not those of extremism, but, instead, of fundamental values at risk. The critical question is why. Why would an ex-Klansman proclaiming a thinly disguised racial message be deemed the preferred candidate by thousands of Americans? Part of the answer, this book suggests, is idiosyncratic—the messenger might be especially attractive; he might find an ideal opportunity and exploit favorable rules and hesitant opponents. Even still, that message ostensibly should have been rejected prima facie. That is what is so remarkable and disturbing about the Duke experience. It is therefore necessary to inquire about the receptivity of the audience. This volume raises the possibility that voter receptivity is not particular to this candidate or to Louisiana, but that it arises from perceptions and attitudes more general throughout American society and more intrinsic to the American system of beliefs.

As with all political occurrences, there are a number of elements to the David Duke story that are particularistic and thus unique. For example,

Duke's attractiveness as a candidate is in part the product of a carefully crafted public persona and of surgically reconstructed photogenic features. His political persistence in part seems driven by a psychological need to gain acceptance from a confusing array of audiences, a temperament most notable in his arrogant appearance before the Populist party convention, his backslapping efforts with Republicans in Baton Rouge, and his continual attempts to woo and win over Elizabeth Rickey. Similarly, Duke benefited from the decision by many, including the New Orleans *Times-Picayune*, to refrain from in-depth, investigative reporting, believing that extremists are best ignored. Duke also benefited from the comparatively weak candidates selected to stand against him, who showed little personal magnetism and said little regarding the issues. Nevertheless, these elements do not add up to a convincing account of the emergence of a viable racist politician. They are certainly insufficient to explain the fervor of many Duke supporters. On the whole, the chapters here conclude, it would be mistaken, even foolhardy, to dismiss the Duke candidacy as maverick, the product of an accidental combination of unique factors from which replication is unlikely and generalization impossible.

David Duke's appeal was augmented by his ability to tap into essential features of Louisiana politics, including the legacy of populism, replete with eccentric characters espousing antiestablishment views, that has predominated in Louisiana since the days of Huey Long. Duke's Senate campaign was made possible by the state's odd electoral laws, which permit many candidates to stand in the primary election and then mandate a runoff between the top two vote getters, regardless of party affiliation, unless someone has received an absolute majority. Furthermore, his legislative victory was dependent on the specific demographic characteristics of District 81, an overwhelmingly white suburb largely populated by middle-class voters who fled from, and fear the complexities of, New Orleans. Duke has taken advantage, as Ferrel Guillory shows, of the southern trend toward Republicanism. Nevertheless, these are only facilitating factors. According to Susan Howell and Sylvia Warren, Louisiana voters are not decidedly different from others nationwide. The white-flight suburbs noted by Lawrence Powell are not peculiar to New Orleans. The decline of political party organizations has opened up most primary elections to personalized campaigns. Again, the David Duke phenomenon cannot be dismissed as something that could occur only within the boundaries of a most unusual and southern state.

The real puzzle remains: why did so many white Louisiana voters listen and apparently react favorably to Duke's campaign? The assertion here is that he successfully struck responsive chords, that something in the symbols, content, or tone of his message was received positively, even enthusiastically, by a considerable percentage of voters. Moreover, through understanding this connection, one understands something universal about American politics and the American citizenry. The chapters in this book focus on three basic aspects of Duke's voter appeal.

One is brute, genetic-based, old-fashioned racism. This is a difficult realization, for Americans ordinarily do not wish to be reminded of the legacy of oppressive slavery and vicious segregation, once entrenched in the fundamental legal and social structures of this nation. Nor do we wish to be shown that a sizable minority among us still would prefer to refuse equal rights to all individuals. According to Howell and Warren, those who expressed strong anti–civil rights attitudes were more likely to vote for Duke. According to Douglas Rose, in contrast to overwhelming anti-Klan sentiments among the supporters of J. Bennett Johnston and Ben Bagert, only slightly more than half of Duke supporters were "very unfavorable" in their evaluation of the Klan. It is certainly wrong to categorize all David Duke voters as overtly racist. Slightly more than half of Duke supporters "strongly" rejected racial separation. Yet this leaves Duke garnering nearly one-half his support from individuals who are, at best, "soft" on segregation. Furthermore, it is possible that the available data underestimate the size of this contingent. First, old-fashioned genetic racism, as Howell and Warren note, has increasingly become socially unacceptable. To the extent that racist opinions are stigmatized, persons might be reluctant to reveal them to an interviewer. Second, genetic racism is manifest in behavioral patterns concerning whom you live near and associate with, whom your children go to school with, and whom you may marry and/or have sexual relations with. By these standards, racism is still prevalent in our society. David Duke, by his background and continued use of coded words, gives outlet for the anger of those among us whose underlying attitudes run contrary to socially sanctioned norms, and he even helps make those attitudes less socially unacceptable.

A second suggested aspect of Duke's appeal is the explicit content of his message, especially his attacks on welfare and affirmative action. According to Moore, at each stage in his political career David Duke has sought to broaden his audience, tempering his language in order to attract wider support. Attacking assistance targeted to the underprivileged and unsuccessful has long been an aspect of right-wing ideology in the United States. Duke has adopted this rhetoric as part of his shift to the Republican party. Yet, in a profound sense, this has meant not the abandonment but rather the expansion of his racial appeal. So-called cultural or symbolic racism, say Howell and Warren, uses the American work ethic in order to differentiate systematic winners from systematic losers. In cultural racism, statistical evidence of inequality by race is explained by the perception that blacks have lower attachment to the American cultural norms of individual responsibility and hard work. Blacks thus should not receive preferential recognition from government programs but instead should complain less and try more to make their way up the social ladder. Voters espousing such views would not necessarily consider themselves racist. Instead, they believe themselves to be articulating fundamentals of Americanism, in which ample opportunity and personal freedom form the sound basis for the individualist race for achievement and reward. This largely explains why cultural racism variables are less effective than genetic racism in differentiating Duke from Johnston and Bagert supporters. Nevertheless, as Rose indicates, voting is often directional. Voters prefer proponents of their side of some categorical divide. David Duke, in a strategic ploy that was not unique, persistently sought to paint his Democratic opponent as a liberal outside the American mainstream. Given the dichotomy and his own outspokenness, he would pull voters further toward the right—assuming that they saw him as a legitimate candidate and not a fanatic. Presumably, once attracted, many voters would remain in the fold. Duke would become their preferred choice, broadening the sympathetic constituency for his divisive message, while establishing his credibility through an appropriation of the American creed.

Finally, a third important aspect of Duke's appeal seems to be status anxiety amid declining economic prospects. According to Powell, Duke's support has been based on the white working and lower middle class, the often-idealized common man, the lunch-pail voter who in previous times felt allied with the Democratic party. This group, quantitatively, has been forced to accept shrinking living standards over the past decade. It has, qualitatively, become increasingly bothered by symbols of decay, crime and drugs, the collapse of moral order, and the erosion of family values. It is a group that firmly believes in the American dream and has played by the rules, but it has been frustrated in achievement and faces diminishing economic prospects. It is the group that most suffers from the contradiction between rising postwar expectations and insufficient present results. The consequence is a deep dilemma. The lower middle class under stress could abandon the Horatio Alger ideal, dominated by a faith in individualism, effort, and performance-based standards of success and failure. Or it could retain the ideal and infer that one simply has to work harder to get ahead. Or it could deduce that something has gone wrong, that the contest for success has become biased and the outcomes have become distorted. Effort and responsibility are not receiving their just reward; others appear to be benefiting unduly. The logical result is anger and resentment. David Duke is not alone among American politicians in tapping such sentiments and channeling them into a form of right-wing populism. Mainstream American politicians, such as Duke opponents John Treen and Bennett Johnston, have given no satisfying answer to the lower-middle-class dilemma and there is no viable left-wing movement to offer an alternative analysis. In a sense, the common person feels alienated in modern America, giving David Duke a cause to exploit.

The writers in this volume give differing emphases to these explanations. There are some disagreements regarding which ones apply and why. Yet I am also struck by the extent of their agreement, especially as reflected in their underlying critical premise. To all of these writers, the David Duke phenomenon is not something that can safely be considered restricted to Louisiana and to the early 1990s. Rather, the general context of voter attitudes and opinions—which provides the fertile ground for Duke's appeal—is universal, or at least nationwide. These are not necessarily attitudes confined to the fringe domain of neo-Nazi fanatics or recalcitrant southern segregationists. Derived from key aspects of the American creed, they have a long history and an entrenched place in American political culture, and that is why, despite extremist readings, they can attract even mainstream support. To say that such attitudes are pervasive, however, is not to say that they are benign. To all the writers in this volume, the basis of David Duke's appeal comes from a frightening emphasis on a distinction between "us" and "them."

However interpreted in the various chapters, the main observation is that social differentiation, to many individuals, is not a cause for celebration, but instead a motive for cleavage, competition, and contempt. The United States has always been home to a dialectic between unity and diversity, assimilation and distinction. As a heterogeneous nation, it has struggled to establish an appropriate balance, sufficient to respect interests while simultaneously securing allegiance. Over our history, nativists have periodically appointed themselves the task of protecting national purity against contamination from some new generation of entrants. Nativists, for whom no reconstituted balance can ever be deemed acceptable, have themselves rarely posed a threat. Nevertheless, they do sometimes find a cooperative constituency among those fearing that a once-desirable balance is being disturbed. Increasingly this is the situation for the United States. In a country where perceptions of economic decline and social decay often coexist alongside those of black political clout and extraordinary government concessions, citizens increasingly believe that centrifugal forces may be overwhelming centripetal ones. The genius of Ronald Reagan rested in his ability to advance the conservative vision of national unity while blithely promising inclusiveness. Not all Americans are as generous, nor as unwilling to eschew exclusivity. It is all too easy to assume that "we" all would be fine if "they" only respected and restored the status quo ante. Diversity within unity is a continual challenge, and there is always a danger that Americans will fail in sustaining this ideal. In unsettled times, there lurk opportunists anxious to accentuate our differences for personal popularity. David Duke is a dramatic and obnoxious illustration of this possibility, but he is not alone in his enterprise. The strongest finding in this volume, therefore, is that he is largely a homegrown creation, and that Duke and those like him take root and thrive in the dark side of the American historic experience.

II

David Duke, in that sense, seeks to bring out the worst that resides in us as Americans—our divisions, jealousies, and antagonisms. Yet it is not automatic that these feelings come to the surface. Nor is it given that politics will become the arena for their articulation. One would hope for leaders who celebrate difference and offer reassurances to those worried about social disintegration. Yet even without such leaders, interest group pluralism usually serves to keep politicians sensitive to heterogeneity. Snake-oil salesmen abound, with pretty faces and deceiving messages, but most do not escape the fringe. The unusual thing about David Duke is that, in just slightly over two years, he was transformed from an invisible third-party candidate for president into a viable contender for the U.S. Senate and a victor over an incumbent in the governor's race. Background conditions need to be exploited and activated. Potential needs to be turned into opportunity. Context alone cannot explain Duke's rise to prominence.

The second recurrent theme in this volume, therefore, addresses the players in the drama and the strategies by which they played. There are, for example, detailed and fascinating stories told of Duke's relationship to the media, the Republican party, and the Louisiana legislature. Here, again, I am struck by the similarities across authors, especially with respect to the key underlying dynamic, which Gary Esolen calls "neat tricks." In his campaigns, Duke has exploited an inherent weakness in the institutional position of others. He has effectively disguised the contradictions in his message, and he has found facilitators among those lacking an interest in exposing those contradictions. He has made into accessories many who would deny cooperative intent. Thus, Elizabeth Rickey concludes her terrifying account of the Louisiana Republican party's refusal to consider a censure motion against Duke with an irate opponent protesting, "Now wait a minute, I never said I liked Nazis!" The tricks help explain how Duke could proceed with little significant challenge, how he could seize the agenda and the rhetorical offensive without the need to defend himself or his views.

Yet at the same time Duke's reliance on those "neat tricks" just might be his weakness. As Douglas Rose shows, his directional support largely depends on prior assumptions of legitimacy, that a candidate does not appear so extreme as to lose credibility. Denying Duke his tricks, and therefore forcing him onto the defensive, should prove effective in denying him legitimacy.

Esolen's trick concerns the news media. Duke needs free publicity, but it must be turned to serve his agenda. The media needs stories and viewers, but it tends to shy away from fanatics. Duke's trick is to be controversial and notorious enough to attract (yet not repel) the media, while delivering a message that denies that he, personally, is in any way notorious. "I am only standing up for equal rights for white people, too," he would say; "why are these people picking on me?" The inherent characteristics of the news media, more comfortable with short quotations than with in-depth analysis or editorial opinion, give little opportunity for rebuttal. In essence, Duke has to be extremist enough to be noticed, and this supplies him with an opportunity to protest that he is not an extremist. The media has been an unwitting facilitator of Duke's trick. By its notions of neutrality and newsworthiness, it is trapped into providing valuable coverage and robbed of the ability to expose Duke's manipulations. An opportunity for public education, the real function of the media in a democracy, has therefore been missed.

Another neat trick concerns the response of Duke's ostensible "allies" in the state legislature and the Republican party. On the one hand, Duke was only one of 144 legislators and a newcomer to Republican politics. He was one among many, in a fragmented system that is designed to keep any single individual from exercising power. On the other hand, Duke was a special case, far more visible than other neophytes and with a remarkable capacity to put all questions in a black-white context and to magnify polarization over issues of race. Duke's neat trick was to play both sides simultaneously, insisting that he be thought of as an ordinary politician while pursuing goals intentionally disturbing to the ordinary routines of politics. Claiming acceptance among state representatives and backslapping like one of the boys, he was clearly interested neither in normal accommodations, nor in a normal legislative career, nor in normal legislative influence. Claiming that he was now an ideological Republican, he joined the party at the last minute to qualify for the District 81 election and showed no obligation to respect the party caucus. His apparent concern was to gain an official legitimacy needed to escape ostracism and censure and to cloak his platform with mainstream respectability.

Here, again, Duke had unwitting assistance, especially from Republican party officials and conservative legislators, who facilitated the trick by refusing to unmask the contradiction. Some wanted to reduce Duke to just one of 144, considering him an opportunist who was best handled by denying him the publicity he craves. Some were concerned about the political cost, to the party or the cause, resulting from the overt recognition and controversial expulsion of an undesirable. Yet others were less naive than conniving, as William McMahon shows, from little matters—voting for a Duke proposal so as to punish black lawmakers for their position on the lottery bill—to major ones. Duke "takes the heat" on ultra-conservative issues, absorbing animosity, while establishing a "comfort zone" for others with roughly similar views. His visible presence on the extreme right, it is believed, establishes a target for critics while deflecting attention away from other attempts to limit welfare or curtail affirmative action. Nevertheless, the users sometimes become the used. Whether the intention is quiet containment or to cast him as a sacrificial point man, Duke apparently finds the arrangement advantageous. Conservatives have had the opportunity to reject a racist in their midst. By failing to do so, an opportunity for the political isolation of David Duke has been missed.

Finally, there is a neat trick that concerns the content of Duke's message; the facilitators of this trick are, ironically, his vocal ideological opponents. Duke is an old-style racist, who requires the label in order to attract controversy and maintain many of his core followers. Yet he grounds his appeal in the language of the American pursuit of success, which is radically individualist in its focus and presumably celebrates effort and achievement regardless of a person's ascriptive characteristics. It is a neat trick simultaneously to exude racism and defend individualism. Similarly, Duke seeks continuity with the populist tradition, defending the average citizen against intrusive government and building a political base, according to Lawrence Powell, "from the bottom up, mixing working-class Democrats with white collarites that he sheared from the lower end of the Republican coalition." Yet he articulates a form of antiestablishment politics that basically ignores the establishment. He defends the little people by directing their anger toward the littler people, not toward the big people, with wealth and privilege, at the top. It is an odd kind of populism that divides the people, rather than uniting them against elites. Again, Duke's appeal depends on a neat trick.

One might think these tricks quite transparent. Presumably, it should not take much for a true individualist to explode the racial stereotypes of welfare —for example, to point out that poverty is most often a short-term episode, that full-time work is increasingly insufficient to bring a family above the poverty line, that the average stay on AFDC (Aid to Families with Dependent Children) is approximately two years, that more welfare recipients are white than black, and that the birthrate in black single-parent households is down while that for whites is up. For a liberal individualist, it should not take much to explain the unevenness of opportunity and the decline of American expectations, and thus the need for government programs to help improve the overall economic climate and to help more people become self-supporting. Equally, it should not take much for a true populist to explode the myth of a divided people, and to highlight the common experiences of those Americans struggling to earn a decent living. The vast majority of us do not have savings sufficient to tide us over the periods of illness or unemployment that so many must experience. For the populist seeking a scapegoat, the dramatic inequality of material prospects in America could provide evidence to revive Sockless Jerry Simpson's distinction between "the masses" and "the classes."

Yet, surprisingly, Duke has hardly been challenged on substance. There have been no ideological opponents ready and willing to debate his views, expose his contradictions, and present contrasting versions of individualism and/or populism. Bennett Johnston, for instance, ran for Senate reelection as a well-mannered moderate who had brought particularistic benefits back home. Governor Buddy Roemer attempted to form a business-led coalition to bring economic development to the state. Duke's more conscious enemies, such as the Louisiana Coalition against Racism and Nazism, are primarily concerned with publicizing his shocking past and racial attitudes. No prominent person (or organization) in the state has been committed to denying Duke his ideological tricks. In pursuing their own agenda, even Duke's opponents have given him a free field for maneuver.

What is remarkable, according to these chapters, is that David Duke can sustain his antinomies and disguise his contradictions, despite the pressures of competitive politics and his own extremist position. It is not as if his tactics are so enormously subtle or so hard to foresee. Yet the conservatives, who might be distressed by Duke's claims of affiliation, the moderates and liberals, who find Duke an anathema, and the media, whose role is public education, all have failed to expose Duke's tricks and often helped facilitate them.

Nevertheless, there are some grounds for optimism. Duke's success largely depends on maintaining a series of difficult tensions: between extremism and moderation in order to exploit the media for free publicity, between association and agenda autonomy in order to exploit his party for necessary legitimacy, between racism and individualism in order to adapt the American creed to his views, and between racism and populism in order to direct mass frustrations against his designated target. These are not such easy tensions to manage. They give to their manager a distinctive fragility. With his lifetime of experience, Louisiana's David Duke is fairly adept at the straddles required, while other would-be David Dukes might find this more difficult. Despite his talent, Duke's contradictions make him vulnerable to confrontation and exposure. It should be possible by cross-examining Duke to reveal his words and actions to be inconsistent, illogical, and shallow. He may play less well on defense than on offense. The luster may disappear as he is forced to justify his particular views and explain his preferences. Although Duke has thrived through his neat tricks, they may just as well be used—dialectically —against him.

III

David Duke is still with us, a force in Louisiana politics with aspirations at the national level. His defeat in the Louisiana gubernatorial election was principally the result of extraordinary voter intensity and record turnout. One cannot simply expect these factors to be replicated. Duke certainly believes that his political crusade is just beginning. He will not willingly go away, and thus the discussion of his emergence will continue beyond this brief volume. There are still many research questions remaining. To my mind, the most interesting among them are comparative. Within Louisiana, how do Duke's voting patterns compare to those of other Louisiana populists, especially Huey Long? To what extent is he capturing voting alignments previously established and to what extent does he threaten statewide realignment? Somewhat more generally, how do Duke's efforts and his constituency compare to those of previous ultra-rightist candidates in America? To what extent are theories of far-right politics developed around the time of Joe McCarthy still relevant, or are new theories necessary? Finally and most generally, what does the rise of Duke teach us about the apparent increase in racism and bigotry, not only in America but also around the world? To what extent is this only part of a widespread and dangerous phenomenon?

No single volume can address all these questions. This one offers a number of substantial contributions. First, it destroys the illusion of the reformed David Duke, showing that his past racial views remain critical to his present beliefs. Second, it examines the context of voter distrust and discontent that is a precondition to Duke's appeal. Third, it discusses the means of legitimation and visibility that help enable Duke to spread his virulent message. Fourth, it explains the grounds of his electoral successes and the causes of his failures. Finally, it has done much to reveal the contradictions in Duke's rhetoric and the problems faced by many ordinary citizens in evaluating it.

There has been considerable progress in understanding the conjurer's tricks, how they work, and why so many are so gullible. Such understanding can lead to strategies aimed at making the world less accommodating and more difficult for the conjurer to operate within.

Contributors

Gary Esolen is a freelance intellectual. A former assistant dean at Cornell University, he has a master's degree from Syracuse University and completed course work for his doctorate at Cornell. An award-winning journalist, he founded *Gambit* newspaper in New Orleans. He is now working as a media and marketing consultant, writer, and television producer. As Executive Vice-President of the New Orleans Tourism Marketing Corporation, Esolen directs advertising and marketing programs for New Orleans tourism. He has been a debate coach for both successful and unsuccessful political candidates, including the current mayor of New Orleans.

Ferrel Guillory is Southern Editor of the *News and Observer* of Raleigh, North Carolina. Since 1972, he has written a weekly column of political and public policy analysis, with a special focus on North Carolina and the South. In addition, he has served as the newspaper's chief state capital correspondent, Washington correspondent, associate editor for editorials, and government affairs editor. Before joining the *News and Observer*, he reported for the *States-Item* in New Orleans. A native of Louisiana, Guillory has also written articles for several national, regional, and state publications, and he appears regularly on the public television panel discussion, "North Carolina This Week."

Lance Hill is Executive Director of the Louisiana Coalition against Racism and Nazism and a graduate student in history at Tulane University in New Orleans.

Susan E. Howell is Director of the Survey Research Center and Professor of Political Science at the University of New Orleans. Her research and teaching interests are in the areas of public opinion, elections, and research methodology. She has published articles in *Public Opinion Quarterly*, *American Politics Quarterly*, *Journal of Politics*, *Social Science Quarterly*, *Political Methodology*, and *Political Behavior*.

Ronald King is Associate Professor of Political Science at Tulane University. He does research on American politics and public policy, specializing in areas of social welfare, fiscal policy, and political economy. He is the coauthor of *Growth with Fairness* (Seven Locks, 1988), the editor of a special symposium on tax reform (*American Political Quarterly*, 1991) and the author of *Money, Time, and Politics* (Yale University Press, forthcoming). He has won research grants from the American Council of Learned Societies and the Russell Sage Foundation.

William B. McMahon is a reporter on state politics and government for the Baton Rouge *Morning Advocate*. Since 1972, he has covered the Louisiana legislature and the administrations of Edwin Edwards, David C. Treen, and Buddy Roemer. He was in charge of election coverage for the 1990 U.S. Senate contest between J. Bennett Johnston, Ben Bagert, and David Duke and for the last three Democratic National Conventions. In 1991 he focused on legislative reapportionment politics and the election for governor. He won the Sunlight Award from Common Cause (1988) for reporting on political action committee (PAC) contributions to legislative candidates and PAC influence in the legislature.

William V. Moore is Professor and Chair of the Political Science Department at the College of Charleston, South Carolina. His major areas of research are extremist politics and southern politics. He is the author of *Political Extremism in the United States* (National Education Association, 1983). In addition, he has published articles on the Ku Klux Klan, interest groups, and political parties in the South. He is presently working on a book on South Carolina government and politics.

Lawrence N. Powell is an Associate Professor of History at Tulane University specializing in southern history and race relations. A former Guggenheim Fellow, he is the author of *New Masters: Northern Planters during the Civil War and Reconstruction* (Yale University Press, 1980), the editor of Frederick Law Olmsted's *The Cotton Kingdom* (Random House, 1984), and the coeditor of volume one of *The Frederick Douglass Papers* (Yale University Press, 1979). The chairman of the Amistad Research Center's 1989 National Civil Rights Conference, "A Continuing American Dilemma," he is a former board member of the Amistad Research Center and a founder and vice-chairman of the Louisiana Coalition against Racism and Nazism.

Elizabeth A. Rickey was elected a member of the Louisiana Republican State Central Committee in 1988 and became active in exposing David Duke. She received the American Jewish Committee's Public Service Award in 1990 for combating bigotry in the political process. In 1991 she received the Cavallo Foundation Award for Moral Courage in Politics. A founder of the Louisiana Coalition against Racism and Nazism, she is currently a doctoral student in political science at the University of New Orleans.

Douglas D. Rose is an Associate Professor of Political Science at Tulane University. He specializes in American public opinion and voting. His investigations of the politics of race include a book in process about New Orleans mayoral elections, "Win, Jesse, Win" about Jackson's Louisiana victory, and expert witness studies in three Jefferson Parish voting rights cases. His most widely cited works are the *American Political Science Review* articles, "National and Local Forces in State Politics" and "Nonattitudes and American Public Opinion."

Sylvia Warren is studying for a doctorate in political science at the University of New Orleans. She is Research Assistant for the University of New Orleans's Survey Research Center, which conducts regular public opinion surveys in the New Orleans metropolitan area and for the state of Louisiana. Her research concerns are public opinion and minority interests.

Index

Watsky, Steven, 122
Wealth, distribution of, 7, 29
Welfare: Duke's criticisms of, xx, 9, 117, 138, 213, 214, 222, 245, 250; racial stereotypes, xx, 33, 115, 164, 165, 250; Duke supporters and, xx, 85, 160, 164, 165, 167, 225, 230; Duke's reform policies, 15, 32, 33, 107, 115, 117, 119, 124–25, 128, 250; "workfare," 15, 124, 130; in symbolic racism, 119, 159–60, 164, 165, 167; Republican party and, 119, 245
West, John C., 4
White, Ed, 43
White flight, 7, 15–16, 244
White Power (Rockwell), 43–44, 45, 48
Whites: and Duke's 1990 Senate campaign, xxiv, xxv, 157, 164, 171, 172, 177, 181, 182, 183, 186, 187, 188, 191, 231; symbolic racism, xxiv, 54, 81, 82–85, 86, 89, 165–68; and Republican party, 3, 8, 16; and Democratic party, 3, 9; working- and middle-class Duke support, 6, 12, 29, 32, 33, 246; political alienation, 6, 170; racial politics and, 8, 9, 12; Duke and racial resentments of, 13, 15, 16, 18, 32, 50, 54, 80, 85, 90–91, 138, 166–67; Duke as champion for, 13, 47, 138, 143, 178, 249; racism and support for Duke, 13, 88, 115, 158, 162, 175, 233, 245; "reverse discrimination" against, 15, 16, 32, 121, 122, 124; and Duke's 1989 legislative campaign, 15–16, 32, 244–45; and white discrimination factor, 85–87, 89, 90; Duke on

genetic threats to, 103, 104, 106, 108; welfare recipients, 164, 250; social marginality, 171; opposition to Duke, 177, 178, 179; and symbolic politics, 190; and Duke's 1991 gubernatorial campaign, 199, 214, 220–21, 225, 227, 228, 230, 231, 232, 233
White supremacy: of Duke, 18, 61, 94, 102, 103, 104, 112–13, 117; Duke's disavowal of, 103–4, 118; in support for Duke, 156, 158, 161–64, 175, 178, 186
White Youth Alliance (WYA), 45–46
"Who Runs the Media?" (Duke), 104
"Why I Oppose Race Mixing" (Duke), 105
Wilder, L. Douglas, 215
Winter, Chris, 66–68
Winter, William, 4
Womack, John Henry, 60
Women, 145, 191, 194–95 (n. 28), 215
Woodward, C. Vann, 2
"Workfare," 15, 124, 130
Working class, xxiii; support for Duke, xx, 32, 33, 34, 246; populism, 20; Duke's appeals to, 22, 26, 29, 32
World War II, 45, 74, 137, 243
WWL-TV, 152

Yockey, Francis Parker, 66, 96

Zatarain, Michael, 42, 43
Zeskind, Leonard, 68, 119
Zionism, 43
Zyklon-B, 73

Tulane Studies in Political Science

Titles in Print